THE MANDATE

T&T CLARK LTD
59 GEORGE STREET
EDINBURGH EH2 2LQ
SCOTLAND

First published 1995

ISBN 0 567 29281 9

British Library Cataloguing-in-Publication Data
A catalogue record for this book is available from the British Library

Typeset by Trinity Typesetting, Edinburgh
Printed and bound in Great Britain by Page Bros, Norwich

THE MANDATE OF HEAVEN

The Divine Command and the Natural Order

Michael Keeling

T&T CLARK
EDINBURGH

CONTENTS

ACKNOWLEDGEMENTS

Grateful acknowledgement is made to the following copyright holders for permission for quotations:

Quotations from the *Revised English Bible* © 1989 by permission of Oxford and Cambridge University Presses.

The excerpts on pp. 200–1, 203, 204 and 206 are quoted here, with permission, from *Befriending the Earth: A Theology of Reconciliation Between Humans and the Earth* by Thomas Berry, CP with Thomas Clarke, SJ, © 1991 by Holy Cross Centre of Ecology and Spirituality (paper, 168 pp. US$7.95), published by Twenty-third Publications, PO Box 180, Mystic, CT 06355, and available in the UK through Columba Books, Dublin, Ireland.

The poem 'Threshold' by R. S. Thomas is quoted from R. S. Thomas, *Later Poems 1972–1982*, by permission of the publishers, Macmillan General Books.

The poem 'Song for Gwydion' by R. S. Thomas is quoted from R. S. Thomas, *Selected Poems, 1946–1968* (published by Bloodaxe Books, Newcastle upon Tyne) by kind permission of Mr Gwydion Thomas.

For thus the royal mandate ran
When first the human race began,
'The social, friendly, honest man,
Whate'er he be,
'Tis he fulfils *great Nature's plan*,
An' none but *he*!

Robert Burns, 'To the Same' (Second Epistle to
J. Lapraik), 21 April 1785

INTRODUCTION

The story behind the use of the word *mandate* in this book really goes back to the year 1966, when Joseph Fletcher set Christian ethics on a new course with the publication of his book *Situation Ethics*. For anyone who was not around at that time it would be difficult now to imagine what a tremendous sense of relief came to many of us as we saw how to throw off a dying system of 'rules' without losing the central urgency of Christian obedience. Of course Fletcher's work had predecessors (what was being called 'the new morality' was condemned by the Vatican in the 1950s), but it was Fletcher's particular interpretation of the Christian response to the modern world, together with John A. T. Robinson's *Honest to God* (1963) popularising the work of Tillich and the later Bonhoeffer, which gave a definite sense of something new.

Situation ethics is essentially the claim that every Christian, and indeed every human being, has the ability and the right to make moral decisions according to the needs and necessities which are present in a particular situation, rather than according to preset rules. Nothing is absolutely right or wrong; the definition of right or wrong is to be determined by those who actually have to act. Only one rule is absolute, which is to act in obedience to a loving God. Fletcher quotes a cartoon showing the stonemasons about to carve the Ten Commandments asking Moses if they can reduce them to 'Act responsibly in love'?

The roots of this apparent reductionism lay in the renewal of the Protestant theological tradition in the 1930s and 1940s in Germany and German-speaking Switzerland by Dietrich Bonhoeffer, Karl Barth and Emil Brunner. Barth argued throughout his life that obedience to Christ required an openness to the new and surprising work of God that could not be constrained within a system of ethics that treated Christian ethical judgments as a set of rules known in every detail in advance of the concrete situations in which actual decisions had to be taken. For Barth, human sinfulness precluded such knowledge of God, except in precise obedience given to the

THE MANDATE OF HEAVEN

Word received in a moment of judgment. In a late essay on 'The Gift of Freedom' (in *The Humanity of God*, 1960), Barth said firmly that even the Scriptures did not constitute a set of ethical rules adequate for every purpose and that it would be a mistake to treat them as such.

In the section called 'The Pharisee' in the fragmentary work *Ethics*, Bonhoeffer said more radically and less defensibly that every attempt to set up a system of ethics, to form our own judgments on the basis of human reasoning, could be considered an act of disobedience. If Bonhoeffer had really thought this, of course, he would not have written much of the *Ethics*, but in the circumstances of the time, in which obedience to rules had led the German people into obedience to the National Socialists' demonic rules, the argument of 'The Pharisee' made a lot of sense, even though it is clear in practice that Bonhoeffer does think that there are quite a lot of useful Christian rules to be had.

The dangers which both Barth and Bonhoeffer were concerned about were those of complacency, of too-easy judgments, and of the use of rules to condemn others without being challenged to consider our own disobedience. In the Europe of the Nazi period the question of the Sermon on the Mount, 'Why do you look at the speck of sawdust in your brother's eye, with never a thought for the plank in your own?' (Matthew 7.3) could literally be sometimes a life and death question. When Christian obedience could sometimes lead to a concentration camp, the temptation to fall back on conventional morality was extremely high.

It was a version of this theology of 'costly grace' that came to be known as 'situation ethics'. Fletcher also challenged 'cheap grace', but in a world in which the alternative did not always seem very costly. It was, in the 1960s, a matter not so much of bearing the cross as of exercising a legitimate claim to self-fulfilment, whatever the rules might say. The message which Fletcher gave the world of Christian ethics was 'You have a right to make your own decisions'. Just as second-generation and later Calvinism accepted the business world as a legitimate forum for Christian obedience, and so gave the world the 'Protestant ethic' as a partner to rising capitalism, so situation ethics gave the green light to a generation which was determined, after two world wars and the economic miseries of the time between them, to seize and enjoy what two generations had fought and died for, the intellectual, moral and political freedoms

of 'the western way of life'. If Calvinism made everybody his own
capitalist, situation ethics took the logic of Calvinism a step further
and made everybody his or her own moralist.

Situation ethics cleared away an enormous amount of dead
wood, but in the long run it became clear that something more was
needed in the way of moral construction than Fletcher had been
willing to supply. This was not simply a matter of people not being
fit to make their own moral decisions, as was suggested by many
critics at the time of publication. On the contrary, the gain from
situation ethics, that we *do* begin our moral work by seeing ourselves
as fit to make our own decisions, is something that needs to be
constantly preserved and exercised.

Nevertheless there was in the end something lacking. This was a
profound sense of moral law, not as detailed rules but as a kind of
'deep structure' underlying detailed moral thought. Though Fletcher
claimed to accept and understand traditional teaching and casuistry
as being among the tools required for ethical decision-making, the
assumption was so vague, and so hedged-about by his polemic
against 'law', that in practice he tended to lead his followers into a
land without maps. In this sense situation ethics, at least in its first
phase, was parasitic upon the older traditions. The older traditions,
meanwhile, were already in the process of disappearing. As Francis
Birrell said to Virginia Woolf about her father, Sir Leslie Stephen,
a leading free-thinker of the previous generation, 'He pulled down
the whole edifice, & never knew what he was doing. He never
realised that if God went, morality must follow' (*The Diary of
Virginia Woolf,* volume 3, 1925–30, Wednesday 24 February
1926). Birrell, of course, approved of the change.

It is only now, a generation later, that the full problem begins to
be clear. John A. T. Robinson, in *Honest to God,* had used the
formulation that love had 'a built-in compass' which will always
indicate the proper ethical response. A compass, however, functions
only in relation to a map, and in truth it is the map which is now
missing, which for previous generations had been furnished by
many traditional means, from the display of the Ten Commandments in country churches to the intensive instruction associated
with the confessional in the Roman Catholic Church.

This is a security to which we cannot now return, for two reasons.
One is that the whole sense of authority in western society has
changed in a more individual direction, even within the churches

THE MANDATE OF HEAVEN

and even within the Catholic Church itself. Today small groups can exercise a 'sectarian' type of authority over their members, but large groups cannot, and there is no general 'Christian' consensus on many issues and no will to hear such a consensus even if it did exist.

The other factor is that our understanding of 'the Bible' has changed so radically in the last one hundred years that no notion of absolute authority can now be sustained from it. This is a problem that now needs to be addressed in detail in the study of particular ethical issues. More generally it can be said that using the Bible in ethics involves a choice of certain organising principles (or as some might say, preconceptions), which help to select what material is relevant and how it is to be read. Though such principles are always present in any reading of the Bible, *there is no absolute basis on which such principles can be laid down.* Every reading implies a viewpoint about the nature of the Biblical materials and the context in which they are to be read. Such a choice can only be 'situational'.

Two themes seem to me to be useful here and have, I hope, been applied fairly consistently in the present book. The first is the position of 'canonical criticism' long advocated by Brevard Childs (most recently in *Biblical Theology of the Old and New Testaments,* 1992), that however much attention we pay to detailed critical analysis of language, form, historical context and literary intention, what remains at the end of the day is a collection of texts, the 'canon' of the Old Testament or of the New Testament, which is intended by the communities which formed it to be read in the form in which they gave it to us, and is intended to be read as a whole. That is to say, there is a responsibility to take seriously the whole history of the text and not just some postulated 'original' form.

The second theme is that this 'canonical' shaping of the texts is not the end of the matter. Later generations of Christians and of Jews also have had the authority of the Holy Spirit to read the texts and in them to encounter God the Maker and, for Christians, Christ the living Word. This is a risky business, but it is a risk that must be taken if Christ is to come alive in our own time. For this purpose we have, as David Kelsey argued in *The Uses of Scripture in Recent Theology* (1975), a further commitment within the church. For every group of Christians which has existed through time has its own tradition of the interpretation of Christ in the Bible. This exists formally in the shape of denominational documents such as the Westminster Confession of 1647 or the Book of Common Prayer of 1662, or the documents of the 'Magisterium', which is the tradition of teaching of the Catholic Church. It exists also more informally in the tradition of particular teachers such as John Wesley or P. T. Forsyth, and also in the traditions of 'how things are done' – and heard – in local churches.

The overall effect of these traditions is to create what Kelsey calls a *discrimen*, a largely subconscious set of choices about what is fitting in this tradition and what is not. To say this is perhaps not to say much more than to acknowledge that theologians and churches are subject to the same social laws as other organisations, that we are governed more than we would like to admit by our past history and by our present culture. Yet without these 'tramlines' we would not in practice be able to function at all, or not for very long. To be free of the constraints mediated in the churches by the power to discriminate what is 'properly' Lutheran or Catholic or Anglican would not produce 'freedom' but 'helplessness'. In this context my own *discrimen* has to be announced as that of an Anglican, heavily influenced by the ecumenical movement, by the demands of social justice and by an outsider's admiration for the Church of Scotland, fuelled by more than twenty years of living and working in Scotland.

It is here that we begin to see the need for the concept of the mandates. The *discrimen* of the particular community needs to be spelled out in the form of an approach to ethics which defines areas of common concern, not only for that community in its own life, but also in its engagement with other Christian communities. The aim of the mandates is to define areas of ethical concern and to indicate some possible common themes within those areas. The mandate is not far off the notion of the *middle axioms* called for by J. H. Oldham in the 1930s.

The notion of the mandates derives from the older concept of the 'orders of creation'. In 1932 Emil Brunner published *Das Gebot und die Ordnungen*, which was translated into English in 1937 as *The Divine Imperative*. Here Brunner undertook the task which had long been neglected in Protestant thinking, of giving an ethical account of the created order. Since the sixteenth-century reformers, Protestant theology had emphasised the gravity of sin, but at the price of ignoring much of the Old Testament teaching on the goodness of God's creation. Brunner, following a lead given by the reformer Martin Luther, distinguished two types of ethical commandment. One was given primarily in the New Testament and described the heroic calling to salvation. The other, the orders of creation, dealt with the fact that Christians, like all human beings, lived in a world given by God, in which certain structures and certain obediences were necessary in order to keep life going at all. We all have to love and we all have to work and we all have to learn and we all have to accept government of some sort – and to centre all these human activities we also, thought Brunner, need the church. God's rules about these basic activities did not save us from sin, nor did they procure our salvation in Jesus Christ, but they were nevertheless good in themselves within the calling to salvation and did provide some essential, though perhaps low-level, ethical guidelines.

The difficulty, of course, in this programme was the separation of obedience in creation from obedience in Christ. Consequently Dietrich Bonhoeffer, in some brief references in the *Ethics*, took the argument a stage further, and changed the terminology, by using the term 'mandates' to signify that even our obedience to the requirements of creation, as Christians, could come only through Jesus Christ. This makes Bonhoeffer's stance more satisfying Christologically, but at the price, which Bonhoeffer did not explicitly recognise, of putting the mandates at some distance from a purely natural law. It has to be said here, however, that neither Brunner's orders of creation nor the Catholic teaching of 'natural law' is truly natural in the sense of deriving simply from what human beings actually are, since both begin with the notion of a creator God who is still actively engaged in making and directing the universe, whose love is expressed through nature but who is not identical with nature.

Bonhoeffer's correction seems to me essential, however much it limits the 'naturalness' of the mandates. It makes the mandate into a term which indicates God's calling to all human beings to explore the potential of social structures as paths of obedience so that a common morality can be sought, but in which there is also a specifically Christian input to be considered. Yes, it is good for people to marry; yes, it is good for people to work; yes, it is good for people to learn and to teach; yes, it is good to have government to create order and peace; yes, it is good to have the church (or another religious commitment) to moderate and give a conscious centre to all these activities. Within the mandate these particular decisions are not simply imposed from the outside: rather they are to be sought together by all human beings in the actual situation of human life.

To say this is certainly to go beyond what Bonhoeffer himself wrote, for Bonhoeffer was concerned with human deputyship in Christ, not with an all-human ethic. But it seems to me to be a possible, and a potentially valuable, expansion of his use of the term mandate to use it to describe *a commission to find the way of Jesus Christ as a path through the ordinary ways of human life, in collaboration with other human beings*. The church has its own markers for those activities – the hope expressed in baptism, eucharist, marriage and funerals – but there are other markers, biological, social and philosophical, which also have to be taken into account.

Karl Barth in 'The Gift of Freedom' has shown the practical way we can work within the mandates. He suggests that in ethics we turn first to the Bible, where the central fact that focuses all our actions is the resurrection of Jesus. The fact of the living Christ is where ethics begins. Then we turn to the church, in which the resurrection is understood and practised daily. Then we can turn to 'expert' help, to the theologians, philosophers, natural scientists, social scientists or whoever is appropriate to the task we have in hand. Finally, however, we carry on our own shoulders the responsibility of the decision, under grace; we alone have the grave responsibility of acting in a situation, or the in some ways even more grave responsibility of daring to give advice to someone else. For Barth it is a particularly perilous responsibility to stand, even for a moment, between someone else and God.

The mandate thus indicates a process in ethics. The balance which Barth describes of fundamental faith with the theological, the ecclesiological, the social and the historical, must be discovered anew for each specific task. The making sense of all of this is always a task for today, which cannot be determined by the past. The four mandates suggest that our responsibility to God must be found principally in the areas of political institutions, of personal obligations centred on the capacity for love and for reproduction, on our use of the material world and on our new capacity to reshape physical human life and the life that surrounds us.

It is also reasonable to suppose that for these separate areas of obligation we need a common centre, a vision at least of the possibility of an harmonious pattern for all obligations, a future resolution of tensions which will lose nothing of what we gain from the interaction of particularities. The home for this vision is the church, in all its various definitions, as the community of those who seek this goal. For the commitment to holy obedience in the four ethical mandates makes no sense unless we are prepared also to sustain a fifth mandate, a vision of the whole earth as a holy community which shares in the envisioned future.

In the excitement which came with the optimism and lively experimentation of the 1960s, the need for this was not fully seen. Only in the last decade or so has the notion of 'moral law' begun to come back on the agenda. Fletcher, of course, did not deny either the existence or the importance of moral law as a guide to individual decision-making, but he did underestimate the extent to which a general knowledge of moral law and a willingness to apply it depended on an inheritance of church teaching which by then was already beginning to disappear.

When *Situation Ethics* first came out Fletcher was accused of being too optimistic about human nature and human ability to make and to carry-through practical moral decisions, without the guidance of judges or priests and without the fear of hell or the rope. That charge, I think, is false. Where Fletcher was too optimistic was in assuming that everybody was already an instructed Christian, or at least living in a world in which Christian principles were, and would always be, part of the general heritage.

Today we face a different task, which is that of being Christians in a society which is largely ignorant of, indifferent to, or actively dissociated from Christian principles and from other traditional moral sources. It is, therefore, necessary today to go back to a notion of 'moral law' to ask whether a notion of moral duty has any basis whatever, and any chance of general acceptance whatever, in the context of what we know about ourselves through all the other relevant sources of knowledge. To put this in Christian terms, we need to ask 'What does God require in the world, not only as a matter of Christian obedience to Scripture, but also as a matter of successful human existence, within the framework laid down by human psychology, human society and human and other biological existence?' Can Christian faith speak realistically to human beings everywhere, with due respect both to expert authority and to other forms of faith, or is its message confined only to those who accept a full commitment to some particular form of the church? Are there mandates for the whole of humanity, or only for the church?

The present book is an attempt to explore what might be involved in defining mandates for the whole of humanity while starting, unavoidably, from a specific and in this case Christian basis, indeed a Protestant Christian theological basis, though keeping open the possibility of ecumenical and inter-faith dialogue. This is an immense and increasingly difficult and increasingly important task, which cannot be done in a single book or in a single generation. All I intend here is a brief sketch of the ground to be covered.

The present study has lasted, in effect, since the publication of *What Is Right?* in July 1969. In that time a vast number of people have contributed to my process of reflection, both at the Ecumenical Institute at Bossey, near Geneva, from 1969 to 1972, and in the University of St Andrews from 1972 onwards. To all these people, too many to thank by name, I offer most grateful thanks here.

Michael Keeling
Pittenweem, Fife
2 July 1994

THE DIVINE ORDER

(i) The Task of Christian Ethics

Christian ethics has been through a time of immense change in this century. Some of this change has come about because society itself has changed, in despite of Christian thinking, in such matters as the loss of the general assumption that marriage is lifelong, or is indeed something that everyone should undertake. Some of the change has come about because of rapid developments in practical techniques, giving new questions to be answered in ethics – this is outstandingly true in the area of bioethics. Some of the change has come as an affirmation of an old truth, partially forgotten in the optimistic 1960s and 1970s, that evil is present in human life in ways that are so fundamental and so deeply horrifying that even the term 'original sin' seems hardly adequate as a description of it. Some of the changes that we shall be considering may point even to the end of human life – or of all life – on the planet.

Throughout all this the task of Christian ethics remains constant. It is to assert that 'Jesus Christ lives; therefore we live also'. What causes confusion, sometimes for Christians as well as for others, is the assumption that this simple affirmation must or can be followed by an equally simple list of activities that are approved or disapproved, attention to which constitutes the Christian life. This is not so.

Christian ethics, in fact, is in the same state as all other serious moral systems, namely that it is trying to deal with intentions and consequences in relation to a number of different moral aims.

We want to preserve the stability of married life, but also we want people to fulfil themselves in love in the way that best suits their own characters and circumstances, married or unmarried, childless or with many children, straight or gay. We want to preserve the sanctity of life and yet techniques of fertility and abortion and the prolongation of life and euthanasia have all come into our hands as practical possibilities which promise increases in human happiness and reductions in human suffering. We want peace on earth, yet we may think that we can achieve it only by waging war. We want justice for all but preferably at little cost to ourselves. We want to preserve the planet, yet the activities and consumption that we might give up also seem pleasant or even liberating to us.

In these dilemmas Christian ethics differs from other moral systems only in the nature of the hope which it offers. This hope is that present life models future life in one single respect – that it offers moral freedom. We have the power now, in each of us, to try to choose the good as it will appear in the kingdom of God. Ethics is a task of discernment, of choosing, but without absolute assurance of the rightness of the choice. Only when we enter the kingdom will we know finally what the nature of our choices has been. As St Paul says, 'At present we see only puzzling reflections in a mirror, but one day we shall see face to face' (1 Corinthians 13.12). When we are face to face with God, then we shall be face to face with our own moral choices. Until then we have to take risks, trusting in the loving power that leads us on to the final glory.

This does not leave us helpless. On the contrary, we are as Christians surrounded by stories – the great stories of Israel and of Jesus and of the history of the church. Around these stories is the story of humanity, which is also an ethical resource. Religions tend to separate as much as they unite, because they want only their own stories to be heard. This is unfortunate, for under the stories of all religions there is a common story, the story of human beings who want also to be moral beings. No matter what the system we are brought up in, whether capitalism or communism, whether rich or poor, whether east or west, what characterises us as human beings is that we recognise a meaning for the words 'good' and 'bad', 'right' and 'wrong', however much we may disagree about particular applications of those words.

Reinhold Niebuhr, one of the most powerful writers on Christian ethics in this century, held that human beings are locked into a dilemma on moral issues. On the one hand we have a human capacity for self-transcendence. The best human characteristic is that we can aspire to change, to do better. We know that somewhere else perfection exists and we feel that it is within our grasp. This is the driving force for moral and social change. 'Onwards and upwards!' we say. On the other hand we have the sad fact of history that all our aspirations somehow get defeated. Mostly this is the result of our own efforts, because we overreach our own abilities. In the search for perfection we forget that we are also limited in time and place, that we are in technical terms 'finite beings'. Hence we mistake self-aggrandisement for the good and the power to act for the right to act.

The tragedy of human beings is that high moral ideals become ways to think well of ourselves. Without the understanding that the completion of any moral act is not our work but God's work, even high moral aims become a source of tragedy, not grace.

Niebuhr delivered his Gifford lectures on *The Nature and Destiny of Man* in 1938, when the tragic tendencies of this century were already becoming clear. He had plenty of reason then to be pessimistic about human endeavours. Today, at the threshold of the third millennium, we have a different historical context but equally strong reasons not to regard human behaviour as immediately perfectible. Rather our question is, How can we learn to live with ourselves? What guidance can we get from the stories of the world and of God? What are the reasons we can give for our hope?

(ii) Hope in Creation

... and God saw all that he had made, and it was very good. (Genesis 1.31)

On the sixth day God brought to an end all the work he had been doing; on the seventh day, having finished all his work, God blessed the day and made it holy, because it was the day he finished all his work of creation. (Genesis 2.2, 3)

Christian ethics is about the task of living in a world that is created by God for a good purpose. It is the task of finding out what is *possible* in such a world and the task of finding out what is *good* in such a world.

The notion of the *possible* is important. Human beings are creatures with short life spans, born into particular circumstances of geography and society and race and sex. As finite beings there is only

so much that we can do. Some people alter their lives heroically in
one direction: they become missionaries in foreign countries or
explore little-known places or land on the moon or move from
Kansas to New York. Even so they achieve only one thing, though
perhaps the thing they most desire. Most people, however, keep the
world turning by pursuing their ordinary lives.

In this important sense Christian ethics is the pursuit of the
ordinary. It is not grand opera, but a village hall amateur production. Now in these circumstances accumulated human wisdom,
from all sorts of moral and religious sources, is likely to produce a
broad agreement on matters such as truth-telling, love and respect
within the family and concern for the neighbour, even if nobody
lives fully up to these ideals and some do not try. What this claim
about a general morality means is that when human beings sit down
and talk seriously about morality, they are likely to agree in principle
that these ways of behaving matter, even though the details of what
is required by truth or love or concern will vary. In this sense the
human moral task is a common task.

It is, on the other hand, also important to know how we can
define some of this detail, to see how we can come to know what is
good. For Christian ethics the *good* is defined as the nature of God,
as known by human beings in history and in personal experience.
The nature of God is affirmed in words taken from human capacities: the words are love, joy, peace, patience, kindness, goodness,
fidelity, gentleness and self-control, as St Paul spells out in Galatians
5.22. We have to start from this kind of human knowledge of life
in order to have any words at all to use in our moral work. In fact,
until another human being makes us the gift of these experiences we
cannot in practice give content to the word 'God' – or alternatively
we may give the word 'God' a false content, as being angry,
dictatorial, punitive or unpredictable, representing the experience
we actually have of human beings.

The human knowledge of God is thus corruptible. When Eve
and Adam chose their own knowledge in preference to obedience to
God, they chose on the serpent's terms (Genesis 3.1–8). This meant
that knowledge was bound to bring dangers. The myth of the 'fall'
sets out the crucial transition in human experience, that the human
species rose through the evolutionary process to the point of being
able to know its own knowing, and so to take responsibility for that
knowing. The knowing self is 'fallen' because the innocence of the

other creatures protects them from moral blame; when a life reaches the moment of self-consciousness, however, it can be held to account.

As we have already seen in Reinhold Niebuhr's account of human nature, the power of choice necessarily leads to sin, because of both our pretension and our finitude. The myth is then not the story of a fall from a condition in which we could and should have stayed, but the story of an essential step in evolution that nevertheless brings us great dangers as well as great opportunities. From now on we are dependent on our own experience to evaluate not only what we are but also what we shall be. In this way it becomes possible to talk about a 'false' and a 'true' concept of God.

The test of the true and the false lies in the interchange between aspiration and experience. Remember here that we are talking about Christian ethics as a practical way of living, but one that is in contact with the truth through worship and prayer. In fact most people have a sufficiently wide experience of human responses at least to be able to begin the task of moral choice. As soon as we begin to wish to discriminate, we are ready to hear a story.

The story is that God acts in love. Rather than being left to find out for ourselves what love is, we are given the task of becoming aware of the love that God already pours out upon the world. Knowledge of this love is found, among other places, in the history of a particular community, the Jews. From there Christians take it on to become the story of a particular individual, Jesus of Nazareth, who was put to death by the political authorities of his day, and came to be called 'the Christ', the one who comes to show, as fully as human life can carry the message, what the nature of God truly is.

Christian ethics is concerned with exploring this story. What the story does most importantly is to locate ethics within an understanding of the creation as a process. That which is seen to be 'very good' in God's initial creative act in Genesis is nevertheless not complete. Israel's experience of life in Palestine, trying to live with the God who creates, led the Jewish people to understand God's work as not only 'creating' but also as 'leading', as 'rewarding' and where necessary as 'punishing', all in order to bring the people to a state where this process would be completed and the fullness of life given once and for all.

This future completion was pictured as the 'sabbath'. The weekly day of rest, the seventh day of the week, represented not only the past, the seventh day on which God rested having completed the work of creation, but also the future hope, that for the whole creation there must be a final state in which 'rest' would mean not a weekly temporary halt to labour, but a new way of living in which the distinction between 'rest' and 'work' would disappear. Then all actions and all relationships would give and receive perfect joy. The Bible of the Jews, the 'Old Testament' of the Christians, is full of the images of this future time of peace, joy and freely-flowing gifts of whatever is needed of material things (as in Isaiah 55).

For Christians this Old Testament idea of the universal sabbath becomes the 'kingdom of God', the time when God's rule will be open and acknowledged by every created being. This kingdom is seen, not as a complete breach with the present, an entirely new beginning, but as a way of life that can begin now. Indeed, the task of Christian ethics is to identify ways of behaving, ways of relating, that are already of that kingdom. In this sense ethics becomes a moving target. The ways of behaving which are appropriate to the kingdom of God cannot be specified as simple basic rules, even though they begin in such matters as honesty, love for family and respect for the neighbour. The kingdom itself demands much more.

So the notion of creation, the initial state of order which leads to the sabbath, gives way in Christian thought to the notion of the *eschaton*, in which the creation is defined in terms of its ending. At the opening of St John's Gospel, the announcement of the presence of Jesus Christ 'at the beginning' (John 1.2) is made, with the comment that 'without him no created thing came into being' (John 1.3). This indicates that in the announcement of the arrival of the kingdom of God through the life, death and resurrection of Jesus the creation finally comes to understand what it has been created to become.

(iii) Hope in Salvation

This new possibility is something which has yet to be defined. 'No one has ever seen God; God's only Son, he who is nearest to the Father's heart, has made him known' (John 1.18). This new commission is undefined because the world in which it is to be done has yet to be built. The Christian life therefore becomes a task of exploration, of pushing to the limits of what can be done through peace, love, honour and joy. Now suffering becomes glory, death becomes life, love becomes not holding-on but letting-go, poverty becomes riches and weakness becomes power. The choice for the kingdom of God is the choice to explore the Christian paradigm, to accept suffering, to wait in hope, to make no demands, to give to those who ask and not to give up hope.

William Countryman opens a discussion of love with these words: 'What God says to you in Jesus is this: You are forgiven. Nothing more. Nothing less. This is the message Jesus spoke and lived' (*The Truth About Love*, p. 1). In this quotation the whole problem of Christian ethics is set out. There are more complicated ways of saying it, and long books have been written to explain the problem. But its essence is that we do not have to *do* anything in order to be loved by God. As Countryman says, this is very different from the general perception that Christian faith says, 'Good news!' If you are very, very good, God will love you' or 'Good news! God loves you. Now get back in line before God's mind changes'.

For the real good news is set out in the First Letter of John, 'This is what love really is: not that we have loved God, but that he loved us and sent his Son as a sacrifice to atone for our sins' (1 John 4.10). This quotation needs more comment, but for the moment we need only note that the Bible is quite clear that love begins with God loving us, irrespective of anything we may have done – or left undone.

This poses quite a problem for Christian ethics, because it tells us that in an important sense Christian ethics is not really any use. The first and only 'achievement' that we need is to accept the love which God already freely gives. Dietrich Bonhoeffer put it even more strongly. He thought that Christian ethics got in the way of accepting the love of God, because it could give 'religious' people a belief, that was really a false belief, in their own ability to make judgments about what was right and what was wrong (*Ethics*, 'The Pharisee'). As Bonhoeffer saw it, the only judgment that we can safely make is that in all really important matters we need to be guided directly by Jesus Christ and not by our own cleverness.

So the first point that has to be made about the task of Christian ethics is that it is a *listening* task, in which our own ideas have to be measured against the primary fact that *God loves*. In this task not only our own ideas but also the ideas of teachers, of books, of church leaders and of the Bible itself have to be put under the single

question, 'Does this measure up to the fact that God loved us first?'
– because we are never, at God's level, 'fit' to be loved. Many
schemes of ethics may fall by the wayside when this question is
asked.

So we come to the second half of the sentence from the First
Letter of John, 'and sent his Son as a sacrifice to atone for our sins'.
The announcement of forgiveness is a liberation. It also serves notice
on us that there is something to be forgiven. This is a notion that we
come to somewhat reluctantly. At the end of the film *Some Like It
Hot*, Jack Lemmon confesses that he is not a girl, but a boy in drag
on the run from the Mafia, to which the besotted Joe E. Brown
responds with the immortal words, 'Nobody's perfect'. A film can
end right there but life goes on and in real life Lemmon and Brown
would probably have a very short future together. Where Christian
ethics does have a work to do is in reconnecting us with life, in
ascertaining the reality principle that life is *thus* and not in some
form that we would wish it to be. This is done, not to disappoint our
hopes, but to establish a firm basis for our hope.

The aim of Christian ethics is to give both true knowledge of what
we are and true knowledge of what we can be. The sending of the
Son is the work of God's initiative towards us. It tells us that we are
never outside the presence of God. As Martin Buber says, 'He who
knows God knows also very well remoteness from God, and the
anguish of barrenness in a tormented heart; but he does not know
the absence of God: it is we only who are not always there' (*I and
Thou*, p. 127).

The 'sacrifice to atone for our sins' rings a deeper note. It says that
what we truly are is a source of pain, to ourselves and to others,
because we do not yet truly act with spiritual knowledge of ourselves
and of others. We are not yet fully in the Spirit of God. But this
painful news would not be received by us at all, if we did not already
have an intimation of it in our hearts.

Existentialist writers refer to the 'anguish' of moral choice caused
by the sense of being alone in a world which always ends in our
death. Jean-Paul Sartre in his lecture of 1945 on *Existentialism and
Humanism* connected this directly with Nietzsche's perception of
the death of God in modern culture. 'Atheistic existentialism, of
which I am a representative, declares with greater consistency that
if God does not exist there is at least one being whose existence
comes before its essence, a being which exists before it can be defined

by any conception of it. That being is man, or as Heidegger has it, the human reality' (pp. 27–8). This perception creates anguish because now whatever is good for the whole of humanity can come only from my own decision – 'in such a moment man cannot escape from the sense of complete and profound responsibility' (p. 30).

Others have been more impressed by all the pain suffered physically in this world, from the Holocaust to the 'ethnic cleansing' of Yugoslavia and elsewhere. As Raymond Aronson comments, Sartre's argument in *Being and Nothingness* in favour of moral freedom can be challenged with the fact that no amount of moral self-assertion would have protected the Jews from being carried off to the death camps in May 1941. 'However free these Jews may have been ontologically, "to consider the anti-Semites as pure objects", it happened that at least twenty thousand of them were shipped to destruction as Sartre was completing his book' (*Jean-Paul Sartre: Philosophy in the World*, p. 77). Aronson's comment on Sartre's life and work holds true of existentialism as a whole, that the theory does not account satisfactorily for the experience of human community: 'sociality itself was left unexplained' (p. 352).

Yet it is also true that existentialism offers human beings the dignity of making their own decisions and standing by them in order to define themselves. Albert Camus in *The Plague*, published in 1947, took up this theme. In Part IV, chapter 3, the novel contains a long description of the death of a child from the plague which is raging in the city of Oran. The death is watched by Rieux, the doctor in charge of the medical battle against the plague, and Paneloux, the parish priest who has preached on the plague as punishment for disobedience to God. The child's death is a defeat for both of them. For Rieux it means that the serum he has been developing has not worked – at best it has prolonged the child's suffering. For Paneloux, as the challenge is put by Rieux, the child was innocent and his death could in no way be comprehended under the heading of divine punishment. In response Paneloux ventures, 'Perhaps we should love what we cannot understand'. But Rieux replies, 'No, Father. I've a very different idea of love. And until my dying day I shall refuse to love a scheme of things in which children are put to torture' (p. 178).

There is no doubt that the world is not a place designed first of all for human happiness. The response of Sartre, that under all conditions we can as individuals assert human freedom, even if only in our own consciousness, is a courageous moral position. It is a defiance of the darkness, an assertion of our own moral right to be selves in the face of an uncomprehending and amoral universe. Sartre sees the courage which is required for such an acceptance, because he knows that in such a universe there can be no question of an appeal to any creating or sustaining power. Such an appeal is only an illusion left over from the Christian past.

The response of Dr Rieux is more immediately practical. It is to abandon metaphysics and to concentrate on what can be done with your own hand and your own mind, and to co-operate for practical purposes with those who are of similar mind. Rieux's reflections on the meaning of hope at the end of Part IV, chapter 4, come to the conclusion that of those who take the risk of living it can be said 'And for some time, anyhow, they would be happy'. Rieux concludes, 'it was only right that those whose desires are limited to man and his humble yet formidable love, should enter, if only now and again, into their reward' (pp. 244–5). Yet the child is still dead after his pain and as Rieux reflects at the end of the book, the plague could bide its time to come again.

Camus' austere moral stance is less comforting than that of Sartre, because he is more aware of the pressures of necessity and of the randomness of hope. Yet in a world in which God is dead it is Camus who is the realist. There is here no point to morality except the acceptance of what is given and its very limited possibilities of love.

The Christian task lies in neither of these options. When the author of the First Letter of John writes of 'a sacrifice to atone for our sins', he is pointing to a conception of the universe which involves faith in the possibility of an interaction between our own moral successes and failures and the givenness of the world. It depends in the end on where you choose to start. The Christian faith asserts, against all reason but not against all experience, that we are finite – bound by the necessities of the world – but also free – able to make moral choices which can and will in time change the conditions in which we live. It is not that our finitude will be removed, but that the nature of our finitude will be changed. Increasingly, as we practise the way, our very limitedness becomes an opportunity for moral choice. So Christian faith regards the world as still morally fluid, still able to be shaped by human moral responses. In this sense Christians believe quite clearly and determinedly in miracles.

Of course, this means that we have to love that which we do not yet understand. The contingency of the world is full of pain. Children are born with diseases which will kill them before they have any chance to grow up. Young parents die and leave their children alone. Those whose lives have become a burden to them find no friend in death as life drags on. Those who began with high hope find themselves frustrated. Those who have no concern except for themselves flourish like a green bay tree. God's universe is too large for our moral comprehension. Paneloux is wrong to make the direct trade-off between suffering and God's justice in his first sermon (*The Plague* II.3, p. 80). But he is wrong also to say in his second sermon that we have to love the pain which comes upon us without a possible moral explanation (IV.4, p. 184). Blind love without judgment is no love at all.

The only reason for loving God *through* the pain of our finitude is the hope that there *is* a moral explanation at the end of it all, even though we cannot yet guess what that explanation might be. In Christian ethics the world is not so much to be explained as a moral system, as lived as a moral experience. If we accept the given as the place to start, what matters is not only that the world is a painful place, but also the more graspable fact that we ourselves are part of that pain.

Where we *do* have choices, our loving can be a painful experience. We can love and not be loved in return. We can love but see the beloved as certainly less than perfect. We can fail to love enough and regret much later that we have not loved enough. And we can refuse love as altogether too risky, to concentrate on something giving more immediate satisfaction.

Yet none of this means that love is not a serious matter, or that we would rather be without it. For love when it 'comes through' is the most glorious thing of all, an experience which really does justify the universe. Even when we have to come down from the heights, to have loved and to have been loved leaves a permanent mark on who we are. It changes the nature of the soul. To mean that much to another person – and to let another person mean that much to me – changes the self. The Christian doctrine of 'atonement' is precisely about this process of being changed by love. It says, simply and practically, that this is what the world is for, that we may learn to be changed by love.

Atonement (or at-one-ment) means learning about love by doing it – and accepting that sometimes the doing will be painful. So atonement is 'a sacrifice' because from the moment we undertake the responsibility of love we realise that there will be a price that will have to be paid. Indeed the most valuable moral learning is in the bearing of the pain of love. What the 'sacrifice' of Jesus promises is that out of the pain will come new life. The cross of Christ is an empty cross because out of the pain of death comes resurrection. The empty cross is followed by the empty tomb and out of the self-emptying of love comes the new creature we are meant to be. The Christian claim is that this is the nature of our moral reality. No amount of argument can substitute for this lived reality of love.

(iv) Divine Order and Human Reality

The primary notion of order is, of course, that of physical order. Ever since the seventeenth century western culture has been trained to think of the world as fundamentally a piece of machinery. We have increasingly made deeper discoveries about the complexity and sophistication of the world-machinery, but the essential image has not changed, the image of a clock. Indeed it was the conquest of accurate time-keeping in the seventeenth century, for the purpose of accurate navigation, that introduced the modern technological world. Today we measure time in seconds and fractions of a second, and feel that we have the world precisely in its place. In the Kazan Cathedral in Leningrad, now St Petersburg, until the overthrow of the communist regime, the presence of God in the Divine Liturgy was replaced by a swinging pendulum, which illustrated the revolution of the globe, symbolising the victory of the science of which communism claimed to be a branch.

Modern developments in physical science have not altered fundamentally this image of order, but they have put it in a new context. Heisenberg's 'uncertainty principle' indicates that we can no longer entertain an expectation of establishing for certain what is happening at the sub-atomic level, but have to talk rather in terms of statistical probabilities. John Polkinghorne calls this 'the cloudy and fitful world of quantum unpicturability' and explains that 'Heisenberg tells us of the particles that make up matter that if we know where they are, we do not know what they are doing; if we know what they are doing, we do not know where they are' (*Science and Creation*, p. 77). Since Einstein, 'time' and 'space' are no longer separate though complementary measurements, but different ways of stating the same measurement. Physics at this level can even play with the possibility of an unlimited number of worlds corresponding to each set of quantum possibilities. Certainly these speculations illustrate a shift in our understanding of the physical universe, from clock-work regularity to something more like a flow of energy, which still obeys rules, but not all of them the rules of clocks. As Polkinghorne again says, 'the matter revealed to the inquiry of modern science is neither inert nor formless. Its pattern-creating dance is in accord-ance with laws capable of astonishing fruitfulness in their conse-quences' (p. 55).

When we move from the physical sciences to the biological sciences, the argument becomes further complicated by the ability of living matter to experiment with itself. Looking back from the emergence of living beings through evolutionary proc-esses to the underlying biochemistry and physics, it has become clear by what processes life was formed. Science has a reasonably coherent story through the various disciplines of ethology, biology, palaeontology and biochemistry. But if we look forward from any earlier stage to the next one, it is by no means clear that the development has to follow. For this reason philosophers and theologians familiar with science a century ago developed the idea of 'vitalism', that life had in it some creative power which emerged in successive developments, and which was able to make the leaps from inorganic to organic matter, from organism to consciousness, and from consciousness to spirituality. These thinkers included Henry Drummond in Scotland and Henri Bergson in France.

The notion of a force emerging through biological evolution to rise to higher consciousness has never quite died out, but more recently the case has been put in a reverse form. Modern biologists such as E. O. Wilson and Richard Dawkins have argued that much that we arrogate to ourselves as the product of human moral choice may more accurately be seen as biological responses to evolutionary necessities. In particular the argument has been made that 'altruism' is not a moral decision but an evolutionary device by which particular gene pools are protected and given a greater chance of breeding success. The use of the term 'socio-biology' indicates the claim that under all our social behaviour there may lie such biological origins.

'Altruism' is an action by which an animal may ensure the reproductive success of the gene pool from which it comes, not by seeking to reproduce itself but by caring for the offspring of a close relative. This has been called 'nepotism' and in this connection John Crook remarks that 'A biological case for "true" altruism does not exist' (*The Evolution of Human Consciousness*, p. 43). However, the project has been extended considerably by the consideration of the existence of 'reciprocal altruism', which may exist both within species and between species, in terms of some sort of co-operation. This can be a successful strategy whenever the net benefits to the 'altruists' exceed those which accrue to those who choose to 'cheat'. Because 'altruists' can remember and discriminate against 'cheaters', in these circumstances the 'cheaters' can quickly be squeezed out. Crook comments that 'Finally, in man, reciprocal altruism is supported by an elaborate psychological system based in friendship, sympathy and moral rules' (p. 43).

Barbara Smuts, studying patterns of friendship amongst baboons, comments that 'Monkeys and apes show highly differentiated, long-term relationships between males and females in the absence of any economic exchange. These relationships are based, instead, on social reciprocity' (*Sex and Friendship in Baboons*, pp. 259–60). Such relationships probably prevailed amongst our hominid ancestors. 'Among non-human primates, exchange of social benefits does not require a pair-bonded mating system, but it does often seem to depend on long-term, affiliative relationships between particular females and particular males (or, in the case of chimpanzees, between particular females and small group of males)' (p. 260).

Smuts notes that to accept the message that our relatives among the primates have complex social systems may be a blow to the conviction that 'only human beings can create rational societies'. But this loss comes with the gain that we can now begin to see our own behaviour in more universal context. If human behaviour is not unique it may be, for that reason, more intelligible.

John Crook has reviewed a variety of human behaviour in the light of sociobiological information about other species and concludes that there are indeed signs of universals in human conduct which suggest the existence of biological constraints on behaviour. This does not mean that such general explanations of conduct fully explain individual actions, nor does it lay claim to more than an interaction between the biological and the social:

The tentative explanation of human conduct that stems from the sociobiological paradigm relates man to behavioural and social evolution in the animal kingdom generally and thus for the first time anchors the study of society in evolutionary biology through a fundamental theory. Nonetheless the enormous variety of cultural processes cannot be interpreted solely by sociobiological explanation. (*The Evolution of Human Consciousness*, pp. 189–90)

Yet this is not to say that God designed the universe in order to produce the planet earth and put human beings on it.

For the argument about 'design' cuts both ways. On the one hand, it might be argued that the universe only seems to be designed for us because we are in fact alive in it. This 'species-centrism' could be argued from the point of view of any species which exists in any universe. On the other hand, given that this actual universe has produced consciousnesses capable of reflecting on order and meaning, it can be argued that the emergence of self-reflective life has been a process of overcoming, leading to higher orders of complexity of organisation, and that this emergence, to the best of our knowledge, has not been explicitly programmed by the necessities of each previous stage. We, therefore, have a choice between seeing the arrival of this complexity and consciousness as a matter of pure randomness, or of seeing it as a process of being overcoming non-being, as Paul Tillich puts it in *Love, Power and Justice*, which is still going on in our own experience.

The fact that there is an observable process, culminating in human consciousness, and apparently not entirely random, does not mean that our own further part in that process is thereby secure. The overcoming of non-being by being may prove to be a temporary phenomenon. At the very least we need to recognise ourselves as part of a process that has no secure results. In Jared Diamond's striking phrase, human beings are the third chimpanzee which has risen alarmingly above its blood relations, the common chimpanzee and the pygmy chimpanzee, and may now be about to experience a catastrophic fall (*The Rise and Fall of the Third Chimpanzee*).

Looking at nature by itself gives us neither moral direction nor moral security. No species has an assured place in the universe. No species has a clear moral purpose. Whatever we do, we do by our own wills, on the basis of our own moral perceptions about the ordered structures of nature within which we live.

The notion of a divine order underlying human reality is nevertheless an ancient one. Early philosophers viewed 'Nature' as a regulating force, though not operating specifically for human good. Some saw the regulating force as the principle of 'Reason', present to some extent in all human beings, but fully present only to (male) philosophers, and largely absent from women, children and slaves. Others saw life as essentially a flow of events without any special purpose, in which human beings had to create their own meaning, using whatever was possible within the limits of their own control of their lives.

The positive notion of a 'natural order' was taken into Christian thought under the influence of the Biblical concept of God's care for the creation. In the Hebrew understanding of the world the rule of God is a personal rule, but not an arbitrary rule. In the contest of understanding between God and Job, at a late stage in the development of this theology, God asks of the human being:

> Where were you when I laid the earth's foundations?
> Tell me, if you know and understand.
> Who fixed its dimensions? Surely you know!
> Who stretched a measuring line over it?
> On what do its supporting pillars rest?
> Who set its corner-stone in place,
> while the morning stars sang in chorus
> and the sons of God all shouted for joy? (Job 38.4–7)

The claim of omnipotence here is primarily a claim to the creation of order. In the Bible order is always the result of God's direct will. The great difference between ourselves and the world of the early church and the mediaeval church is that in the ancient world the universe was regarded as essentially a fixed order. Even God's act of creation has, so to speak, its own fixity. Human beings might damage the given order by the misuse of their wills, in defiance of rationality, but anyone who accepted the discipline of rational thought could both see what the world was meant to be and follow through the moral indications which arose from that fact.

St Thomas Aquinas put this view into the form which became fundamental to both the mediaeval and the modern Catholic understanding of the moral world. In his theory of 'natural law' St Thomas argued that although all of nature was damaged by the fall of human beings, which infected all created organisms, yet God's intention for nature remained within the reality which had been created. Rocks and plants and insects and the lower animals and human beings all showed their original purposes, as planned by God, in exercising their daily being.

Human beings were more severely wounded in their behaviour than other creatures, because the fall of Adam and Eve affected the moral consciousness, by which through reason human beings were able to respond consciously to the glory of God. Nevertheless, human beings could return to the fullness of God's plan by the exercise of rational thought, since it was still possible to see from the creation as it existed the moral ends which it was intended to serve. Though the fullest knowledge of God, the knowledge of the salvation offered from sin in Jesus Christ, required also the divine revelation of Holy Scripture, nevertheless the 'natural law', the law given in nature when we perceive ultimate purposes there, still provided a sufficient moral basis for daily human existence.

The great difficulty with the theory of 'natural law' in Christian theology is that it became, almost inevitably, the preserve of ecclesiastical authority. The immediate temptation was to press the theory beyond a general concept of order and intention in creation to make it a set of quite specific rules of behaviour. Now it is clear that the initial assumption of 'natural law' thinking, that we can perceive the purposes of structures of life from their present form, does not lead on to widely agreed detailed rules in terms of human moral life. Though many ethical precepts would find wide acceptance among human beings generally, others, such as the control of contraception or possibly of abortion, are a matter of controversy, even among Christians.

The temptation to make the definition of 'natural law' an act of authority is, therefore, very great. In the encyclical letter *Humanae Vitae* in 1968, Pope Paul VI made clear his view that the content of the 'natural law' was a matter for the 'Magisterium' of the Roman Catholic Church (Section 4). The subsequent trials of various theologians, in particular that of Charles Curran, have made clear that the current temper of Rome is towards ever more rigorous control of expressions of dissent from the established teaching, especially on questions of detailed moral judgment. In the documents concerning the case of Charles Curran it is made clear that neither theologians nor laity have the right to argue publicly, either against papal teaching or against anything normally taught by the bishops. All the dissent that is permitted is, on the basis of conscience, to have a private doubt which is not publicly proclaimed (*Faithful Dissent*, pp. 268–9).

This particular ruling, repeated in the trials of other theologians such as Leonardo Boff, has now been given general authority in relation to Catholic moral teaching by the encyclical letter *Veritatis Splendor* of Pope John Paul II, published on 6 August 1993, twenty-five years after *Humane Vitae*. The letter opens with a sustained exposition of the story of the rich young man who asked Jesus what he should do to be saved (Matthew 19.16–26), which expounds the Christian life as a response to the goodness of God and emphasises the unity of the commandments to love God and to love the neighbour (Sections 6–24).

The difficulty with the letter for those who are not Catholics is that it then proceeds to affirm the status of the 'Tradition' of the Roman Catholic Church as the source of authoritative teaching on Christian life and locates this authority specifically in the 'Magisterium' of the Church, which today means the Pope and the bishops (Section 17). This really brings to an end many of the possibilities of discussion of the concept of natural law between Catholics and Protestants and also some possibilities of discussion within the Catholic Church itself.

Underlying this doctrine of authority is a more fundamental problem, which is the notion of 'objective morality'. This theory holds that while the intention behind an action and the foreseeable consequences of the action have to be taken into account, it is the moral nature of the act itself which defines whether it is a good or bad action. '*The morality of the human act depends primarily and fundamentally on the "object" rationally chosen by the deliberate will* ... The object of the act of willing is in fact a freely chosen kind of behaviour' (Section 78). The letter goes on to quote the new *Catechism of the Catholic Church*, saying that 'there are certain specific kinds of behaviour that are always wrong to choose, because choosing them involves a disorder of the will, that is, a moral evil'. Such a position, leading as it must to the preparing of detailed lists of actions which are held to be objectively wrong under all circumstances, can be sustained only by a hierarchical system of authority such as exists in the Catholic Church, culminating in an unchallengeable, because infallible, peak.

For other moral thinkers in the Christian tradition, the morality of actions depends on intention, circumstances and consequences. There are many actions which can be seen to be difficult to justify except under the most extreme circumstances. For some this would be true of abortion or the death penalty; for most it would be true of torture or doing harm to children; for most it would be true of apostasy. Nevertheless, no action can be seen to be good or bad absolutely, irrespective of the conditions which govern it at the moment of choice.

Joseph Fletcher's phrase, 'Act responsibly in love' has received, and has needed, much criticism since he first offered it, jokingly, as an alternative to the Ten Commandments (*Situation Ethics*, p. 28). In fact Fletcher nowhere suggested that we should ignore the Ten Commandments or any other source of moral enlightenment. What he meant was that all information and instruction, in the context of serious moral decisions by members of Christian communities, has nevertheless to be weighed by the conscience of those who have to perform the action and to bear its consequences, and that here – and only here – can authentic moral decisions be taken.

This remains the key statement of the Protestant understanding of ethics in our time. Fletcher himself quotes Luther on this point.

> Therefore, when the law impels one against love, it ceases and should *no longer be law*, but where no obstacle is in the way, the keeping of the law is a proof of love, which lies hidden in the heart. Therefore, you have need of the law, that love may be manifested; but if it cannot be kept without injury to the neighbor, God wants us to suspend and ignore the law. (*Situation Ethics*, p. 62)

The great pity of the development represented by *Veritatis Splendor* is that we really do need a concept of moral behaviour as a general human task. The two great Protestant thinkers on ethics of the inter-war years, Emil Brunner and Dietrich Bonhoeffer, both saw that common human tasks exist as part of our activities in a created universe. So, in a more limited sense, did Karl Barth. These tasks inevitably imply the existence of some moral imperatives.

Brunner in *The Divine Imperative* called these moral imperatives the 'orders of creation', following Luther's use of the term. For Brunner these 'orders' were the necessities of the organisation of the family, of labour, of government, of culture (science, art and education) and of the church.

Bonhoeffer in his *Ethics* used the term 'mandates', rather than 'orders', since he was not so ready as Brunner to separate the moral requirements which arise from our created nature from the moral requirements which arise from our salvation. For Bonhoeffer, all true moral callings come to us in a sense through the revelation of Jesus Christ.

In this sense Jesus Christ is always at work ahead of us in the created order, forming it in advance even of his own act of salvation. The traces of morality in the creation are for Bonhoeffer, therefore, already indications of the presence of Christ. The mandate of the church Bonhoeffer saw as 'deputyship', the point where the action of God in creation and the action of God in salvation are brought together. The church has a task of proclamation, but in the exact moment that the proclamation is made, it is also fulfilled – Jesus Christ is present on earth. 'This means that, precisely through its willingness to be merely the instrument and the means to the end, the congregation has become the goal and centre of all God's dealing with the world' (*Ethics*, 'The Commandment of God in the World', p. 266).

If this is really the task of the Christian Church, then its reflection on the natural order will take the form suggested by some recent Catholic thinkers. Richard M. Gula has noted that the natural order is not simply the same as the moral order. Natural law is the product of human reflection upon nature and it is characterised by 'a critical effort to grasp the whole of human reality in all its relationships' ('Natural Law Today', in Curran and McCormack, *Natural Law and Theology*, p. 375). The word 'natural' then becomes a kind of shorthand for 'the total complexity of human reality taken in all its relationships and with all its potential' (p. 379). Consequently there are no particular guarantees given in advance about the outcome of this process of reflection. As Gula says, 'A moral position developed from this approach will reflect the tentativeness of historical consciousness and the provisional character of moral knowledge' (p. 386). It is, of course, exactly this kind of reflection that *Veritatis Splendor* sets out to suppress.

All those who accept a God-ordered view of the universe can perhaps agree on this, that it rests with religious believers in particular to accept the ethical task of making good whatever promise there is in nature of the possibility of a harmonious human existence. In the life of the gathered communities of all religions we can at least see the beginnings of the knowledge of what a true order of creation would be. It is this tentative human response in community that can truly claim to be a 'natural order', though as Enda McDonagh has wisely remarked, 'The traditional notion of natural law persists in a genuine way in such an approach (*i.e. through Christian community*) to moral theology, but in an important sense it is neither natural nor a law' (*Invitation and Response*, p. 37).

The main danger of Christian ethics is still the temptation to want to provide complete answers for everything. The illusion of completeness is the particular sin of 'objective morality'. It exists, however, in all forms of Christian ethical theory. John Kent in his biography of William Temple remarks that:

> In *Mens Creatrix* he took for granted that the final victory of the ideas of equality and co-operation over those of acquisitiveness and competition was to be interpreted as progress to a higher stage of human existence. This progress did not mean, in his opinion, substituting socialist politics for the Christian gospel, but moving away from secular politics towards the politics of the kingdom of God. (*William Temple*, p. 53)

Mens Creatrix, in fact, was written in the middle of the First World War and published in 1917. Temple was not buoyed up on a moment of false optimism. Rather he was determined to assert the rule of God at the lowest point of human existence, with a view to a better time to come. But the 'politics of the kingdom of God' is not a practical programme for post-war reconstruction.

As the young Reinhold Niebuhr said in *Moral Man and Immoral Society* in 1932, we need such religious illusions in order to encourage us to go on working for change, but we should not expect to see them realised in this world. Reinhold Niebuhr can properly be accused of making too sharp a distinction here between religion as a personal commitment to sacrificial love and the practical possibilities of the world of political and economic institutions, where we can expect only rough justice, but the practical point remains, that 'love' is not a sufficient prescription in the work-a-day world.

The point was better put by Reinhold's brother, H. Richard Niebuhr, in 1951:

> Without loyalty and trust in causes and communities, existential selves do not live or exercise freedom or think. Righteous and unrighteous, we live by faith. But our faiths are broken and bizarre; our causes are many and in conflict with each other. In the name of loyalty to one cause we betray another; and in our distrust of all, we seek our little unsatisfactory satisfactions and become faithless to our companions. (*Christ and Culture*, pp. 253–4)

H. R. Niebuhr had more faith than Reinhold in Christ as 'the transformer of culture'; Reinhold was always more aware of our human capacity to over-reach ourselves. But Richard also refused to come to 'the conclusive result that would enable us to say, "This is the Christian answer"' (p. 231). For such a human decision would be 'an act of usurpation of the Lordship of Christ', which would destroy Christian liberty and foreclose the Christian future (p. 232).

This brings us back to 'situation ethics'. For with all the information which the world can provide about how human beings work, think and love, and how the world around them is ordered, and all the agreement we can find about general moral principles, the specific human act always depends upon a specific human decision, and this is always taken in a moment which brings us under the possibility of judgment. Every moment of serious moral decision-making is a *kairos*, a moment when we stand before God and reveal who and what we are. Our very lack of equipment for this task means that our decisions must be relative and individual, but as H. R. Niebuhr says, 'They are made, it appears, on the basis of relative insight and faith, but they are not relativistic. They are individual decisions, but not individualistic' (p. 234).

It is in this sense, and only in this sense, that we can seriously set out to seek 'the mandate of heaven'. It is not that, after all these centuries, the human race has been missing something which we can now reveal. It is rather that, throughout the centuries, the task stands to be done again and again, because for each generation in turn, it is *our* task, and no one else can predetermine it for us.

2

THE MANDATE OF HUMAN DIGNITY

(i) The Problem of Order

There is no doubt that at the present time the possibility of order, both in human social life and in human dealings with the rest of nature, presents a profound problem. We may indeed be at a crisis-point for the possibility of a continued human occupation of the planet. The human capacity for disorder, the incapacity to take seriously the fact of our finitude, is now a factor working against survival. What in another context is called the Christian virtue of humility, willingness to be subjected to limit and to regulation, is for the whole species now a question of the recognition of our status in creation as special but not infinitely protected. The belief that we are here as masters of the universe is what earlier generations of western civilisation would have had no difficulty in seeing as 'original sin'.

This failure is, of course, partly a failure of political will. The Chinese in ancient times used the term 'the mandate of heaven' to indicate that an earthly ruler was always dependent, not only on the human power that she or he could summon up in support of the reign, but also upon the will of heaven that decided whether the ruler remained within the norms that heaven required for all its creation. While this was not a covenant in the Biblical sense of God's personal agreement with the people of Israel, it reflected a human concern that what made life possible was order and that order needed constantly to be renewed by some sort of power in the universe beyond the powers of human beings.

At a point in human history when human beings seem to be about to exceed the mandate of heaven for their life on the planet earth, it is worth looking again, in the context of Christian ethics, at the concept of order in our world, to see what this can tell us about our own possible future. If the mandate of heaven is indeed withdrawn,

23

then we have no future, though other species no doubt will continue; but if we can learn to live within our mandate we may yet have hope. Not a law of nature but a programme for nature, including our own nature, is our own best hope.

All human social arrangements are in a certain sense arbitrary. They exist primarily as a means of avoiding disorder. At the beginning of a discussion of the concept of pollution, Mary Douglas remarks that 'As we know it, dirt is essentially disorder. There is no such thing as absolute dirt: it exists in the eye of the beholder' (*Purity and Danger*, p. 2). There may be good scientific reasons for some rules of simple hygiene, but these do not cover the whole range of our reactions to dirt. Social anthropologists have long identified our underlying structures of avoidance and acceptance as being located in the sphere we generally call 'religious'. That which is dangerous, polluting, upsetting of order is 'taboo', not to be approached except with severe caution: this is the area of the sacred. That which can be handled safely by everybody without undue concern is the profane: this is the area of daily life. Daily life also depends upon the sacred, but is not so dangerously a direct contact with its power.

Emile Durkheim argued in 1912 that what was then called a 'primitive' religious understanding of life, such as the totemism of the Australian aborigines, was a first attempt at deciphering the universe by categorising phenomena and establishing relationships between them, in terms of what was to be treated as 'sacred' and what was to be treated as 'profane'. When the aborigines organised their world in terms of relationships to a 'totem', a sacred object, they recognised themselves as being of the clan of the crow or of the kangaroo, or of a rock or a tree; in so doing they also defined their place in the whole creation, from which all other relationships flowed, including the blood relationships of biological kin and the place of the whole people under the sun and the moon and the stars.

Durkheim viewed this effort of self-classification as the beginning of the whole process of scientific interpretation of the world. 'Religion sets itself to translate these realities into an intelligible language which does not differ in nature from that employed by science... . In this regard, both pursue the same end; scientific thought is only a more perfect form of religious thought' (*The Elementary Forms of the Religious life*, p. 429). He, of course, expected religion eventually to give way to social science in the organisation of the human social world.

Few would share this positivist vision today, if only because of the difficulty which Durkheim already saw, that the sciences, like religion, exist only as social facts. 'In the last resort, the value which we attribute to science depends upon the idea which we collectively form of its nature and rôle in life; that is as much as to say that it expresses a state of public opinion' (p. 438). For Durkheim's argument about society notoriously reduces itself to a situation in which 'truth' is a function of a society worshipping a 'collective representation' of itself. If this is the common basis on which both science and religion rest, we might indeed be better off with the old 'world religions' as independent functions in human experience.

Few also would now share Durkheim's view of primitive religions as an early stage of social evolution, to be overtaken first by more complex religions and then in our own day by scientific method. So little do we now have confidence in a purely scientific solution to the problem of order that many are turning to elements of the so-called 'primitive' religions for a renewed and humbled understanding of our place in the world. It is, however, good to remember here Rosemary Radford Ruether's comment that 'Those people for whom Taoism or Pueblo Indian spirituality are their native tradi-tions are those best suited to dig these roots and offer their fruits to the rest of us. Those without these roots should be cautious in claiming plants not our own, respectful of those who speak from within' (*Gaia and God*, p. 206). We can no longer imagine that we can move simply into the whole thought world of the Australian aborigines or Native Americans from the thought world of modern Christianity, or of modern atheism – nor for that matter can we move into the thought world of Confucius, of Buddha or of Jesus in his own time.

What we can do, however, is to recognise from all these sources that the problem of order is a religious question. Mary Douglas points out that order necessarily starts from disorder:

> Granted that disorder spoils pattern; it also provides the materials of pattern. Order implies restriction; from all possible materials, a limited selection has been made and from all possible relations a limited set has been used. So disorder by implication is unlimited, no pattern has been realised in it, but its potential for patterning is indefinite. This is why, though we seek to create order, we do not simply

condemn disorder. We recognise that it is destructive to existing patterns; also that it has potentiality. It symbolises both danger and power. (*Purity and Danger*, p. 94)

A world in which there is no disorder would be regulated but also sterile, without change and without purpose beyond itself. In terms of the Biblical myth, we needed the 'fall' in order to become changers of the world and of ourselves.

On the other hand, a world in which we try to produce too much order can lead to some strange mistakes. Colin Thubron tells the well-known story of a Chinese contribution to agricultural advance. Seeing some songbirds in cages in Beijing, he comments:

The orioles carol here with little competition. In the 1950s, in one of those mass feats of which the Chinese are peculiarly capable, the whole population of the country turned out to destroy its birds, which were thought to be consuming too much grain in the fields. For twenty-four hours on end the people beat tin cans and blew whistles, so that the startled flocks took off and found nowhere to alight, until they fell from the sky in their millions, dead of heart failure. (*Behind the Wall*, p. 38)

Whether the Chinese drove their birds to death by heart failure or simply ate them into extinction, the loss would have been not only in bird-song but also in insect control, almost certainly leading to crop losses more severe than those caused by the birds themselves. So one kind of rationality becomes another kind of madness.

There are three major theories which have been put forward to account for the present forms of social order in the west. The *Marxist* theory sees different social structures in history as part of an inevitable process of evolution towards a final state of happiness. The *functionalist* theory sees social structures as a means to efficiency rather than happiness, within systems about which questions of fundamental change are not asked. The *social action* approach is not so much a single theory as a recognition that all theories are complicated by the desires and decisions of individual human actors: we would like to achieve happiness and existing social structures are the not always very happy results of our fumbling attempts to achieve it.

The expectation of social change bringing happiness begins with the moment in modern thought when society begins to be seen as something which can be manipulated and changed in the interest of general human objectives. Through most of our written history 'the way we are' has been seen as something given, not really open to change except in small particulars. It might be possible to assassinate a bad ruler, but this one would be replaced by another who might or might not be as bad. It might be possible to relieve merchants or peasants of a particular tax, or at least to riot for such a change, as in John Ball's peasants' revolt, but new taxes would eventually appear. It might be possible to obtain a charter of rights, as in the English 'Great Charter' in 1215, but making those rights effective was another matter.

In none of this past history could we take 'society', the whole complex of interlocking social structures, and reshape it in our own way. The enormous optimism and daring required for such an enterprise had to come from two new sources. The first was the centring on human achievement which came about in the sixteenth century. This was a mixture of explosive chemical elements: the rediscovery of the humanism of the ancient world, the excitement of the new natural sciences, and the loss of moral authority by old structures and the assertion of the rights of individual conscience which followed the Reformation. All of this opened hearts and minds to what seemed unlimited possibilities, not only for speculation but also for action.

The second source was the process of actual social change which followed in the seventeenth and eighteenth centuries. Technological change revolutionised societies. From the upheavals of the enclosure of common land for private profit to the swelling numbers of people, many living in vile conditions, in the new industrial centres, human beings were brought face to face with change that was rapid, unplanned and often devastating in its effects. Industrialism knew no boundaries and respected no persons.

All this change began to be thoroughly analysed in the nineteenth century. Amid many competing words, one mind now stands out as having grasped the fundamental challenge of such change. Karl Marx may not in the long run be judged to have changed the social and industrial structures of the world profoundly, as he and his followers have hoped. But he is likely to be remembered as the thinker who most firmly grasped the moral questions at the heart of the industrial system.

The *Manifesto of the Communist Party* dramatically declared in its opening words in 1848, 'A spectre is haunting Europe – the spectre of communism' (Marx in Kamenka, *The Portable Karl Marx*, p. 203). The communist programme was essentially one of centralisation. It included the abolition of property in land, a progressive income tax, the abolition of the right of inheritance, the nationalisation of banking, communications and transport, the equal obligation of all to work, the unification of town and country, free education and the abolition of children's factory labour. The main point about this 'spectre' is its hopefulness, culminating in the romantic final cry:

> The proletarians have nothing to lose but their chains.
> They have a world to win.
> Working men of all countries, unite! (Kamenka, p. 241)

The programme is nevertheless wanting in many respects. In particular it fails to see that the concentration of power will make it difficult, if not impossible, to call the organs of power to account. There is here a kind of faith in what one might call 'the immaculate conception of the working class' which assumes, without argument, that the workers and their leaders will never be mistaken or given to greed and selfishness in pursuing their individual interests. The notion of the proletariat as a kind of moral wellspring from which no evil can come is entirely comprehensible in that the sufferings of the poor are a primary source of moral concern about the social order. But it ignores the fact that those who come to hold power are no longer 'the poor' in that sense, whatever their personal origins or group ideology.

This naivete, then, springs from a profound moral indignation at what industrialism was doing to the new industrial working class. In Marx's analysis it is the condition of 'alienation'. The theory is complicated, if only because it was never clearly set down as a single theory. The central point, however, is quite simple. It is that the nature of industrial production under the capitalist form of ownership is such as to impose burdens upon the workers which destroy their humanness.

In the essay 'Alienated Labour' in the *Economic and Philosophical*

Manuscripts of 1844, Marx gives a number of reasons for this. One is that the work is in effect *forced labour*: the labourer must work to live, but the employer, supported by the state, sets all the conditions of work and pay. The labourer has no control over the hours or conditions of work, the wage earned or the design and purpose of the product. Another is that, without choice, the worker has no possibility of the expression of human *creativity* in her or his labour. Industrial labour destroys that fundamental sense of freedom to act which Marx calls our 'species being'. Worst of all, *co-operation* between workers is made impossible. Instead they are forced to compete against each other for employment, in order not to starve. Here again the fundamental humanness of the worker, the fact that co-operation in work is one of the ways in which we know ourselves to be human, is denied.

This analysis is neither more nor less than a practical reflection on what was actually happening to human beings in early industrialism. In the twentieth century the dilemma has become more complex. On the one hand we have deep concern about the plight of the 'underdeveloped' countries, where poverty – perhaps the result of climatic change or population growth or bad government – has also been seen as resulting from a lack of industrial power. Certainly from the 1960s onwards industrialisation was seen as the major answer to 'Third World' problems. Yet the most successful industrialisation has tended to bring with it the same problems of a suffering proletariat.

Consequently, what Marx saw may not have been a necessity of capitalist organisation but a short-term result of rapid industrialisation. On the other hand, it may be that in the more 'mature' industrial nations the development of the countervailing forces of trades unions and of democratic representation has successfully modified what would otherwise have been the natural tendencies of capitalism. For mature capitalism the returns are not yet in.

The positive analysis of the modern capitalist industrial society comes from the approach known as *functionalism*. Emile Durkheim, whose work on religion has already been mentioned, was also one of the first to attempt a structural analysis of the social changes involved in the development of industrial society.

In *The Division of Labour in Society*, first published in 1893, he suggested that the process of the division of labour into increasingly specialised tasks has two effects. Economically, as Adam Smith had pointed out in the previous century, it gave a vastly greater efficiency to production, so that goods could be made in large quantities at low costs. In this sense a whole society becomes richer, even though relative inequalities remain. Politically the division of labour had two effects. By reducing the tightly-controlled relations between people which are the rule in traditional societies it gave greater freedom of choice to individuals. At the same time this greater individualism tended to weaken all the ties which bind a society together.

Durkheim's first interest was in the relationships between different institutions in a society, rather than in the relationships between individuals and institutions. In the first edition of *The Division of Labour in Society* he was concerned mainly with the way in which different parts were held together in a society which no longer had the unchallenged customary rule of traditional societies. The autonomy of institutions in modern society could easily become what he called *anomie*, a situation in which a society becomes 'an aggregate of disconnected parts that fail to co-operate with one another' (p. 304).

This Durkheim regarded as an abnormal condition of society. In the normal course of events the division of labour should produce a harmony visible even to the individual worker. 'The division of labour supposes that the worker, far from remaining bent over his task, does not lose sight of those co-operating with him, but acts upon them and is acted upon by them' (p. 308). In this way the worker is not a machine, but 'feels that he is of some use'.

Nevertheless Durkheim recognised that the speed with which change had taken place from agricultural to industrial forms of production created in fact a moral problem about the aims and methods of social organisation, which he described as 'an appalling crisis' (p. 339). For the harmonious working of an industrial society required that 'social inequalities express precisely natural inequalities'. By this he meant that workers should not only be free from forced labour but also that 'no obstacle whatsoever prevents them from occupying within the ranks of society a position commensurate to their abilities' (p. 313). This was a formidable requirement and one which Durkheim increasingly recognised as not being achieved.

By the time he came to write the preface to the second edition, Durkheim was greatly concerned about means to ensure this 'spontaneity', not through the state, but through intermediate organisations which would combine solidarity with flexibility. In fact he had the same problem as Marx, of how to ensure that the new society worked. When Marx and later Lenin put their trust in central control by a party élite, Durkheim had no such illusion of a godly rule. Consequently the problem remained without a solution.

The functionalist successors to Durkheim were, therefore, left with no option but to tinker with a society that could not produce fundamental satisfactions. Either that or to posit a spurious harmony which could only exist as a cover for what was in fact still a form of forced labour. As Durkheim grimly commented at the end of *The Division of Labour in Society*, 'The new life that all of a sudden has arisen has not been able to organise itself thoroughly. Above all, it has not been organised so as to satisfy the need for justice that has been aroused more passionately in our hearts' (p. 339). These words, first written in 1893, can stand for the whole social experience of the twentieth century.

This brings us to the third approach to the study of society, the *social action* approach which derives mainly from the work of Max Weber, a near-contemporary of Durkheim. Weber argued that the modern world, beginning with the Reformation and early capitalism, was based on an almost entirely new form of organisation, the rational-legal form, as opposed to the forms based on tradition in older societies, and the charismatic form of organisation, based on a personal response to an outstanding leader, which would occasionally break out in opposition to the tradition. Modern society is based neither on tradition nor on personal leadership, but on rules and to some extent on competition according to merit. The prevailing institution of the modern form of society is bureaucracy.

Wilbert Moore points out that today we can see that this modern form is fundamentally flawed:

> The limits to secularisation are symptomatic of the limits to rationalisation generally. In addition to the inescapable significance of human emotion and of affective patterns of interaction, there are collective or system-oriented limits to rationality. Rationality describes a calculated choice of effective means for given ends but is not the basis for the ends pursued ... Bureaucratic organisation lends itself at least as well to warfare or internal repression as it does to producing

cars or distributing welfare benefits. ('Functionalism', in Bottomore and Nisbet, *A History of Sociological Analysis*, p. 356)

Modern society, in fact, is essentially unstable. Social systems, lacking a proper means to incorporate and express collective values, 'are no longer self-equilibrating entities but rather systems in constant disequilibrium because of deliberate change, unintended consequences of change, and the very unequal susceptibility of segments of conventionalised behaviour to the master process of rationalisation' (p. 356).

In this situation conflicts may or may not give good outcomes, but we cannot hope to live without them. Individuals choose goals and undertake actions in order to get to the goals. Systems produce results which may be neither beneficial to particular individuals nor intended by those who run the systems. Harmony and stability may then be false social aims because they depend on the assumption that there is only one 'right' social outcome to any situation. This is indeed an intrinsically authoritarian assumption, no matter who makes it or to what purpose.

As Alan Dawe puts it, our experience of the major institutions of modern society is contradictory. 'On the one hand we are "nothing more than a machine". On the other hand, against these massive odds, we persist in our stubborn refusal to be less than "just human"' ('Theories of Social Action', in Bottomore and Nisbet, *A History of Sociological Analysis*, p. 365). The conclusion is that we have to accept the necessity of an ambiguity at the heart of our social life. On the one hand we fear chaos and really do have a need of 'systems' to protect us from it. On the other hand these same systems are always also enemies of human creativity and moral promise.

(ii) Dehumanisation

Chepe Mozote was 7 years old at the time, one of a group of children taken by the soldiers to a playing field near the school. He told Mr Danner: 'I didn't really understand what was happening until I saw a soldier take a kid he had been carrying – maybe 3 years old – throw him in the air and stab him with a bayonet. They slit some of the kids' throats, and many they hanged from the tree ... The soldiers kept telling us: "You are guerrillas and this is justice. This is justice." Finally, there were only three of us left. I watched them hang my brother. He was 2 years old. I could see that I was going to be killed soon, and I thought it would be better to die running, so I ran... .' (Anthony Lewis, 'No Denying the Deaths of El Mozote', *International Herald Tribune*, 7 December 1993, reprinted from *The New York Times*)

Mr Lewis' article is a report of the account by Mark Danner in *The New Yorker* of the previous week of a massacre carried out in December 1981 in El Salvador by troops trained by the US government, a massacre which was persistently denied by the Reagan administration in the USA, despite a report by its own ambassador, Deane Hinton, that such an event had probably taken place (the government of El Salvador refused to allow embassy investigators to enter the area). Lewis comments that the priority of the US government was not to establish the truth, but to ensure that the Congress would continue military aid to El Salvador. The final irony was that far from being inclined to the guerrillas, 'In fact El Mozote was a stronghold of evangelical Christians, who were fiercely anti-Communist.'

The 'truth' of this small massacre in El Salvador was thus defined by a political point of view. This practice of bayoneting babies, or the choice of ignorance about this fact, could, to serious-minded and well-informed people, seem justified in resisting a different ideology, or in keeping down an ethnically distinct people, or simply in not raising complicated questions about economic and political programmes that were profitable to many people. This is the human dilemma, that such choices are possible.

The realities underlying policy are usually concealed from us under broad generalisations. It does not make much difference what the political colour of the concealing government may be, except that the 'democratic form', not least in the USA, does have a commitment among some of its citizens also to discover 'truth'.

The mandate of human dignity, the fundamental moral demand that arises out of our existence as moral beings, lies in this commitment to truth. Yes indeed we need order in society, but not beyond a certain price. The level at which the price is set, by our existence as rational beings capable of knowing and of loving others, is that we

should never let another human being fall below this basic requirement of dignity, that we should recognise them as an other like
ourselves.

Once the human being is made into an object, as 'a Communist',
'a supporter of guerrillas', an 'enemy' of some sort, the moral game,
the game of being human, is already lost. This is the point at which
it becomes possible to speak of 'objective morality', that the process
which denies human dignity is always an evil. This is the base line
of Fletcher's 'act responsibly in love', the one commandment, to
love God and to love the neighbour as the self. So the *fatwa*, the
condemnation to death for 'blasphemy' against the author Salman
Rushdie by Iran's Ayatollah Khomeini in 1989, is a profound moral
evil; so the hatred of 'Communists' has been a profound moral evil;
so is all ethnic and religious hatred.

The trouble is that the capacity for these evils is well-embedded
in the general human consciousness. The inhumanity of the El
Salvador massacre or the Iranian *fatwa* is latent in all of us. We all
have the capacity to treat others as less than human, though it may
take a lot of pressure to bring us to this point. Then it is the self which
is lost. We do indeed see the other as 'like ourselves', but the self we
project is the self which is capable of bayoneting a child or condemn-
ing another to death. The urgent need for 'moral authority' in
society is not to protect us from the (often imaginary) potential for
attacks from others, but to protect us from the self that we have the
potential to become through fear. Moral duty is the acceptance for
ourselves that there *is* a level below which, by the way that we behave
to others, we cannot be true human selves.

In this perspective the use of violence becomes intelligible as a
denial of the personal reality of the other in a way which makes the
other easier to handle and also affirms, falsely but for the moment
effectively, my own superior moral reality. Since most human
beings emerge from their family upbringing without a wholly stable
sense of personal existence – since indeed the achievement of such
stability is the adult human task – we always present a danger to one
another. Violence and denial of the other are basic human possibilities.

Consequently the experience of the use of power to exercise
violence runs in an unbroken chain from domestic violence and the
abuse of children to mass destruction in warfare. Closed institutions
are particularly vulnerable to this sort of damaging use of power. A

young man alleging abuse by the staff at a home for young offenders in which he had once been an inmate said, according to a recent report, 'The routine physical abuse ranged from a punch in the face, strangulations, suffocation, canes, hair-pulling, pushing, banging heads on walls, kicking while on the floor, being kicked in the genitals, being grabbed by the genitals, to being hit by the black-board' (*The Observer*, 13 September 1992). This allegation had not been proved in court at the time of writing, but anyone familiar with social affairs in the period since, say, 1945, will find the possibility of such behaviour all too recognisable.

People in closed institutions are, of course, often difficult to deal with. That is why they are there. But as a consultant psychiatrist wrote in a letter to *The Observer* about violent and disturbed long-term prisoners in British prisons, 'The majority were abused at home, at school, in children's homes, in Borstals', and quoted one as saying, 'Since the age of eight, not a day went by when I do not think of killing myself' (15 July 1993, p. 42). This interplay between crime and violence in society and crime and violence in its 'remedial' institutions can sometimes be little short of demonic, but this is not necessarily because of any particular evil in the people who work in such places.

On the contrary, many who work in such institutions may take a keen interest in improving the welfare of their clients. A report in *The Independent* about a young man called 'Simon', in Feltham Young Offenders Unit, who came from a broken home, started his criminal career at the age of eight, was taken into care at the age of nine and had a string of offences to his credit, ends with the young man saying of the training programme, 'Barriers between staff and inmates are broken down. They take you back to your earliest problems. There is a lot of support. I'm taking a diploma in social studies and I am allowed out to do support work at a local day centre ... I'm not going to offend any more. I have caused a lot of people harm ... But now I am helping others' (27 July 1993). In the same issue a report from the Home Affairs Select Committee of the House of Commons noted that 'It is clear that economic and social disadvantage, whether in family background, education, employment or housing, is intertwined with the roots of criminal behaviour by young people.'

None of this is new knowledge. Indeed 'Simon's' chances of going straight on release from Feltham must depend very much on the possibility of his finding work and affordable accommodation on his release. The real difficulties are, on the one hand the sheer complexity of the issues involved in organising society so that work and a place to live *are* available to those who need them; and on the other hand the fact that the cost of dealing with a young offender such as Simon, with fully trained staff in sufficient quantities to have a chance of making a breakthrough in terms of his own self-understanding, is not directly related to the costs incurred by society if the breakthrough does not occur and he goes on with a life of crime.

In other words, we have an *economic* problem about ways in which society is dysfunctional, as well as problems about the *psychology* of crime and the issue of moral choice. To restrict the problem solely to the question of moral choice is to delude oneself that the social issues of identity do not exist. This is not to say, of course, that the problem of individual moral choice is explained away entirely by environmental factors. The individual act is always also a willed act, except in rare cases where mental breakdown prevents any moral responsibility (a condition that is notoriously difficult to define). We have to reckon also with the element of the demonic which lurks within each of us as a potential for harm. The random murder of children may be done by people who are sexually and socially inadequate and who have themselves been abused in the past. But of all those who are inadequate and abused, those who murder are the ones who have also responded to that demon of violence in themselves.

We therefore have a potential for action of various sorts, meant to protect and enhance our social destiny, which is also available for negative use. Every step of this road, from group self-assertion, to territorial defence and other devices of closure, including the creation of negative stereotypes and the controlled use of violence, is intelligible and is available as part of our normal consciousness. When stability in a society breaks down, the negative side of these defences can go into overdrive. On a small scale, this happens in domestic violence. When dislocation occurs on the larger scale, whole societies can become destructive. On Easter Island in the Pacific Ocean the problem apparently began with the ecological error of destroying the forest with which the island was covered, partly as a result of the religious practice of making and erecting the great statues which are still to be seen there. Deforestation caused soil erosion, reducing the possibility of growing crops, and also reduced the ability to manufacture canoes for fishing, reducing the available protein even further. As Jared Diamond tells the story, 'As a result, the population was now greater than Easter could support, and island society collapsed in a holocaust of internecine warfare and cannibalism' (*The Rise and Fall of the Third Chimpanzee*, p. 297).

It does not seem necessary to go back as far as in-built biological responses to account for human group aggression, since there are such clear social reasons available. Jared Diamond stresses the newness in human history of the experiences of having to meet groups of strangers frequently. In field studies in New Guinea he experienced precisely the situation in which most human beings have lived during most of our history:

> Whenever I go bird-watching in New Guinea, I take pains to stop at the nearest village to request permission to bird-watch on that village's land or rivers. On two occasions when I neglected that precaution (or asked permission at the wrong village) and proceeded to boat up the river, I found the river barred on my return by canoes of stone-throwing villagers, furious that I had violated their territory. (*The Rise and Fall of the Third Chimpanzee*, pp. 206–7)

On another occasion, wanting to cross the territory of the Fayu tribe, the Elopi people among whom he was staying 'explained to me matter-of-factory that the Fayus would kill me if I tried'. He comments that it was a reasonable expectation for the New Guineans that, if allowed in, 'Strangers would just hunt their game animals, molest their women, introduce diseases, and reconnoitre the terrain in order to stage a raid later' (p. 207).

Similarly John Crook, writing of the reciprocal altruism of baboons, says that 'Genetic control of such a complex system of behaviour is obviously not at all direct', but adds that low genetic relatedness and greater geographical or social distance are likely to produce 'negative rather than positive reciprocity'. He comments 'The anxieties of strangers in foreign lands are not without foundation, one suspects' (*The Evolution of Human Consciousness*, pp. 177–8).

David Riches refers to studies which suggest that aggression, from large-scale warfare to individual violence under the influence of alcohol, serves specific purposes. He notes that 'few societies are without norms stipulating how violence should be organised – specifying, for example, the sorts of weaponry that might be used against particular adversaries' (*The Anthropology of Violence*, p. 9). We may note in passing that this fact indicates that there is still a place for the continuing use of the concept of the 'just war' in the armoury of Christian ethics, however difficult this may be in the face of both nuclear war and guerilla war.

Riches identifies four basic properties of violence as a specific social resource. The first is that 'violence is inherently liable to be contested on the question of legitimacy' – it is neither accepted nor intended as a 'proper' act. The second is that violence is always an unambiguous act. It is seen to be and meant to be the 'contestable giving of physical hurt'. The third is that 'The practice of violence is highly visible to the senses'. The fourth is that 'The performance of violence to a moderate degree of effectiveness requires relatively little by way of specialised equipment or esoteric knowledge'.

The use of violence as a political act, therefore, is in the widest sense a natural act. It may be modified by various rules and expectations, from family relationships to general social assumptions, but as we have already noted in the quotation from Jared Diamond, it can quickly come into use when we are dealing with people who are outside these limits. It should be emphasised again that violence is primarily willed behaviour. Riches himself concludes that, 'Whilst a biological component to violence need not be ruled out, I believe that much in human violence is perfectly amenable to explanation in terms of the human being's unique mental capacities' (p. 21).

This is true even of one of the great acts of apparent insanity in world history, the attempt by the Nazis to exterminate the Jews of Europe, which in large part succeeded. Here deep social stresses in German national life, arising from the defeat of 1918 and the associated mistrustful feeling of having been betrayed by hidden enemies, and from the economic suffering caused by the reparations demanded by the victors, were exacerbated by the general economic distress in the western world caused by the slump of 1929. All of this then combined fatally under Hitler with a long-standing ideology of racial purity and racial hatred.

Lord Russell of Liverpool, one of the lawyers involved in the Nuremberg war crimes tribunal, says, 'From the very moment

Hitler came to power he and the Nazi Party began to put into execution the common plan or conspiracy whose aims had already been set out in *Mein Kampf* and which included the commission of crimes against peace, war crimes and other crimes against humanity' (*The Scourge of the Swastika*, p. 13).

This plan depended on an ideology of race: 'In *Mein Kampf* Hitler had written years before, "A stronger race will drive out the weaker ones, for the vital urge in its ultimate form will break down the absurd barriers of so-called humanity of individuals to make way for the humanity of Nature which destroys the weak to give their place to the strong"' (p. 11).

Lucy Dawidowicz points out that the Holocaust, the systematic destruction of the Jews in Germany and in occupied Europe, was a carefully planned undertaking. 'The National Socialists regarded this mass murder as nothing less than an ideological war and its prosecution was synergised with the conventional military war' (*The Holocaust and the Historians*, p. 9). The ideology was one of racial purity, and for this ideology six million Jews were murdered, along with hundreds of thousands of patients from mental institutions, of all races, and perhaps a quarter of a million of the Gypsy population. In all this, the Jews were a special case. 'They obsessed Hitler all his life and their presence in Germany, their very existence, preoccupied the policymakers of the German dictatorship. The *Judenfrage* – the question of the Jews – riveted all Germany' (p. 11).

Lord Russell quotes Hans Frank, Governor-General of Poland during the occupation, speaking in his own defence at his trial in 1946: '"We have fought against Jewry for years", he said, "and have indulged in the most horrible utterances – my own diary bears witness against me ... a thousand years will pass and this guilt of Germany will not have been erased"' (*The Scourge of the Swastika*, p. 197).

National Socialism and the Jewish extermination programme had specifically German roots, including a long history of anti-Semitism and of romanticisation of the state. Nevertheless the Holocaust stands as an indictment for the whole of humanity. For Jews and Christians it is, as Arthur Cohen says, 'a radical interruption and break in the continuous unfolding of the divine-human nexus from creation to redemption' ('In our Terrible Age: The *Tremendum* of the Jews', in Schüssler Fiorenza, *The Holocaust as Interruption*, p. 15).

Cohen interprets the event as 'the tremendum', a sign to be pondered-on and feared, but not explained away. It is a reversal of the sign of the rainbow given to Noah. For the Jews were abandoned both by their fellow human beings and by God. Susan Shapiro asks whether language itself has been broken by this event and whether the notion of God can persist? 'What does it mean to be human in a world that performed and passively witnessed such destruction? And how can we now imagine or conceive of a God who did not save under those circumstances? In what sort of language might we even frame these questions and to whom might we address them?' ('Hearing the Testimony of Radical Negation', in Schüssler Fiorenza, *The Holocaust as Interruption*, p. 3).

Rabbi Dan Cohn-Sherbok reviews and rejects a number of ways of dealing with the Holocaust within Judaism, including Arthur Cohen's *tremendum*, and concludes that:

> Contemporary Jewish theology is thus in a state of crisis both deep-seated and acute: for the first time in history Jews seem unable to account for God's ways. This means that for many Jews the Holocaust is a decisive refutation of the traditional concept of a providential God who watches over his chosen people. If Judaism is to retain such a fundamental belief Jewish theologians will need to find a more adequate explanation for the events of the Nazi period. (*Jewish Faith and the Holocaust*, p. 18)

For many the only possible conclusion is that of Elie Wiesel in the words of the narrator of his story *Night*. 'Never shall I forget that nocturnal silence which deprived me, for all eternity, of the desire to live. Never shall I forget those moments which murdered my God and my soul and turned my dreams to dust. Never shall I forget these things, even if I am condemned to live as long as God himself. Never' (p. 43).

Yet even the Holocaust can be understood as a response to a specific situation. Zygmunt Bauman has argued that modernity as a political and economic system is not only incapable of generating social values but also destabilises the ability of other institutions to generate values. In particular the irregularity of capitalism, with its rapid swings from booms to slumps and its unpredictability in terms of personal progress and security, necessarily creates the situation which Emile Durkheim described as *anomie* or 'normlessness', the feeling of not being sufficiently guided and formed by society as a whole. In the resulting breakdown of social order, the capacity for pluralism, the greatest of democratic safeguards, breaks down and is replaced by the authoritarian personality expressed in all totalitarian systems. As Bauman says, paradoxically 'The voice of individual moral conscience is best heard in the tumult of political and social discord' (*Modernity and the Holocaust*, p. 166).

(iii) Racism in Britain

Paulo Freire, the Brazilian Catholic educator, has suggested that concern for 'humanisation' has become 'an inescapable concern of our era' (*Pedagogy of the Oppressed*, p. 20). Though groups have ruled, or attempted to rule, over others in all periods of world history, the significance of the twentieth century is the systematic and pervasive way in which domination has been put into effect by small groups over great masses everywhere. Indeed the century of 'the common man', as the phrase once was, has been the century above all others of stress on division into superior and inferior on grounds of race or religion. In this last decade the century has even invented a new and malevolent term for this habit, the euphemism 'ethnic cleansing'.

Racism is always purposive. 'Ethnic cleansing' is a term designed to conceal the economic and political purposes it serves. The denial over many years that Britain has a problem of racist attitudes in the majority population served to delay the giving of serious attention to real structural and attitudinal obstacles to the full citizenship of Black* people and to put off the perception of any need for change. As the Swann report *Education for All* on the education of children from ethnic minority groups concluded in 1985, the problem lay not in the diverse ethnic groups, but in the host society. The

---

*I am aware that there is a problem about using the word 'Black' to cover West Indian, African, Indian, Pakistani and other ethnic groups. It is, however a useful convention in this context, provided the real variety of experience behind it is also borne in mind.

Committee on Education of the Church of Scotland Board of Education commented in 1990, 'The problem for Britain was not its multiracial character but its racism' (*Multicultural Education*, 1.3, p. 1).

The Committee on Education adopted a definition of racism given by Michael Banton:

> Racism is the doctrine that a person's behaviour is deter-mined by stable inherited characters deriving from separate racial stocks having distinctive attributes and usually consid-ered to stand to one another in relations of superiority and inferiority. (Banton, 'The Concept of Racism', p. 18, cited in *Multicultural Education*, 3.1, p. 3)

This, as the Committee rightly states, is a false doctrine. Genetically there is only one 'race', the species *Homo sapiens*. What we call 'racism' is for most people not this implausible ideology, but a cover for group purposes aiming at some sort of domination.

We could, of course, in Britain have attempted to learn much earlier from the American example what the nature of 'racism' really is. In Mississippi in the South of the USA in August 1955 a fourteen-year old black boy, visiting from Chicago in the freer North, was murdered by two white men, Millam and Bryant. As James Campbell tells the story in his life of James Baldwin:

> Accepting a dare from some friends, Emmett Till had gone into a store and asked the young woman behind the counter for a date. He called her 'baby'. She told her husband Roy Bryant about it, and he and Millam went to the house where Till was staying and drove him away in a car. After torturing him for several hours, they murdered him and threw the body into the river. (*Talking at the Gates*, p. 122)

Millam and Bryant were acquitted for 'lack of evidence', but later told their story to *Look* magazine. As Campbell comments, this killing was 'not by any means an isolated incident'. It was, in fact, part of a sustained and systematic attempt, which ultimately failed, to maintain white supremacy in the South in the face of the growing Civil Rights Movement.

I think that we were misled in Britain in the 1960s by the fact that this sort of outrageous violence was not visible among us. Consequently the people who should have been concerned, including most people in the churches, concluded that we did not have a problem. We did, however, have a problem, but in a slightly more subtle form. This was well documented in the 1960s, in such works as Henri Tajfel and John Dawson, *Disappointed Guests* and E. J. B. Rose, *Colour and Citizenship*. But the general stereotypes were not seriously challenged.

Today, as the situation has worsened and as the challenge from the Black community has sharpened, we can identify three areas for particular concern: these are employment, racially-motivated violence, and a general refusal to admit the existence of an institutional problem of racism in Britain.

In the area of employment, two points can be made. The first is that there is clear evidence that ethnic minority groups have more difficulty in finding employment than the majority group. The Church of Scotland Committee on Education quotes research by the Policy Studies Institute on youth employment:

> The 1985 Labour Force Survey showed that over thirty per cent of West Indian men, twenty eight per cent of Indian men and thirty seven per cent of Pakistani and Bangladeshi men in the sixteen to twenty four age group were unemployed, compared with less than twenty per cent among white men. As for women in the same age group, thirty three per cent of West Indian and twenty per cent of Asian women were unemployed, compared with roughly fifteen per cent among white women. (Colin Brown, *Black and White Britain*, p. 72, cited in *Multicultural Education*, 7.7, p. 18)

That this is not only a British problem is confirmed by the report of a consultation organised by the World Council of Churches in 1975, which said that 'We are faced with overwhelming evidence from multiracial societies throughout the world that being black or white results in significantly different levels of access to and participation in education, employment, housing, health and all the other amenities society has to offer. Power, in short, resides overwhelmingly with the white members of these societies' (*Racism in Theology and Theology Against Racism*, p. 12).

While it is essential, in order to understand our society, to distinguish the specifically Black experience of disadvantage in employment opportunities, it is important also to see this as part of a wider experience of disadvantage, in which the white working class have already accepted that there must be someone – a lot of people – 'at the bottom of the heap':

> At this point, they are in an unperceived alliance with the members of various nations within Britain who are disenchanted with the current political options and who seek a political ideal which is more relevant to disadvantaged minorities. This is a development in the understanding of democracy which is urgent and essential if we are to be a just society. Black people have made the problems more identifiable within Britain, but even without them the standard understanding of democracy has become inadequate. Perhaps the sharpest question which has come to us in our investigation is this: is it possible for a British type of society to exist except as a heap with a group of people at the bottom? Is it possible to be so interested in success, without a group of failures to make success credible? (*The New Black Presence in Britain: A Christian Scrutiny*, p. 24)

Even in 1975, when a British Council of Churches' Working Party made this statement, it was possible to recognise forms of domination that were implicit in the economic structures prevailing in Britain and the danger not only to community relations but even to democracy itself of the pursuit of unrestrained greed. The Black community posed the question with particular sharpness, but it was a question for every citizen.

The second major issue is that of violence. The report of the Church of Scotland Committee on Education begins with a reference to 'the racist killing of a Somalian student in the Cowgate, Edinburgh' in 1989. Further on it notes:

> A survey by the Scottish Ethnic Minorities Research Unit of 100 people of minority ethnic origin in Glasgow in 1986 found that forty nine per cent of Pakistanis and fifty five per cent of Indians had experienced damage to their property; that over eighty per cent of both groups had experienced racial abuse; and eighteen per cent of Pakistanis and twenty two per cent of Indians had experienced physical attack. (*Multicultural Education*, 3.7, p. 4)

The Committee also notes that 'the media are themselves open to censure for being racist, either actively or passively' (3.8). It adds a comment from an article on the Edinburgh murder:

> It is one thing, though bad enough, adjusting to the knowledge that isolated gangs of racists might attack you late at night on a dark street. It is another to realise that nobody cares, that your murder would not even merit a line in a national newspaper, especially when you know full well that had it been the other way round – had a gang of black youths murdered an innocent white – there would have been screaming headlines in every tabloid in Britain. (Callum Macrae, *The Observer*, 15 January 1989, cited in *Multicultural Education*, p. 5)

Since 1989 more attention has been paid to this issue by police forces. It certainly has to be recognised that Britain is a society with a very high level of acceptance of violent acts. *The Independent* on 30 December 1993 reported that in a survey 'only' 2 per cent of 3,000 teachers surveyed had experienced physical aggression from pupils *in the last week*. A union official estimated that about 3,000 teachers a year suffer some form of assault. It is generally accepted that this problem is getting worse.

In this context it has to be recognised also that the police themselves suffer a good deal of violence and are in the front line of whatever is going on in our society. Nevertheless it is clear that there is a very substantial general problem of mistrust between the police and the young in the Black community, which is part of, but also distinct from, the general mistrust between the police and almost all the young working class.

Behind the specificity of this problem lies the deeper fact that official attitudes, particularly in the Home Office, the government department responsible for police forces, have an inbuilt racist bias, which is most clear in the immigration laws and procedures:

> Most conspicuous amongst those measures sustaining a political climate hostile to ethnic minorities are the immigration and nationality laws. They were passed in circumstances which made it clear that the government intended to keep out non-whites, with the implication that the very presence of these people was somehow problematic. Away from the public gaze the restrictive and discriminatory measures are

implemented in an oppressive and, at times, cruel way. Children are kept from their parents, adults are prevented from caring for their parents, spouses are separated and visitors are removed before seeing their friends. These practices are not accidental or simply tolerated, they are institutionalised (*Multicultural Education*, 7.1, pp. 16–17)

As the Committee also notes, 'The enforcement of the immigration laws since the mid-1960s has, in itself, also been a major factor poisoning police attitudes towards the non-white population' (7.3, p. 17).

Kenneth Leech notes that the riots in Brixton in London and in Moss Side in Manchester in 1982 which led to the Scarman report were not race riots. 'Certainly the racial element was crucial, but they were not conflicts *between* races. In Brixton there was a fair cross-section of black and white people. In Moss Side the majority of those arrested were white' (*Struggle in Babylon*, p. 107). Nevertheless much of the impetus for these events came from a build-up of hostility to black people on the side of the police. Leech quotes from Gabrielle Cox's report, *The Church of England and Racism – and Beyond* (1982):

Young people from ethnic minorities fear the police. They do not respect them. Their fear springs from experience: they are often stopped in the streets to be questioned or searched; many are racially abused; some are beaten in police custody; and others are criminalised on the perjured evidence of policemen. Parents of these young people have gradually come to realise that a Christian upbringing and the instilling of standards of honesty and integrity do not safeguard their children from such practices since racism discriminates in terms of colour not behaviour. This is not the judgment of blinkered political extremism: it is a sad and bitter witness of church members from multi-racial inner city communities throughout the country. (Cox, p. 23, quoted in Leech, p. 109)

The difficulty that the white community has in admitting all this is the third major issue of British racism. It is a deep-rooted human habit to protect the boundaries of our groups by creating stereotypes, pictures of the other and of ourselves which simplify our judgments and justify our attitudes. As Roger Brown remarks, stereotypes have a rational basis in the sense that they perform an intelligible function in the world. 'Natural category formation is a very primitive process and also a non-deliberate, almost effortless process that requires nothing more than attention to an array of instances' (*Social Psychology*, p. 594). Stereotypes can, in particular circumstances, be overcome by education, through specific information, but ethnic stereotypes are, so to speak, community operations which are difficult for individuals to overcome by themselves.

For this reason anyone who is white in Britain has to accept themself as a racist at least in the sense of being the holder of community stereotypes which have their force from being largely unrecognised as such. Stereotypes are fed down from parents to children, and from older children to younger children, in defiance even of the child's own positive experiences of children of other races. Where the child is from a minority community, white children may feed-in a negative self-image.

Canon Wilfred Wood has said 'The outstanding need in the Black community is to adjust to a strong self-image. The outstanding need in the White community is to adjust to a proud Black man, and here the concept of charity is a stumbling block. There is a stifled resentment of Black people asserting claims to rights as distinct from favours' (quoted in David Sheppard, *The Black Experience in Britain*, p. 14). Help 'from above' which keeps control out of the hands of the Black community is not real help. The churches have not been much better at learning this lesson, so far, than anyone else, except some in the inner-city areas. The sad fact is that stereotypes are challenged most effectively face to face. The churches consequently still need a long period of listening hard to what Black leaders are saying to them. Even a genuine commitment to Jesus Christ, as a white person in a white community, does not in itself qualify anyone to know what the Black experience is.

What is needed, on the part of the white community, is not charity, but the simple recognition of the equality of Black people in every respect in our society. This is not a matter of goodwill, though it begins with goodwill, but of taking actions to see that the institutions of our society do not work in the wrong direction. In employment this means two things.

The first is a concern for 'equal opportunities', the provision of a level playing field in which Black people can get jobs on the basis of the same qualifications as whites. Today this needs a clear policy by all organisations, including churches, to inspect their own practices and to account for the results. It has been clear for a long time that Black people are under-represented in Parliament, in the law, in medicine, in the military and in the police. The consistency of this bias is such that it cannot be brushed away as accidental or accounted-for by anything other than racial bias, including those biases in the educational system against all the inhabitants of the 'inner cities' which add to the problems of ethnic minorities.

Alongside the provision of equal opportunities there is the need also for 'affirmative action':

> Affirmative action does not mean giving someone a job, just because he is Black, even though you know he is not competent to do it. It means that special and appropriate training should be offered to those who are at a particular disadvantage, to help them reach the starting gate; and there should be sensitive support for those who are holding posts which have not been filled by Black people before. If this subtle and widely pervasive discrimination is to be removed, there needs to be a persistent programme of persuasion by every employer and every Trade Union. (David Sheppard, *The Black Experience in Britain*, p. 12)

As David Sheppard also says, 'If we are to reflect the righteousness – *tsedeq* – of the living, eyes-wide-open, God of grace, the righteousness which topples over in favour of those at a disadvantage, we should argue unashamedly for policies which will intervene on behalf of those in special need.'

The situation in Britain today in terms of race relations is not good, but in one sense at least it is better than it was twenty years ago. Largely because of the challenge from the Black community, and the white community's own loss of faith in its symbols and institutions, from the Crown to the police, from the political parties to the law courts, from the newspapers to Lloyds of London, there is greater readiness than ever before to accept that there are problems of racism. The American example also shows us daily that there is no such thing as 'benign neglect' and that the impoverishment of one part of the whole community will sooner or later affect all the others as well, in terms of the rise in the use of drugs and in crime and in the corruption of public life. The problem of 'order' is, in the end, a seamless garment. Only if all are properly served can any be properly served.

(iv) Human Rights

One of the most effective barriers to the unjust use of power is a proper understanding of human rights. There is an immediate problem here for theological discussion, in that the notion of human rights is a recent concept and one that comes from secular sources. The fundamental theological notion is of the human being as a creature made by God and therefore owing duties to God. In the face of God the creator there can be no notion of 'rights' as such. The obligation of one human creature to another arises from the common origin, the fact of creatureliness. As creatures all, we cannot have power over another except to further God's purposes on earth.

This Biblical view works within a further notion of social order as given by God. The Old Testament certainly contains evidence of concern about social changes affecting social justice. The looking back to the ideal of the life in the desert, the dispute about the introduction of kingship and the civilisational way of life, and the constant concern that the poor and the weak are not being looked after – all these themes imply that the Old Testament writers do not simply regard the existing social order as just and given by God.

In the New Testament the emphasis shifts to the citizenship of the future kingdom, the event of the visible reign of God. At the same time it is made clear that this kingdom is for every human being. All that is necessary is to accept the way of Jesus, not as an arbitrary condition, but as a recognition precisely of the rights of others and of the dignity of the self. The German theologian Hans Küng caused a stir at a UNESCO conference in 1989 by stating that 'only a religion that promoted true humanity, *humanitas*, could be a true and good religion ... what matters in the end is that a human being should behave in a truly humane way towards fellow human beings. In this sense, true humanity is indeed the prerequisite of true religion.' In reflecting on this experience, however, Küng now adds, 'But the converse has also become clear. True religion, in so far as it is directed in this form at one's fellow human beings, is the

fulfilment of true *humanitas*' ('Towards a World Ethic of World
Religions', in Küng and Moltmann, *The Ethics of World Religions
and Human Rights*, pp. 117–18). Küng argues that not only
Christians but all the major religions are already in agreement on the
most basic ethical commandments. He lists them as:

> Thou shalt not kill the innocent.
> Thou shalt not lie or break promises.
> Thou shalt not commit adultery or fornication.
> Thou shalt do good. (p. 116)

What is necessary now is to give some substance to such concepts
through political practice. In the western Christian tradition there
have been two main areas of concern about what can broadly be
called human rights. They are the rules for justice in warfare and the
notion of fundamental political rights in the form of 'natural rights'.

The rules which were developed in the Middle Ages about the
'just war' required that it should be declared by a properly-consti-
tuted authority, for a legally sound cause, and with a clearly-defined
goal; that it should be conducted in a manner proportionate to that
goal (i.e. a moderate use of force), and that the innocent (civilians
generally and women and children in particular) should not be
treated as combatants. While elements of this argument continue to
have force, the general propositions have been weakened by the
modern acceptance of the notion of total warfare, by the massive
forces of destruction now available up to and including atomic
weapons; and by the development of guerrilla warfare and terror-
ism, to which it is difficult to make such rules apply. In this area it
seems now that the proper Christian moral approach would be to
find alternatives to the use of force rather than to justify it.

It was the experience of the two world-wide wars of 1914–18 and
1939–45 that led to the formulation of the 'Universal Declaration
of Human Rights' in 1948. The notion of 'natural rights', that
human beings, as rational creatures, are born in a state of equality
among themselves with regard to the basic features of existence, and
that, therefore, they should also enjoy political equality among
themselves, were first stated in a legal, rather than a theological, form
by Hugo Grotius in the seventeenth century. Human rights acquired political force with the American 'Declaration of Independence' in 1776 and the French 'Declaration of the Rights of Man and

of the Citizen' in 1789. Because these first modern political revolutions were overthrowing established rule in the name of some more fundamental order, they needed to lay down a claim which did not depend on past history. As the French Declaration puts it, 'Man is born free and equal in rights. Social distinctions can only be founded on general usefulness' (Hans Küng and Jurgen Moltmann, *The Ethics of World Religions and Human Rights*, p. 3).

The United Nations' Declaration of 1948 was an ambitious attempt to put a great deal of detail into this general notion. Though it was not itself a legally binding document, Sean MacBride comments that 'Certainly, by now most international lawyers of repute regard the *Universal Declaration of Human Rights* as forming part of international customary law' ('The Universal Declaration – Thirty Years After', in Alan Falconer, *Understanding Human Rights*, p. 11). The attempt to make the Declaration effective by means of a system of regional courts of human rights, culminating in the World Court, set up by international legal agreements, has been a major step in making human rights a realistic concept. The practical working out of such a structure, however, still depends on the goodwill of governments, since these courts have no powers to compel compliance and their rulings have been ignored by countries ranging from Albania to the United States of America.

There is also the problem of different cultural interpretations of the very wide social and cultural 'rights' of the later paragraphs of the Universal Declaration. Nevertheless, what has begun to be established by the existence of this document and the first faltering means of putting it into practice is that states cannot in principle expect to go unchallenged in future about what is done within their own borders. The theory of the 'just war' said that states are not necessarily to be trusted in their own acts of territorial defence and offence. The theory and practice of the 'Universal Declaration' establishes, in Sean MacBride's words, that 'no matter how well intentioned or democratic a State may be, it is nevertheless necessary to provide effective machinery for the protection of the rights of the public or of individual members of the public' (p. 17).

MacBride spells out the necessary minimum structures within a state:

1. A watchful parliament with an effective and courageous opposition.

2. A free press which will not hesitate to expose injustice.

3. A constitution which spells out the rights guaranteed and delimits clearly the powers of the executive, the legislature and the judiciary.

4. An independent judiciary, not subject to direct or indirect pressures by the Executive or by Parliament, charged with the function of upholding the constitution and enforcing its provisions.

5. An 'ombudsman' directly responsible to parliament and/ or administrative tribunals with full power of investigation of complaints of maladministration. (p. 18)

The question of theology follows on from the question of structure. Both the notion of the 'just war' and the notion of 'human rights' represent an acceptance of the fact that to be human is to experience conflict. The work of Christian faith is to recognise our own contribution to the tally of sin, as individuals and as churches, but to recognise also that our calling is to enter into situations of conflict for the good of the humanity of all human beings. As Alan Falconer puts it:

> God continues to be a 'scandal' to us. He challenges us through the situations of conflict, which are presented to us as claims to human dignity, and for acceptance with the differences inherent in being human. The challenge to Christians is to respond to the 'word of God' as presented to us through human beings who have specific needs as they strive to affirm their humanity. ('Theological Reflections on Human Rights', in Falconer, *Understanding Human Rights*, p. 216)

Conflict in inescapable, but God is to be found in the conflict. There we must be also.

It is not the business of theological ethics to lay down the specifics of human rights, either the detailed claims or the means of putting them into practice. That has to be a task for the whole of humanity. But theology can and must state the fundamentals of the issue. Hans Küng records that at a 'World Conference of Religions for Peace' at

Kyoto in 1970, the assembled delegates declared that a universal ethic might be:

> a conviction of the fundamental unity of the human family, of the equal dignity of all men and women;

> a sense of the sacrosanctity of the individual and his or her conscience;

> a sense of the value of the human community;

> a recognition that might is not the same as right, that human might cannot be self-sufficient and is not absolute;

> the belief that love, compassion, selflessness and the power of the mind and inner truthfulness have, in the end, more power than hatred, enmity and self-interest;

> a sense of obligation to stand on the side of the poor and oppressed against the rich and the oppressors;

> deep hope that good will, in the end, triumph. ('Towards a World Ethic of World Religions', in Küng and Moltman *The Ethics of World Religions and Human Rights*, pp. 118–19)

The battle for human rights is not in the end a battle for particulars – it is a battle for the right to exist, as a human being, in a world which is our common property under God, the creator to whom all moral obedience is owed, and to whom answer must be made for every action that is less than fully just.

3

THE MANDATE OF THE SANCTITY OF LIFE

(i) The Christian Moral Perspective

The primary task of living is, of course, that of maintaining life itself. St Thomas Aquinas said that one of the first rules of the natural law was that every being 'seeks its own preservation according to its own nature' (*Summa Theologia*, I–II, Qu. 94, Art. 2; D'Entrèves, p. 123). Yet for the animals that we are with human consciousness, this cannot be the complete answer. For we know that our lives must end in our deaths. This is the fact that makes life, in the existentialists' sense, 'absurd'. The ethical task, consequently, is to deal with life in such a way as to make it no longer absurd, but meaningful.

Here Christian ethics parts company decisively with some other forms of ethics. For it says that the purpose of life now is to prepare for a future life, more glorious but also more difficult, since the future life has higher ethical demands than the present one. The task of the present life is to 'foresee' the future life and to bring it into being now. In this way we prepare for a future which must sooner or later become our own present, the life beyond death.

The quality of life today is to be measured by the degree of its preparation for this future, not by success on any present terms. A good life is one which leads most directly into the future life of the kingdom of God. Death is not the collapse of our hopes, but the gateway through which our hopes must become realities. The death which matters is the possible death of the soul. As Ray S. Anderson says, 'for Christian theology the answer comes to us in the middle of life, not at its boundary' (*Theology, Death and Dying*, p. 11).

At the same time death remains arbitrary, beyond our control. It approaches in unpleasant ways. Very naturally, we wish to take whatever measures we can to seize control of both the beginning and

54

the end of life. Our ways of doing so are the subject of this chapter. Before we get on to the technical possibilities, however, there are two moral observations to be made.

Unfortunately for those who like things to be cut and dried, the Christian hope of the kingdom does not produce any very clear-cut rules on the issues of life and death. But two general principles can be laid down, of *responsibility* and of *compassion.*

The first moral command is that we are responsible for life, human and non-human. Though we do not directly create it, we are nevertheless answerable for it. In Christian thought this stems directly from our responsibility as members of the future kingdom, to which all life belongs. Even humanly, however, as bearers of moral consciousness we may have a responsibility to honour life as a potential which we should help to come to fulfilment wherever possible. Even if that potential consists of no more than its contribution to a food chain, it should not be destroyed or altered wantonly.

As human beings we need the earth and for our own sakes we need to preserve that which is not us, to preserve our own sense of being within a system of co-operation and co-dependence. We are not random powers. As Jesus says in the Gospel of Matthew, 'Are not two sparrows sold for a penny? Yet without your Father's knowledge not one of them can fall to the ground' (Matthew 10.29).

The second moral command is that of compassion. A moral concern which is restricted to the rational thoughts of an autonomous being is not enough. Within the kingdom the moral requirement is to feel for the other as for the self. All the moral systems which relate to a single centre of consciousness, be they Christian or Jewish or Islamic or Buddhist, have this at their heart. Both the God of the Christians and the experience of the Buddha lead us to see every pain and every joy as something to be shared and gone beyond, though they have very different ways of describing the process. For Christians every human life must be respected, not only for its potential to grow, but also for its present share in the divine glory. Full human life is the power to love and suffer and rejoice with other human beings and with other created life.

Christian ethics sees the extension of compassion from human to non-human life as a process not of right but of the duty of attribution. Compassion does not seem to be a non-human attribute (one might say that other creatures in creation have not yet risen to this moral stance). Yet those who have the power of compassion have a duty to use it as widely as possible, and certainly to use it towards other species than ourselves. It is 'attributed' because the non-human cannot call for compassion on a basis of equality, but this act of giving care is a necessary part of human experience. It is, however, relative to the purposes of creatures, since we do not yet live in a situation in which all is already perfected. As God says in the address to Job:

> Who provides the raven with its quarry
>   when its fledglings cry aloud,
>   croaking for lack of food? (Job 38.41)

Food chains are also part of the practical 'divine plan'. The whole creation is a process leading into the growth of moral consciousness, perhaps for all of life, but we are not yet at that moment. Meanwhile the basic mechanisms of survival and of evolutionary change remain.

(ii) Aiding Fertility

The most dramatically changing area of ethics today is that of bioethics, which refers to the ways in which we can change the workings of living organisms. Today we have the technical means to aid or to prevent fertility, to identify medical conditions in which it might be appropriate to bring about 'a good death' and to change the design of life itself through genetic engineering.

In most of these changes the interest lies in what we can do to our own particular organism, the human body. Where 'western' standards of medical care can be obtained it is now possible to give hope to the infertile, to prevent pregnancy for those who are fertile, to bring an end to a life beginning to form in the womb and to intervene through surgery, drugs and machinery to maintain life to the point where some are now beginning to demand the right to die. All of this arises from human capacities which are good in themselves. Both the vision of change and the technical capacities which make it possible are achievements which call for admiration and awe, whatever the moral difficulties which follow on from these triumphs. Nevertheless, the question remains, have we now come dangerously close to fulfilling the ancient human ambition of replacing God with our own intelligence and moral sense?

In the Bible reproducing the species is the primary command given to the newly-created human beings. 'God blessed them and said to them, "Be fruitful and increase, fill the earth and subdue it, have dominion over the fish in the sea, the birds of the air, and every living thing that moves on the earth"' (Genesis 1.28). In the theory of 'natural law' the right to reproduce its own kind is seen as part of the basic gift which makes every living being what it is. In human beings the gifts of intelligence and moral sense mean that the reproduction of ourselves through the sexual act continues through the carrying of the child and the moment of birth into the nurture of the child and on to the beginning of the adult human being. The self-fulfilment of individuals is thus also an act of co-creation, a sharing of the divine power of ordering the universe.

Consequently, one of the major challenges to bioethics in this century has been to give help to those couples who want to have children but are unable to do so. This is not merely the meeting of a human whim, nor is it only the rational fulfilment of an abstract 'right to have a child', if such a right can be asserted. Rather it is the meeting of a pain which is not unlike, though perhaps not as deep, as the loss of a child who is already born. The human need which is felt here is a profound example of the inter-relation of the physical, the emotional and the spiritual life. If technique can help to achieve what is, theologically, a calling to share in God's work of creation, then that technique must be assumed to be good unless strong arguments are produced against it.

Here a digression is necessary into some basic biology. Human reproduction is essentially a matter of bringing together two cells which are specially designed to join together, one from the female and one from the male. These gametes form the beginning of a new human being. In the male the gamete is the sperm, produced in large quantities and designed to travel after the sexual act inside the female body to meet and penetrate the female gamete in the fallopian tube. The female gamete is the ovum or 'egg', which is produced at the tips of the two fallopian tubes which lead into the womb. Unlike the sperm the ova are not manufactured by the body in an on-going process. All the eggs that will become available in the fertile years are already present in the female body at birth. In the fertile years, during which the woman is able to conceive and carry a baby, the eggs ripen and are released at the rate of one or two in each monthly reproductive or 'menstrual' cycle.

Human females appear to be unique in the animal kingdom in having the possibility of conceiving a child throughout the year, rather than in restricted periods of fertility, but are also unique in not having any outward sign of when in the month they are fertile and when they are not. This has always made it difficult to plan the conception of a child. This difficulty is increased by the fact that even in the fertile period the task of the sperm in finding and penetrating the fertile egg is relatively hard – the sperm have a long way to travel, are easily damaged and may not be present in sufficient quantities in the male emission for some to make the full journey and for at least one to penetrate the egg.

It is this problem that most techniques for aiding fertility are designed to overcome. Artificial insemination at its simplest involves taking some of the sperm from a male and helping it on its journey in the woman's body by medical techniques, for example to get past a blockage in the fallopian tubes. Between a husband and wife (or otherwise committed partners) this technique seems to raise little in the way of moral problems. The fact that the fertilisation is not the result simply of the natural sexual act needs to be noted, but so long as it is done within a committed and loving relationship, most Christian moralists would see the act as a gift of technique which enables the couple to fulfil the 'order of nature' for their own happiness and that of the child.

The moral situation changes, however, when we move on to the next possibility, which is the use of donor sperm with this technique. Here two questions arise. One, the more fundamental, concerns the biology of reproduction. In fertilisation, the two gametes, the ovum and the sperm, each contain half the information needed to construct a human being. The normal human complement of 46 chromosomes, the strings of the genes which define particular characteristics, is halved in the gametes. In fertilisation each chromosome finds and links up with its 'pair' and decisions are made along the strings of genes about the characteristics that each pairing will produce in the adult human being, such as the colour of the eyes, the height and weight (which obviously depend also on environmental factors such as feeding in childhood) and even possibly the time of death (again allowing for environmental factors such as war, plague, pestilence and famine!). While this may sound complicated, the basic point is that the donor of the sperm has a half share in all these decisions which derives from his own bodily characteristics, including whatever is the bodily basis of intelligence and feeling. It cannot be said, therefore, that the donor is not present in this process.

The other question, rather more manageable, is that of the donor as a personal presence. Should the couple who want the child know who the donor is? Should the donor know what child he has helped to produce and even have a right of access to it? Should the child have a right to knowledge of and access to the donor?

In Britain the Committee of Inquiry into Human Fertilisation and Embryology, chaired by Dame Mary Warnock, recommended in its report in 1984 that donors of gametes should have their anonymity preserved, except in private arrangements between relatives or friends (4.22). The Committee recommended also that the parents and child should have the right to a minimal genetic 'profile', giving only basic information about 'the donor's ethnic origin and genetic health' (4.21). These recommendations have been given effect in the *Human Fertilisation and Embryology Act 1990*, which puts the control of all details of procedures involving donors into the hands of a statutory body, the Human Fertilisation and Embryology Authority.

The need for such action became clear in 1978 when, for the first time, an egg was fertilised outside the human body and the resulting embryo was transferred to the mother's womb, where it successfully implanted and came to live birth. The birth of Louise Brown, the first 'test tube' baby, led to a widespread use of the technique. The Warnock Committee recorded that at the pioneering Bourn Hall clinic, 'By May 1984 the clinic knew of 439 pregnancies, of which 131 were ongoing. 215 children had been born since it opened, including 18 sets of twins and one set of triplets. Among these infants there had been no major congenital malformations' (5.14). It should be noted that there is at present no follow-up programme to monitor IVF children for possible longer-term genetic effects.

Once 'in vitro fertilisation' had been established as an acceptable procedure, the issues of donation applied also to the donation of the female gamete. Leon R. Kass summarises the new possibilities which became available as follows. 'With the technology to effect human *in vitro* fertilization and embryo transfer comes the *immediate* possibility of egg donation (egg from donor, sperm from husband), embryo donation (egg and sperm from outside the marriage) and foster pregnancy (host surrogate for gestation)' ('"Making Babies" Revisited', in Shannon, *Bioethics*, p. 464).

This certainly sharpens the moral concern about donation, but does not fundamentally change the issue. If donation is seen as a gift, under the conditions of anonymity and a limited 'right to know' for the parents and child, then the donation of the egg rather than the sperm, or the donation of the whole embryo, does not change the nature of the gift. If, on the other hand, emphasis is laid, as in the Roman Catholic moral tradition, on the undesirability of any intervention in the natural process of procreation, then any form of donation is out of the question. On the whole it seems preferable to view the donation of gametes as a gift which enables the creative intention of God to be carried through for a couple who genuinely wish to extend their relationship into the care of a child and who cannot otherwise do so. It is clear, however, that this is a question on which Christian opinion is going to remain divided.

What Kass in the quotation above calls 'foster pregnancy' is a more difficult matter. 'Surrogacy' is the carrying of a child by one woman in order to give it to another after birth. Where the woman carrying the child does not provide the egg, but has the child placed in her womb as an embryo, this is sometimes called 'womb-leasing' (here both gametes may come from the couple who wish to be parents). The additional problem in surrogacy, compared with the donation of gametes, is that carrying a child for nine months in the womb is generally thought to have the potential to set up a relationship between the child and the woman who carries it, which is then denied or rejected when the child is handed-over at birth. There is anecdotal evidence which suggests that where the parties are known to each other as relatives or friends, no psychological problems need arise for the surrogate mother (Kass, p. 478, note 8). The majority of the Warnock Committee took the view that the problem of potential relationship made surrogacy a morally and socially undesirable activity (8.17).

What is clear to all parties, however, is that surrogacy should not be encouraged as a commercial practice. In Britain the *Surrogacy Arrangements Act 1985* lays down that commercial agreements for surrogate births cannot be enforced at law, in the sense that a mother cannot be forced to hand over a child to a person who has made such an arrangement, nor can payment be enforced. To make a surrogacy arrangement for money, however, is not in itself a criminal act. The main moral concern in this legislation has been to protect vulnerable women from agreeing to carry a child simply for the sake of the money, and in particular to protect those who may change their minds and want to keep the child when the moment comes to hand it over. In addition, the *Human Fertilization and Embryology Act 1990* now defines the 'mother' as the woman who is carrying or has carried a child, and her husband or consenting partner as the 'father', in relation to any donation of gametes or embryo [Sections 27 and 28].

These techniques for aiding human fertility give rise to a number of other issues, including 'superovulation', the use of 'spare' embryos, the freezing and storage of gametes or embryos, and the use of embryos for experimentation.

Some of these questions permit easier answers than others. Superovulation is the use of drugs to enable a woman to produce more ripe eggs at a given time than she would normally do. This can involve either the natural sex act or IVF techniques. Having more ripe eggs available increases the chances of successful fertilisation, but this means either that more babies are conceived than are required (up to six have been known), or that in the IVF process spare embryos are created and discarded. Superovulation involving multiple births may be undesirable in so far as it affects the life chances of each child, but is not otherwise a problem.

In the early stages of the development of the IVF process additional embryos were indeed created in the laboratory (an attempt would be made to fertilise several eggs in order to ensure the fertilisation of at least one of them). This immediately made the process problematical for those who saw the embryo as having all the moral rights of a human being from the moment when the sperm penetrated the egg. Others argued that no embryo is on its way to become a full human being until it has successfully implanted itself in the wall of the womb, and that the discarding of fertilised eggs is not substantially different from the body's normal process of discarding sperm and eggs, even some fertilised eggs being discarded before or after implantation. More recent refinements of IVF techniques mean that fewer 'spare' embryos are created, but the ability to produce embryos other than for the purpose of implantation has to be recognised as a fact about the IVF process.

The ability to freeze both embryos and male sperm for later use represents another set of opportunities and their associated problems. At present female eggs are not stored in this way, as the risk of deterioration of quality during storage, leading to possible genetic defects in the resulting child, are thought to be higher for ova than for sperm or embryos. The main advantage of freezing biological materials is that it gives control over the timing of the birth process. In the case of freezing embryos it enables the birth to be timed more or less exactly. It can also enable the spare embryos arising from the IVF process to be stored and given to other mothers when they require them. A man intending to have a vasectomy as a form of contraception to prevent him fathering a child accidentally might decide nevertheless to have some of his sperm stored in case of a later change of mind – for example if he remarried.

So far this is not problematical, if the aiding of fertility at all is accepted. Questions, however, can arise about the ownership of and the right to give permission for the use of stored material. In the USA the Tennessee appeals court in September 1990 refused a woman permission to use a frozen embryo, fertilised by her former husband, against his will. In Britain control over the use of all stored gametes and embryos is in the hands of the Human Fertilisation and Embryology Authority, set up under the 1990 Act, which will no doubt have due regard to the wishes of donors. The Act itself devotes close attention to issues of legal rights of inheritance arising from these techniques. It also lays down a maximum storage period for human gametes of ten years and for embryos of five years [14(3), (4)].

The Authority in its first code of practice has set age limits for sperm and egg donations of 18–35 for women and 18–55 for men; a limit of ten children resulting from the donations of any one individual; and a limit of three eggs or embryos to be used for a woman in any one monthly cycle.

A further problem opened up at the end of 1993, with the possibility of eggs taken from aborted female fetuses being used in fertility treatments. This suggestion raises a number of issues about the nature of a 'donor'. For those who object to abortion in principle, of course, the question of the use of such eggs cannot arise. What is initially an evil act, the abortion, cannot then be put to this use. To do so would only encourage the evil. For those who accept the practice of abortion under some circumstances, problems still remain.

The first is that a dead fetus cannot consent to such an action, as even a live child could not do so, nor could its parents do so on its behalf. Consequently the donation cannot be considered to be a gift of the donor, though it might be considered a gift of the parents of the fetus. The second point is that the situation is not analogous to the donation of organs, since it concerns the creation of an entirely new life, not the sustaining of a life that is already in being. Because the genetic presence of the donor continues throughout the span of the new life, the notion of who the donor was cannot be entirely absent from the situation. Yet the donor in this case is not a 'person', and even the basic genetic profile would be more speculative than that of a normal donor. For these reasons it seems possible – and even desirable – that this particular technique should not be permitted. The decision, however, is still to be made.

The question of experiments on the human embryo is the most difficult of all. It is difficult because immense benefits may be gained from such work, while very strong moral inhibitions suggest that we should not do it. Let us be clear about what 'experiment' means in this case. At present the embryo can be kept alive in laboratory conditions, which is to say that the cells will continue to divide and to grow, for something less than 14 days. The primary form of experimentation has been simply the observation of this process. Beyond this, however, lies the possibility of introducing drugs into the nutrient solution to see what they do. As a test for possible effects on the embryo of drugs given to pregnant women, this could lead to a substantial increase in the safe use of drugs. Clearly if it becomes possible to keep the embryo alive for longer periods – perhaps even until birth in an artificial womb – the possibilities of experiment will increase vastly.

The question which has faced the law-makers is whether the entity which exists up to 14 days or so is effectively different from the child to be born, and so open to being experimented on. The Warnock Committee took as its practical criterion the first appearance of the specialisation of cells in the embryonic disc. This is the 'primitive streak', a dark marking which appears 14 or 15 days after fertilisation. Up to this point the embryo is a relatively simple collection of cells, which can still divide to form identical twins (Warnock 11.5). Beyond this point it becomes an increasingly complex organism. The *Human Fertilisation and Embryology Act 1990* accepts the Warnock recommendation that experiments on the embryo should be allowed up to 14 days after fertilisation (not counting any period in frozen storage), for the purpose of securing information about the treatment of infertility, the causes of congenital disease and miscarriages, more effective techniques of contraception and methods of detecting gene or chromosome abnormalities in embryos before implantation [Schedule 2, Paragraph 3]. Embryos may be created for the purpose of research [Schedule 2, Paragraph 3], but donations for this purpose must be separate from donations for fertility treatments [Schedule 2, Paragraph 4 (2) (a)]. The Act also forbids the placing in a woman of an embryo or gametes from an animal other than a human being, the placing of a human embryo in any (other) animal and the replacement of a nucleus of a cell of an embryo with any other nucleus [Section 3 (2) (a), (b); 3 (b), (d)].

One possibility which comes under the heading of experiment is cloning, the division of the embryo into two or more identical embryos. In October 1993 it was reported that American scientists had divided human embryos into twins and kept them growing for a short time. The embryos used were chosen because they suffered from genetic defects and had no chance of growth to birth. The value of this experiment is disputed. Some experts argue that because the mass of the human embryo is so small it can probably never be divided into quantities which will enable both parts to grow to birth as twins. Others argue that this possibility may remain for the future and that at some time mothers will be able to bear 'twins' some years apart.

Finally it should be noted that embryos used in the IVF process can now be tested for a wide range of genetic defects by the removal and examination of a single cell. This technique, 'blastomere analysis before implantation' or BABI, reduces the risk of producing children with genetic defects by the IVF process. Whether a single cell counts as an 'embryo' from a moral point of view is a difficult question. Certainly it does not have the practical possibility of growing into a fetus, even though at this stage it contains all the genetic information available in the cells which form the embryo.

At the border line between 'aiding fertility' and 'preventing fertility' we can also note one more technique, that of influencing the sex of the child by sorting the sperm before fertilisation to increase the proportion that are likely to give a child of the desired sex. While this involves the destruction of sperm, it does not involve the destruction of, or experiment upon, the embryo.

The moral question is whether, once again, we have the right to make such a decision about a child. If we accept the possibility of making decisions at all, across the whole range of techniques, this one does not seem to be immoral in itself. Rather it raises social questions about the balance of populations and the different esteem given to female and to male children. In the very long run, of course, a change in the balance of the population between the sexes should also lead to a change in the esteem given to each. This, however, would be 'social engineering' on the grand scale. In the short run, on the other hand, it might seem to be a practice which is better than the abortion or exposure and death of female children in societies which give preference to the male.

(iii) Contraception and Abortion

While some people need help to achieve the conception of a child (about 10 per cent of couples are infertile for one reason or another and IVF techniques help about 5 per cent of these), many more are interested in ways of preventing conception or in preventing the progress of the fetus to birth, that is to say in means of contraception, sterilisation or abortion. Like fertility treatment, these activities also raise questions about the nature and rights of the fetus and the significance of relationships between parents and children.

There are two natural methods of contraception which are generally accepted as not raising moral problems. The first is abstention from sexual intercourse, which as the *Dictionary of Medical Ethics* wryly remarks, 'is infallible' (p. 118). The other is the restriction of sexual activity to the time in each month when the woman is infertile. It is said that this 'rhythm' method can now be used with considerable accuracy, given proper record keeping. It offers the advantage of not requiring drugs of any kind, with the associated expense and risk of harmful side effects.

The disadvantage of both these methods, however, is that they require the application of a restraint and foresight to the sexual act which is not entirely compatible with the spontaneity of love. If physical love-making is a proper part of the totality of love, without every act having a reproductive intent, then even the rhythm method may not provide enough opportunity for a married couple to express themselves sexually at moments when real opportunities occur. Family life does not always fit in to a monthly rhythm. Once the intention of non-reproductive sex is accepted, there is no good moral reason for not considering other forms of contraceptive action.

Other forms of contraception fall into two kinds – those which prevent the sperm meeting the egg, and those which prevent the egg from proceeding to implant in the womb. Some forms of the female pill, possibly the intrauterine coil (IUD), and the pill RU486, which is taken after the sexual act and requires medical supervision, all have the latter effect. They may, therefore, be reckoned technically to be forms of abortion rather than contraception. Leaving this point aside for the moment, the choice rests on the various personal and medical issues that arise from each method. Apart from the Catholic Church, which opposes any intervention in the reproductive process at any point, most Christian thinkers accept non-reproductive sex as a good in itself within a family that does not reject the idea of children altogether, and leave the method to the couple's own choice.

Sterilisation is more problematic because in the woman it is not reversible – it involves removal of the ovaries. In some men the operation – the sealing of the vas, the channel through which the sperm comes – may be reversible, with the additional problem that in some men the operation may reverse itself spontaneously and without any warning, leading to an unplanned child. Given these facts, a decision in favour of sterilisation, taken freely and with moral seriousness, may still be a morally proper one in particular medical or other personal circumstances. That is to say, a decision to be sterilised simply to avoid inconvenience and to widen sexual opportunities would not be taking sufficiently seriously either the human body or the sexual act. A carefully-thought-out decision in the context of a family would be a different matter, and cannot be ruled out as a moral possibility within the general context of human freedom to choose how to use our own bodies.

The moral difficulty comes when this freedom obstructs the moral freedom of another person. Even in some contraceptive acts the possibility arises that we may be destroying the moral freedom of another person, once the egg is fertilised. To investigate this possibility further, in the context of contraception, of abortion and of experiments on the human embryo, we need to return to some questions of basic biology.

What is the precise nature of this entity, the zygote or fertilised egg? It begins as a single cell, consisting of a membrane which holds it all together, a body in which nutrients are digested and used and wastes excreted, and a nucleus which contains the genetic information necessary for these processes to take place. The nucleus also holds the instructions for dividing and so reproducing the cell. For the moment this cell division into identical, related units is the main work of the cell. While this multiplication takes place the cluster of cells moves from the fallopian tube to the womb, where it implants itself in the wall of the womb, putting down roots, so to speak, and beginning to draw nourishment directly from the mother's body for the enormous tasks ahead.

There is a generally accepted estimate that about half of all naturally fertilised eggs fail to implant, and that after implantation some spontaneously abort in a short time. It is suggested that these failures may be a response to defects in the genes or chromosomes which would make the fetus not viable in the long run. Implantation is also the point at which the cluster of cells can no longer divide to form two embryos, which will be identical twins (non-identical twins are formed from the fertilisation of two separate eggs). It has been observed in mice, though not in human beings, that before implantation such identical twins can also recombine to form a single embryo.

Once implanted, the cluster of cells fulfils two purposes. The embryonic disc forms the amniotic sac, the environment in which the fetus will live, and within the disc the fetus itself begins its long task of increasing specialisation. Even in these early stages, the zygote / embryo is a living being. As Leon Kass puts it, 'First of all, the zygote and early embryonic stages are clearly alive. They metabolise, respire and respond to changes in the environment; they grow and divide' ('"Making Babies" Revisited', in Shannon, *Bioethics*, p. 457). There is no doubt that from the beginning the zygote, the cell formed from the egg and the sperm, is in this sense an independent, self-directing entity.

After implantation the embryo quickly takes on recognisable features of being a human body. Richard Higginson describes the process from the moment of fertilisation:

> After three weeks, activity of the heart begins. After five weeks there are reflex movements in the spinal cord. After six and a half weeks (about the time abortions begin to be done), fingers and toes have formed and major organs such as heart,

lungs, guts and kidneys are all there in rudimentary form. The brain has already developed to a size where it swamps everything else. Between eight and twelve weeks the fetus doubles in length, grows fingernails, starts sucking its thumb, develops sexual organs and – in many cases – is capable of registering brain waves (this is the peak period for performing abortions; from eight weeks the term 'fetus' replaces that of 'embryo'). ('The Fetus as a Person', in *Abortion in Debate*, p. 40)

Live birth is possible, with the best modern techniques, from about 24 weeks onwards, though full pregnancy lasts for nine months. Even live birth, however, is not an absolute threshold, in the sense that the child is still dependent for its life on others and has much physical, mental and emotional development to come before it can be accounted a full adult 'person'.

The biological evidence about the nature of the zygote / embryo / fetus is thus at best ambiguous. There is no doubt that it is *human* in the sense of being created from human genetic material. There is no doubt that given success at the moment of implantation, freedom from major genetic defect, and a favourable environment, it has the capacity to grow into an adult human being. Yet as a fertilised egg, a bundle of identical self-reproducing cells or an embryo in the earliest stages of differentiating itself from its container, it is not a human being in precisely the same sense that this term is applied to an adult of the species. The most that biology can lead us to say is that the human embryo demands great respect. As Kass says again, discussing the status of the blastocyst (the three to six day old embryo present in the laboratory dish in the IVF process):

> In the blastocyst, even in the zygote, we face a mysterious and awesome power, a power governed by an immanent plan that may produce an indisputably and fully human being. It deserves our respect not because it has rights or claims or sentience (which it does not have at this stage), but because of what it is, now *and* prospectively. ('"Making Babies" Revisited', in Shannon, *Bioethics*, p. 459)

This respect for the life of the embryo becomes in religious traditions a respect for the creative action of God. That the Biblical tradition, Jewish and Christian, does not specifically condemn abortion is, as it were, an accidental fact. The presumption in favour of procreation and of the God-givenness of life is so strong that the consequent prohibition of abortion nowhere comes to be stated. It remains nevertheless a clear moral fact that there is no licence to kill embryos or fetuses anywhere in the Bible. This means that the stance that abortion is morally neutral, something which a woman has a right to do to her own body, is ruled out from the start by theology and is a dubious proposition even on the biological facts.

On the other hand Biblical references to the child in the womb, such as Psalm 139.13 'You knitted me together in my mother's womb', are too far away from modern biology to do more than support the general theological principle that all life is given by God. Exodus 21.22–25 refers to the accidental causing of a miscarriage, not deliberate abortion, but it is certainly possible to read it as meaning that the loss of the fetus is less serious than injury to the mother would be. The theological principle of incarnation, that in Jesus of Nazareth God takes on fully our humanity in order to give us the fullness of salvation, adds a specifically Christian emphasis to the Jewish tradition of respect for human life. None of the Biblical material in itself answers the further question, 'Are there nevertheless situations in which the life of the embryo or fetus may be taken for another moral purpose?'

Here two positions are possible within Christian thought. The first is that the embryo or fetus is to be treated at all times as having the full moral right to life of an adult human being, even though in most respects it is as yet unable to exercise or claim that right for itself. On this view the fetus may be removed from the fallopian tube or from the womb, or with the womb, when the continuation of the pregnancy would inevitably end the mother's life. Such situations would include an ectopic pregnancy, when the embryo has implanted in the fallopian tube instead of the womb, or when cancer develops in the womb. No other conditions would justify abortion. This is the Catholic position, of which the strict formulation is that the doctors must strive equally to save the life of the mother and of the fetus.

All other claims to justify abortion depend on some form of the argument that the fetus is potentially a full human being but not yet a full human being. Certain clarifications can be made at the start. From the point of view of being biologically a member of a species it is clear that any living entity which is conceived from human gametes is a member of the human species. An immediate presumption is then created that it may be 'a human being' in other senses. Equally it is clear that a fetus in the womb is not yet a 'human personality' in any sense which requires consent, memory, foresight and the forming of relationships. In this sense the status of 'human being' may be given to the fetus by courtesy in view of its projected future development, but the status does not yet belong to the fetus as a right by virtue of what the fetus already is.

There are two difficulties in the approach to the status of the fetus as a potential human being. The first is the absence of biological thresholds to mark degrees of potential. From the moment of implantation the biological process is an unbroken development; only the beginning of the formation of the central nervous system in the appearance of the primitive streak offers any possibility of an argument for a threshold, very early in the developmental process.

The other difficulty is that the range of conditions which can be claimed as justifying an abortion is so great that the protective effect of granting the fetus the status of 'potential human being' can be reduced to almost nothing.

The British legislation on abortion makes this latter point clear. The *Human Fertilisation and Embryology Act 1990* states the main grounds for abortion as being not only a threat to the woman's life, but also a threat to her long-term physical or mental health (this would include the continuance of pregnancy after rape), or a threat to the future life of the family [Section 37]. While many moralists would recognise rape as a special case, as a pregnancy which results from a violent intrusion, the other grounds give little value to the 'potential' of the fetus.

A separate problem in the 1990 Act, as in the original legislation of 1967, is the provision for abortion of the fetus on the grounds of 'a substantial risk' of physical or mental abnormalities which would make the child to be 'seriously handicapped' [Section 37]. This is in effect aborting the fetus for its own good, in the sense that the Act requires a decision to be made about the future quality of life of the child to be born. It may also, of course, imply a decision about the capacity or willingness of the parents to care for a handicapped child.

A recent *Instruction* of the Congregation for the Doctrine of the Faith sets out the basic Catholic teaching on all aspects of the control of human fertility. 'The inviolability of the innocent human being's right to life "from the moment of conception until death" is a sign and requirement of the very inviolability of the person to whom the Creator has given the gift of life' (*Instruction on Respect for Human Life in Its Origin and on the Dignity of Procreation*, Introduction, Section 4; in Shannon, *Bioethics*, p. 594). The *Instruction* adds a quotation from Pope John XXIII, 'The transmission of human life is entrusted by nature to a personal and conscious act and as such is subject to the all-holy laws of God: immutable and inviolable laws which must be recognised and observed. For this reason one cannot use means and follow methods which could be licit in the transmission of the life of plants and animals' (*Mater et Magistra* III, 1961; in Shannon, *Bioethics*, p. 594).

This teaching has the advantage of being clear and, within the area of fertility and abortion, consistent. It affirms two things about all these questions: that their central reference point is the personal relationship of two people which has the capacity to lead on to the birth of a new life; and that certain moral truths follow inevitably from the physical and personal facts.

The first of these points is indeed determinative for all Christian moral thought on these issues. It can lead to a conservative, even defensive, stance, not only for Catholic theologians but also for Protestant ones. Oliver O'Donovan has protested that the ability to promote fertility through IVF techniques, donation and surrogacy has moved procreation from a personal decision within a highly personal act to being the sort of decision one might make among supermarket shelves. 'Now that we have successfully attacked the bond of necessity ... we have destroyed the ground of our knowledge of the humane. From now on there is no knowing what a parent is' (*Begotten or Made?* p. 48).

This tendency to dehumanise a deeply personal act must indeed be a matter of concern to any serious Christian thought. Nevertheless there are things to be said on the other side. The problem lies in the second part of the quotation from Pope John XXIII on the existence of 'immutable and inviolable laws'.

In the first place, as some Catholic authors such as Charles Curran have had the courage to remark, Catholic natural law theory ties itself too tightly to the physical process of sex and reproduction, without allowing sufficiently for the question of intention (and therefore also of the personal). Curran himself lost his licence to teach in a Catholic university for this and other statements, but to a non-Catholic his point about 'biologism' remains true. ('Natural

Law', in Charles Curran, *Directions in Fundamental Moral Theology,*
pp. 127–37). Both the suppression of individual theologians and
the encyclical letter of Pope John Paul II, *Veritatis Splendor* (1993),
make clear that the determination of natural law is in the end a
matter of the teaching authority of the Catholic Church. For those
not bound by this authority it is simply a fact that the modern
biological understanding of the processes of reproduction does not
lead to immutable and inviolable moral laws.

The second difficulty about the teaching of the *Instruction* lies in
the notion of 'the innocent human being'. Clearly the fetus is
innocent in the sense of not yet having made decisions and carried
out actions of its own. This, however, might be argued to indicate
not so much innocence as immaturity. Immaturity is also a ground
for defending life, but the defence of life then has to be recognised
as something that is less than absolute. Richard Higginson sees this
point and tackles it by denying that it can ever be right to kill the
'innocent', even when these are adults rather than fetuses. This is a
well-established Christian position for those who are absolute
pacifists and do not accept a right to kill under any circumstances
whatever. For those, like myself, who accept the necessity sometimes of killing in war, there can be no absolute 'right to life', for wars
do in practice kill innocent people. Higginson's response is to say 'I
would regard the killing carried out in a just war as essentially a
killing of guilty parties' ('The Fetus as a Person', in *Abortion in
Debate*, p. 45). This, however, cannot be right. Even if it be
admitted, for the purposes of argument, that we can identify some
wars as 'just' (not only from our own point of view, but from the
point of view of some neutral observer), that cannot make every
soldier on the other side a person *deserving* to be killed. If the
innocence of the fetus can only be preserved at this cost, then it
cannot be preserved at all.

It is no longer possible to regard the male sperm as a mass of
homunculi, miniaturised human beings, and the female womb as a
seedbed in which they grow until birth, as some thought in the
ancient world. Nor can we presume that a soul is put by God into
the male fetus at forty days and the female fetus at eighty days, as
Christian thinkers supposed in earlier times. Indeed biology now
reverses this patriarchalism in seeing the male embryo or fetus as a
'female-minus', a female embryo or a fetus which has not developed
full female characteristics, a failed female. No doubt males will say

that no moral conclusions should be drawn from this. It does illustrate, however, the extent to which biology leaves us on our own to decide what the fetus is, morally and theologically. The question of 'ensoulment' at this point is in practice irrelevant, since we can have no knowledge of such an act. Those of us who are dualists have to be content with the possibility that God puts a soul into the body either at fertilisation or at birth – or at any point in between.

The Christian conscience, therefore, has to decide two separate things. The first is, 'What are the limits in my personal life?' Given reasonable health, a stable family life and a secure income, it is not difficult to conclude that abortion is wrong except to save the mother's life and perhaps after rape. This indeed is the primary ideal, as lifelong monogamous marriage is the primary ideal of sexuality. In practice we all have to recognise the reality of marital breakdown and to make choices about moral responses to it. So it is with abortion.

Only those who face, for example, the reality of carrying a child with an indication of severe handicap – or even the possibility of a second such child – have the moral authority to make that decision for that child. Only they are *in* the reality. Instructed Christians will regard a decision for abortion as a very serious decision. There is nothing in biology or in Christian theology which makes it an absolutely impossible decision. Certainly moral instruction must stress the seriousness of the decision, but the idea that one can legislate for all in so complex and controversial a mater is a delusion. The authority of the Holy Spirit lies in the whole people of God and every Christian carries the authority to make these serious decisions for her or himself, in the context of the thinking of the whole Christian community, when the whole Christian community does not have a unanimous view on these matters.

The one point in the 1990 Act which is not covered by the discussion above is the production of human embryos for the purpose of research. Here the argument that personal necessity may sometimes overrule the presumption that the embryo should live does not apply. Leon Kass takes the view that we should not experiment even on embryos which are produced in the course of fertility treatments and are surplus to the requirements of that process. 'Invasive and manipulative experiments involving such embryos very likely presume that they are things or mere stuff, and deny the fact of their possible viability. Certain observational and non-invasive experiments might be different' ('"Making Babies" Revisited', in Shannon, *Bioethics*, p. 461). This also, of course, implies that embryos ought not to be created for such purposes, and this might be right as the 'bottom line' of this whole issue, except that it is also probably now too late to go back on this point.

For, as Oliver O'Donovan points out, the development of the IVF process itself is the result of such research. 'IVF is not the gift of a fairy-godmother; it is the gift of researchers' (*Begotten or Made?* p. 80). If we will the end, we must also will the means. The restriction in the use of embryos in research to the purpose of improving fertility and increasing the understanding of congenital disease can still be argued for. That the human embryo is an essential experimental subject in research on human fertility does not necessarily mean that it need be viewed as an essential subject of any other kinds of research.

All of this will not be satisfactory to those who ask for a 'strong lead' in moral matters. All I can say is that for me the requirement of human freedom, given at the hand of God, is that we should take responsibility for our decisions, even though these may sometimes be wrong. The desire for absolute moral certainty is an infantile desire, which blocks our moral progress and prevents us from seeing the open and changing nature of the world in which we live. Modern knowledge has made the exercise of our freedom much more difficult, but this is no reason for refusing either the knowledge or the task.

(iv) Euthanasia

Just as the creation of human life has become an area for human decisions in a way that would have been unimaginable a century ago, so the end of human life is becoming a matter for specific decisions. Here again the cause is the advance of techniques, in this case techniques for delaying or for redefining death. As death has become less 'natural', as something over which we have no control, so a demand has arisen that death should be determined in the context of a need for 'human dignity', and it has been said that this is not the same as living until breath finally leaves the body.

Three recent court cases in Britain illustrate this demand.

In the case of 'Baby J' in October 1990 the Court of Appeal

upheld the judgment of the lower court that all available means need not be used to maintain the life of a child born prematurely, severely handicapped and with a life-threatening condition:

> Baby J was born very prematurely at 27 weeks' gestation. He was not breathing and was placed on a ventilator and a drip and was given antibiotics to counteract an infection. A month later, he was able to come off the ventilator but remained very sick and severely handicapped. He has suffered recurrent convulsions and breathing failures and has had to be put back on a ventilator a number of times.
>
> Despite a slight improvement, his long term prospects are not good. His brain is severely damaged. He appears to be blind, will probably be deaf and is unlikely ever to be able to speak or to develop even limited intellectual abilities. But he will probably feel pain as much as a normal baby. His life expectancy extends at most into his late teens. (*The Independent*, 23 October 1990, p.19)

The court ruled that the physicians were not obliged to put Baby J back on the ventilator if he stopped breathing again; if he developed a chest infection he should be treated with antibiotics and maintenance of the saline drip, but again no special effort should be made to keep him breathing.

This decision was clearly based on two principles. The first was that beyond a certain point 'it is not in the child's best interests to subject it to treatment which would cause increased suffering and produce no commensurate benefit'. The second was an implied distinction between treatment that constitutes normal care and treatment that was in some sense 'extraordinary'.

The second case was that of Dr Cox, who in September 1992 was found guilty of deliberately killing a patient, Mrs Boyes, a lady of 70, 'who was terminally ill with acute rheumatoid arthritis and in agonising pain' and who 'had asked him to help her die' (*The Independent*, 22 September 1992, p. 3). It was common ground that Mrs Boyes' pain could not be controlled, that her medical condition could not be cured and that the injection which Dr Cox gave to her had no purpose other than to end life. In this case the court reaffirmed the existing legal principle that no doctor may deliberately end a person's life. The court recognised that Dr Cox's action was one of compassion for a dying patient 'who had become an admired and cherished friend'. For this reason Dr Cox received only a twelve month suspended jail sentence and was subsequently allowed to continue in practice. In effect Dr Cox had directly challenged the law on a serious moral issue, which was recognised to be such, even though under the current law the challenge had to fail.

The third case was that of Tony Bland, in which the Court of Appeal decided for the first time in English law to allow doctors to end the provision of food and liquids in order to allow a body to cease functioning (it appears that Scottish law already allowed medical staff this discretion). Tony Bland was injured in a disaster in Hillsborough football ground in 1989, when his brain was starved of oxygen and he entered a coma, a 'persistent vegetative state', in which the body continued to function but there was no possibility of the recovery of consciousness. In this case it was possible to say that part of the brain was so badly damaged that consciousness could never return. In November 1992 the Court ruled that doctors could discontinue 'ventilation, nutrition and hydration by artificial means' (*The Independent*, 20 November 1992, p. 33). As the judgment reported, 'Scans revealed no evidence of cortical activity. He had suffered cognitive death but could continue to breathe and reacted in a reflex manner to painful stimuli. He is fed artificially by a naso gastric tube'.

This decision does not automatically apply to all coma patients. In the case of Tony Bland it could be argued that in a clear though technical sense he was already dead since part of the brain had disappeared. Other patients in a persistent vegetative state may be argued to have 'no reasonable chance' of a return to independent life after three months without change, as John Collee argues (*The Observer Magazine*, 4 August 1991, p. 42), but this is not always so clearly revealed by a scan. Tony Bland died within ten days of kidney failure, apparently without discomfort. Others argue, however, as in the case of Nancy Cruzan in the USA in 1990, that it is not always possible to assess from the outside what level of sentience and therefore of discomfort there may be, and that the dying may in fact be a painful process. Some would argue that it would be better in such cases to go a step further and end life directly.

These three cases between them raise almost all the main issues, practical and moral, in the area of euthanasia. Is it ever permissible to end life directly? Is it permissible sometimes to decide not to use 'extraordinary' or 'disproportionate' means to preserve life? Is it ever permissible to end life, not by direct killing, but by withdrawing the means of sustenance, which will inevitably lead to death over time? To all of these questions it is now possible to give the answer 'Yes', though with complications about the issue of the consent of the patient.

In some cases the question is no more than that of defining 'death' accurately. For patients whose consciousness has already gone, the definition of 'clinical brain death' shows by means of specific tests that the body can continue to function for only a short time. This definition has relevance to the removal of organs for transplant operations, since a successful transplantation requires both that the organ should be functioning at the point of removal from the donor body and also that the donor body should be in a real sense dead. The definition has relevance also for the switching-off of life-support machinery, which does not then count as 'killing' the patient, though it does obviously raise serious pastoral questions for medical staff and relatives.

Some comatose patients, however, are not near death and can live for many years. In the case of Karen Quinlan in the USA, the first person in an irreversible coma for whom a court gave permission for the withdrawal of a ventilator, spontaneous breathing began after the ventilator was removed and Quinlan lived for several more years, still in a coma, but clearly not 'brain dead' in the technical sense (Frank K. Veith, 'Brain Death', in Shannon, *Bioethics*, p. 182). Here it is clear that the decision might have included also the cessation of feeding and hydration, even though Quinlan was not in the strict sense 'dead'.

The issue of consent seems to be crucial. While it is proper and desirable for medical staff to have the right to say, in consultation with relatives or guardians, that 'there is no medical benefit in initiating such-and-such a procedure', it is quite a different matter either to initiate a procedure or to discontinue a procedure where it is clear that this *must* result in the death of a patient who is not terminally ill. Where such a patient cannot consent to the action, but has not lost all capacity for consciousness, there would seem to be no moral ground on which death could be initiated. To kill, for example, senile patients, by an active decision, such as injecting a drug, or the decision to discontinue feeding, when these patients can

neither consent nor know what is being done to them, is to do
something that is not required by the medical facts and that does not
lie within the responsibilities of family or guardians.

For this reason some argue for the legal recognition of an advance
declaration, or 'living will', in which a person able to give consent
can declare that at any future time in which they are not able to give
consent, they wish to exercise the option to refuse medical treatment, or even not to be fed, in order not to have their life prolonged
beyond the point at which it ceases to have meaning for them. The
doubt which would remain with such consent in advance, however,
is whether the patient would in fact be of the same mind at the
moment that the decision is taken not to continue treatment or
feeding. Even the renewal of the advance declaration at regular
intervals while the person is able to give consent cannot remove this
doubt altogether. Such advance declarations do not have the force
of law at present in Britain. On the other hand it is clear that the
possibility of such an advance declaration would come as a great
relief to many who are worried about their own future health.

For the patient unable to consent, however, there still remains
the very grey area of means which may be held to be 'extraordinary'
or 'disproportionate'. It is not clear, for example, why the court in
the case of 'Baby J' thought that antibiotics were proper to be used,
but mechanical or manual ventilation was not. In the natural order
antibiotics might be considered equally 'artificial' compared with
food and drink. Indeed, even food and drink might be considered
'artificial' when pumped into the body through a tube. It seems
that here we have a distinction which is clear in theory but not in
practice; and which yet we need in order to express a common-
sense feeling that we ought to keep people 'comfortable' without
going on trying to 'cure' them when we think a 'cure' to be
impossible. It seems to me that the practical solution here is the
one that the courts have not yet arrived at, which would be to insist
that terminally ill patients who are not in great pain should be kept
comfortable while they live, but that the question of ending
feeding and hydration is properly a matter for medical staff and
relatives or guardians, not for the courts.

If the 'right to live' should not be the right to be kept alive by all
means available, then the 'right to die' by one's own choice is also
controversial. In the case of Mrs Boyes this right was simply denied
by the court. So far in the argument it has not been necessary to

appeal to specifically Christian morality, but here we come to a point where only a religious stance might deny the 'right to die'. While the definition of death and of proportionate means is primarily a matter of medical judgment, the claim to a right to die seems to run counter to a basic theological principle, which is that life is a gift of God, and can neither be given nor taken away on human decisions alone.

What should a Christian say about death? The first necessity is the right to know the truth about my condition. This can be seen as a general human right. In the Christian context, however, it involves the need to prepare for death, not as a dissolution of what has gone before, but as an entry into a new stage of life. The need to make peace between the self and God, and between the self and relatives and friends, is a proper part of the process of dying, as this has been analysed by Elizabeth Kübler-Ross and others. So is the need to prepare oneself for the journey and to ask for God's protection on the way. All this requires consciousness, so far as this is consistent with the control of pain. Indeed, after knowledge of the facts, the control of pain is the next priority. Not everyone has the chance to prepare for death in this way. This may be one of the worst aspects of senility, though it is also a Christian belief that others can share in this task, both with us and for us.

Where death can be approached in this way there may be no 'right' to die; rather there may be a duty to carry through the process. But not every death is of this kind. Where there is pain that cannot be controlled, where the illness is terminal within a short period, and where, perhaps, the next step is a descend into loss of consciousness and of bodily control, there can be a case for saying that the consenting person has a right to choose the exact moment to die in an otherwise inevitable process.

The current practice in the Netherlands provides that a person can choose euthanasia where three main conditions are present: when there is a terminal illness, a pain not able to be controlled and a repeated request for euthanasia which is made with a clear mind. It is probable that similar legislation will follow in other countries in Western Europe in the next few years. This is, from any point of view, a very substantial breach in the western legal tradition of the protection of life, yet it is not necessarily contrary to the Christian faith.

The Christian argument against this position is the belief that life is a gift of God. As John Mahoney says, this is not to be seen as an unreasonable demand by a distant power:

> ... dying is not, at heart, a lonely struggle in isolation from a distant God whom one longs to join; it is a final stage in that pilgrimage which is surrounded and bathed in God's friend-ship, in which, the Christian believes, as throughout life, he is sustained by God's 'everlasting arms'. Viewed in this context, euthanasia is not an injustice towards the Lord God, but a disappointment of his personal trust and a rejection of his abiding presence. (*Bio-Ethics and Belief,* pp. 42–3)

On the other side of the argument it might be said that sometimes the Christian argument against euthanasia, as also against suicide, underestimates the degree of distress that people may suffer before taking these paths. While suicide can often be construed as an aggressive act, legal euthanasia on the Dutch model, with counsel-ling and consultation with relatives and friends, is not necessarily and always a wrongful act. The right to choose may arguably lie within God's gift of freedom to human rationality and human will.

The most serious arguments against such a right to choose lie in medical ethics and in the social effects of such an ability to choose, rather than in a theological principle.

For many medical staff the problem of euthanasia is that it is contrary to the ethos of the medical profession, whose task is to cure. As Hans Jonas puts it, 'it is prohibited by the innermost meaning of the medical vocation, which should never cast the physician in the role of a dispenser of death, even at the subject's request' ('The Right to Die', in Shannon, *Bioethics,* p. 203). It should be noted, however, that even Jonas would accept that the termination of life in a case such as that of Tony Bland can be argued to be permissible within this ethos, when there is only a 'lingering, residual life with the patient's personhood already extinguished'. In any case, Jonas' objection is not shared by all the medical profession, as both the Dutch example and surveys of opinion in other countries show.

The second argument, and perhaps the stronger, is that the Dutch practice creates a serious risk of establishing a presumption in favour of euthanasia which might put intolerable pressures on those who would not wish to choose this path for themselves, but

who might find themselves socially driven to it. Even the anticipation of such a situation at some future stage of life might be a heavy
burden on the old or the chronically sick. It remains to be seen
whether the restrictions surrounding the current practice in the
Netherlands will reduce this problem to manageable proportions.
In any case there is some reason to suppose that actual practice in the
Netherlands has been, and will continue to be, much wider than the
legal theory allows.

(v) Genetic Engineering

The greatest power to come into the hands of human beings in this
century has arguably not been the power to make atomic weapons
– though that is terrifying enough – but the power to change our
own genetic structure and that of other living creatures. From the
earliest times of agricultural settlement human beings have been
involved in altering natural organisms for their own advantage,
domesticating animals and selecting forms of grain and other plants
to cultivate. From this came breeding programmes for plants and
animals, first selecting favourable variations among those that
occurred naturally and later crossbreeding between these varieties to
induce variations from which some might be selected for continued
production.

This human practice of designing nature has been immensely
successful, as every flower garden testifies. Some problems also lie in
waiting with these processes, such as the loss of natural varieties in
selecting only a few stocks to be developed, the loss of vigour or of
disease resistance in cultivated stocks (listen to any gardener on the
relative power of weeds to grow compared with cultivated stocks),
or a tendency to grow for show appearance rather than efficiency in
life, as with the monster marrow or the dachshund's long back.
Nevertheless, from the human point of view our interaction with
natural selection in other species over the centuries has been an
overwhelming gain, and has even made up to some extent for our
equally overwhelming ability to extinguish other species.

What is new in this generation is that we are now beginning to
have the power to alter the fundamental genetic design of ourselves
and other animals by operating directly on the biological 'memory'
or the design which is held in the genes. The cells which are the

building blocks of living creatures are programmed for their tasks of survival and reproduction by the genes, which are units of information stored as chemical sequences in the nucleic acid known as DNA. As David Suzuki and Peter Knudtson put it, 'A *gene* is life's way of remembering how to perpetuate itself' (*Genethics*, p. 7).

Although every cell in a human body in principle carries all the genetic information needed to grow that whole human body, when the cell takes up its specialised function of being in a specific part of the body all the information not relevant to this task is blocked-off. This *somatic* or body cell, in most parts of a healthy body, can reproduce itself exactly in its given location by growing in size and then dividing.

This offers the first possibility of 'genetic engineering', *somatic cell change*, which is to change the functioning of a particular part of an already existing human body. In the simplest form, new cells can be supplied on a temporary basis, repairing the functioning of the body but needing renewal from time to time. Such a procedure is now on trial for cystic fibrosis. This is a problem of the lungs becoming clogged with mucus, which offers a breeding ground for bacteria. As reported by Tom Wilkie and Ann Barrett in *The Independent*, 'The defective CF gene fails to control the passage of salt and water in and out of the body's cells. In the lungs, this failure results in the sticky mucus. By replacing faulty CF genes with normal ones the defect can be corrected' (26 August 1993). In trials in the USA the 'engineered' gene was introduced into volunteers by an altered version of the common cold virus, but this caused inflammation. In British trials, 'fat globules, called liposomes, are used to carry the gene', and it is hoped that this technique will avoid the problem.

The other possibility of therapy on somatic cells would be to introduce a new gene into a location where the body would then begin to manufacture the gene for itself. The process of identifying genes which cause problems such as muscular dystrophy is now under way. Once the gene is identified and reproduced or 'engineered' in its proper working form, the problem of getting it into the body remains. Professor Sir David Weatherall said in 1992 that 'The real success will be to insert normal gene cells into cells which are self-renewing, such as the cells that make blood cells in the bone marrow, so that a lifetime's treatment, or only two or three in a lifetime, would be given' (*The Independent*, 16 January 1992).

It can safely be assumed that somatic cell changes cannot be passed on by sexual reproduction, because the cells which are changed do not connect with the gametes or reproductive cells. A different series of changes, however, aims precisely to introduce changes into the *germ* cells, the gametes themselves. In *germ cell therapy* new DNA is induced to 'recombine' in the gamete DNA. In this way it might be possible to change the genetic profile of a child of parents who are carriers of a genetically based disease, even though the parents themselves are not helped by the change, by putting a new gene into their gamete DNA, in place of the defective one. In this case, once the new gene is recombined in the living record, it can be reproduced over many generations. In experiments on animals, this has led to the introduction of the race of 'supermice', which were given a growth hormone which increased the size of succeeding generations by 50 per cent above the norm, and of the 'oncomouse', a breed of mouse designed to develop cancer, for use in drug tests.

The problem with altering germ cells in this way, both in other animals and in human beings, is threefold. In the first place, the altered gene, once released, cannot be recalled. Recombinant DNA becomes a living part of the host body and its successors. Secondly, this means that, like natural DNA, it becomes liable to random mutation. It may be, indeed, that engineered DNA will be more liable to random change or to deterioration than natural DNA.

The third problem is the fact that genes interact in their effects. Many characteristics seem to be produced by a combination of genes, rather than a single gene. We have no way of knowing in advance what changes through the whole set of human DNA relationships may be introduced, over several generations, by the introduction into the human reproductive system of manufactured genes. This is not an argument in favour of doing nothing, but it is an argument in favour of exercising extreme caution in making human germ cell changes. In particular it is an argument for strict international control of all such procedures. Many scientists would go further than this. David Suzuki and Peter Knudtson put forward the principle that 'While genetic manipulation of human somatic cells may lie in the realm of personal choice, tinkering with human germ cells does not. Germ-cell therapy, without the consent of all members of society, ought to be explicitly forbidden' (*Genethics*, p. 163).

Another complication about this area of research is the economic power that accrues to those who hold the knowledge. The Human Genome Project is a team effort to map the location and functioning of every gene in human DNA. All the information discovered by the team will be the subject of patents, that is to say that it will be 'owned' by specific persons or corporations. Attempts are also being made to patent specific changes, such as the oncomouse, and in the USA one corporation patenting a change to the cotton plant has attempted to have the patent cover any future such changes, irrespective of who makes the experiment. In this case the corporation would simply own 'the cotton plant' as a whole. It remains to be seen if this latter effort will succeed.

An association of charities which have an interest in human genetic disorders, the Genetic Interest Group, is opposing the patenting of aspects of human genes. Alastair Kent, its director, has said, 'Our view is that there is something fundamentally unacceptable about any institution, corporation, or individual having ownership over part of a human being' (*The Independent*, 17 November 1993). It is possible that the European patent authorities may be less willing than those in the USA to accept such wide ranging patents, which tend to restrict the exchange of scientific information in a highly undesirable way. On the other hand it can be said in defence of genetic engineering corporations that they do have a need to recover the costs of their research. But they also have their eye on profits which are potentially very large indeed.

Now that we have acquired the ability to cut up DNA and transfer it from one body to another and even from one species to another, it is by no means clear where the boundaries may or should lie. What is to be regarded as worthy of 'cure' and what will be the effects of such changes on our social functioning? The progress now being made on the Human Genome Project makes this an urgent question. In a review of an account of the project so far (*Genome* by Jerry Bishop and Michael Waldholz), M. F. Perutz comments:

> Genetic screening could be beneficial if it were to be restricted to the most common life-threatening diseases, or to cases where there is a family history of congenital disease. Otherwise, we might finish with a society of genetic hypochondriacs ... Some years ago, the Swedish Government decided that much ill health could be avoided if new-born

babies were screened for [*a deficiency predisposing to emphy-sema*], and parents of affected babies were told to warn them later on to avoid smoking. In fact, this screening led to so much morbidity as a result of guilt, recrimination between married couples, and quarrels with in-laws for having brought a deleterious gene into the family, that the Swedish Govern-ment had to abandon it. (*London Review of Books*, 16 September 1991, pp. 3–4)

There may indeed be a 'right not to know' arising from processes of genetic screening.

The knowledge arising from genetic engineering will also tend to benefit some at the expense of others. In general, highly technical research favours rich societies which have the resources both to pursue the research and to put its results into practice. Equally, it favours richer groups or social classes within societies at the expense of smaller or poorer ones. So Keith Buchanan comments that the use on cows of the genetically engineered bovine growth hormone to increase milk yield by 20 to 40 per cent and feed efficiency by 10 per cent will tend to reduce the number of smaller dairymen as a few large producers take on the necessary capital investment and tech-nological expertise, including 'computerised monitoring to optimise feed nutrient levels and controlled environments which will reduce the impact on already stressed animals of abnormal weather condi-tions' ('The Ultimate Arrogance', p. 40). The high-tech cow, in fact, will be a high-tech problem, giving cheaper milk to a market which is not particularly elastic.

'All these developments promise increasing profits and power to the handful of giant pharmaceutical firms which are developing the hormone', says Buchanan (p. 40). Others have also expressed concern about the effects of commercial investment in genetic engineering. Jonathan King's view that companies will tend to concentrate medical research on products which alleviate symptoms and therefore have to be taken regularly, rather than products and processes which remove the primary causes of diseases, is quoted by Birch and Cobb, who add that there is a general objection that can be made to 'the development of expensive medical technologies that are available only to the few and which deprive others of basic health care' (*The Liberation of Life*, p. 228). M. F. Perutz, in the review already mentioned, concludes:

It worries me, though, that the billions of dollars to be spent
on the Genome Project are likely to benefit only the people
in the rich world who are already very healthy, but will do
nothing to rid the vast majority of people in the poor world
of the host of crippling and deadly parasitic diseases that are
the real scourge of mankind. On these very little money is
being spent, and there has been no clarion call to stir scientists
to action. (p. 4)

As with medical research, so with consumer products. Keith
Buchanan gives the example of the development by genetic engineering of a new sugar substitute, thaumatin, which is 100,000
times sweeter than sugar and presents a threat to the work of sugar
cane growers in poor countries. He forecasts that 'The development
of bioengineering substances threatens a far more massive devasta-
tion of third world peasant societies than did the development of
chemical substances' ('The Ultimate Arrogance', p. 41). Both
internationally and within particular societies the ability to reinvent
the creation promises to increase divisions as well as bring practical
benefits. We may conclude that the scientific powers which we now
have are awesome. The doubt is whether our social institutions and
our moral perceptions are adequate for the decisions which we now
have to make about the use of those powers.

(vi) The Meaning of Health

Theologically the notion of health relates first to our spiritual
condition. It is the ability to make our bodies the place where the
Spirit of God acts for our good and for the good of others.
Everything else comes under the heading of 'contingency', the brute
facts of life which happen to be in *this* form and not another form.
We may live long lives or short ones; we may be physically fit or
given over to illness; we may have wide life-opportunities or very
narrow ones. All of this is simply the working material from which
'life' is constructed.

Much in life seems unfair because we start from ourselves as the
centre and feel that all possibilities ought to be given to us. But there
is no 'ought' in the natural world. Health is whatever we happen to
get. In this context the long Christian tradition of emphasising the

positive value of suffering has been a way of saying that what counts for spiritual health is always the act of the human will, the decision to be 'for' God. This is the decision to take a positive view (not to 'explain', for explanation is often not possible) of the current state of health. The Christian tradition also says that help is always at hand, not necessarily to cure, but to enable the person to come to a positive act of acceptance of what life brings. The Spirit of God always comes when called upon, though not in the form or the measure or for the purpose that we try to define.

Such trust in the Spirit of God does not mean that suffering is always ennobling. To be ill is often to be tired, confused, bitter, irritable or unable to cope. It can also be a time for dark thought, for feeling the absence of God, for retreat into childhood or into the womb, and for refusing self-knowledge. The offering of the gospel as a direct cure for all this may simply be insensitive. Those who care for those who suffer need first of all to offer their own presence, nothing else. The Spirit comes to us in paths that are not necessarily marked 'religious', even for those who are dying. In these circumstances the affirmation of the Spirit is through care for the other, not through conversion. Many religious needs are approached most directly through simple love.

The other wrong conclusion that might be drawn from faith in the Spirit is that no great effort ought to go into some of the ways of preventing ill health or changing the world to promote physical and mental well-being. On the contrary, the same judgment that accepts contingency as setting the necessary boundaries within which we have faith also sees the contingent as precisely a set of conditions which may under some circumstances be altered. The Spirit of God who gives faith and consolation in suffering also gives intelligence and energy to change what can be changed in our lives. The commission to use human intelligence and human energy to change life seems to me to be absolutely clear, provided that it is expressed not merely on the basis of the immediate objective ('can do, will do'), but also in the wider context of the moral capacities of human beings. What sort of people shall we be if we agree to this change? is always a legitimate question. The difficulty lies in the prior question, How do we decide what sort of people we want to be?

The earth is not a place of health in itself. Rather it is a place of competition for living space and for evolutionary advantage, in which human beings are equally caught up with other species. While it is obviously better to be healthy than ill, and while it is obviously good to give resources to health care and to research into cures, it is the moral results of life rather than the physical results which are the reason for our existence.

Consequently, health resources are first of all a question of justice. Do we have enough resources to give adequate health care to all? Or do we not care enough about the health of all to devote adequate resources to it? The many advances we have made in medical possibilities, from new types of surgery, through new drugs, to organ replacements and scans of all sorts, all increase the political problem of cost. It is already clear that some medical care, even in 'advanced' countries, is being refused to those who are not considered to be in some sense 'fit' – too old, too confused or too poor to demand or receive the right to care.

It is also clear that some medicine is dealing with ills that are the byproducts of poor social conditions, the results of poor housing, poor diet, polluted air, or the stress of poverty and unemployment. There is no good physical health without good social conditions. In the nineteenth century in Britain the rising middle classes understood that the health of the poor was also their concern, both to produce an efficient workforce and to prevent the spread of disease among themselves. Out of both fear and love there came campaigns for better drainage, clean water and improved housing. This sense of our belonging together is a lesson we are in danger of forgetting again.

Some medical problems also may not yield to whatever we can bring against them. Premature senility (known in some of its major forms as 'Alzheimer's disease') is one of the largest problems in terms of numbers and demands on resources, but no answer to it is yet in sight. Some conditions cannot be dealt with because the cost is too high in other respects. So malaria is returning to many parts of the world, because the environmental effect of killing the mosquito which is the carrier is too dangerous in putting the pesticide DDT into the food chain and poisoning the species at the upper end of the chain, including ourselves, which feed off smaller species which accumulate the chemical.

Some diseases can be cleared away completely, as appears to have happened with smallpox. Others are simply waiting to happen, as was the case with the Human Immuno-Virus (HIV) associated with

Aids. Nature is, after all, a vast experimental laboratory, and the combination of the breakdown of traditional restraints on sexual activity in many cultures, freedom of travel and a lack of education about and concern for the fitness of our bodies, provided a clear opportunity for an aggressive disease to appear. Other new diseases will appear. Other old ones, such as tuberculosis, are already making unexpected reappearances in communities that thought them gone for ever.

Aids (Acquired Immune Deficiency Syndrome) is not strictly a disease, but a specific liability to succumb to a range of diseases because the immune system can no longer repel intrusions. In most of the world it seems to be associated chiefly with promiscuous heterosexual activity; in Western Europe and North America it has been associated more with drug abuse and with homosexual promiscuity. As such the sufferers have been the target for a considerable amount of moral condemnation.

Yet in the homosexual community in particular Aids has prompted a good deal of moral reflection among both sufferers and carers. In the first place, it has illustrated the unreadiness of our society to contemplate the fact of death. That a death sentence could so suddenly be pronounced upon the young and healthy, as it were out of nowhere, revealed the element of the unexpected, the sudden presence of the unknown, which always underlies our lives. For not only the 'guilty' suffered, but also the 'innocent', the relatives and friends who found themselves on the verge of bereavement, and even those who were infected unknowingly by loving partners. Suddenly the language of the Book of Common Prayer, 'In the midst of life we are in death: of whom may we seek for succour, but of thee, O Lord, who for our sins art justly displeased?' seemed appropriate again, not only for the sick, but for all the human race.

Three positive lessons have come from this experience. The first is the wealth of compassion that has been drawn upon by sufferers and carers, making the approach of death a positive experience for many. As Stephen Pattison says, 'We cannot accompany one another beyond the moment of death. But the subversive memory of life in death suggests that we can learn and live together up to that point, refusing to relinquish hold of one another and so wresting some kind of new life from the living void from which we sprang and to which we all return' ('To the Churches with Love', in Woodward, *Embracing the Chaos*, p. 17). The second has been the reconsideration of the nature of our commitment to one another, especially in relation to sexuality – we have been reconnected with our bodies in a matter of serious moral obligation. The third has been that the moral seriousness of sexuality should not be limited narrowly to traditional Christian marriage. It was because the churches did not take sexuality seriously enough that there was no teaching, no 'education' indeed, about the realities of sex, of love and of embodiment which could have prepared us to deal with the event of Aids and even to have avoided beforehand some of its worst effects. As Edward Norman asks of traditional Christian attitudes to homosexuality, 'What sort of God is envisaged, who sends his children into the world with compulsive instincts, which they do not choose, and who then denies them the affection and consolation of shared sexual experience?' ('AIDS and the Will of God', in Woodward, *Embracing the Chaos*, p. 89). One might add, that this is true not only of homosexuality, but of sexuality in general. The British government's lamentable lack of serious effort at open sexual instruction about HIV and Aids, both on television and elsewhere, compared with many other European countries, is a sign of a deep-rooted hypocrisy and lack of moral seriousness in this country on these matters.

For the morality of sexuality is really about the affirmation of meaning in our deepest experiences, both of life and death. The notion of health is the notion of being able to be 'real', to acknowledge the truth, both to ourselves and to others, of our human situation of being 'persons', body and spirit, driven to one another for whatever brief time, to take what consolation we can in one another's humanness. No theology, and no notion of health, is any good which does not address this reality as we actually experience it. True 'health' is to know ourselves as we are today.

The question of health is now not simply a question of the human longing for life without pain or physical limitation. It is a question of the health of the whole creation. Human life is absolutely dependent on the well-being of the whole interlocking system of species, animal and vegetable, bird and fish and insect, which makes up the 'biosphere', the fragile envelope of life on the surface of the planet earth. No amount of technology can replace this system. No prayer can heal us which is not located in this system. For we are it and it is us.

The 'health' of a human being is to be a part of the biosphere as one having responsibility for it. There are no purely human aims which have validity without respect for the wholeness of creation. There are no spiritual aims which take us outside the system or place us in isolation within it. At the same time the biosphere is not a moral or a spiritual absolute. It too does not have moral autonomy. The lives of animals and plants are not moral lives in any human sense. Their morality comes from their integrity within the system, that they do the work of birds or of bees or of mosquitoes, both in co-operation and in competition with other species. Their morality is the maintaining of the dynamics of the living world.

The spiritual responsibility of human beings is to be responsive to this system. We are to be aware of its fullness, of its beauty, of its fragility and above all of its 'purposes' as something other than our own moral aims. A fox is not 'for' anything but to be a fox. When human beings live at the level of subsistence, they too claim their 'rights' over creation simply in order to be able to survive. When we move above the level of subsistence the opportunity for 'play' arises, the opportunity for culture, for chosen aims. So we can hunt foxes for pleasure, cut down trees to make books, level hills to make roads, use earth and water and fire and air for our own dominion.

We can also now alter ourselves for our own pleasure and profit, or simply to rejoice in our own skills. Keith Buchanan quotes an official of the US Patent Office as remarking that 'a horse is just a temporary situation – it only represents a certain amount of (genetic) information and that can now be changed' ('The Ultimate Arrogance', p. 37). It seems that the same may now be true of a human being. The range of choices for those who have the resources to enter into the new technologies is awesome. The restrictions on those who have not the resources are also awesome. The sin of Adam and Eve is now clear: they asked for knowledge and we have received it, pressed down and flowing over.

It is not entirely clear to me that this is a system which can continue for very long. The sort of use of resources to which we now seem to be committed may prove not to be sustainable, even though some of our inventions may save resources rather than destroy them. In that case the system, which some call 'Gaia', the living earth, will have reasserted itself at our expense. Before 'Gaia' moves, however, we have a chance, though not a very big one, to take charge of ourselves more responsibly. It will be a hard course to take. It will require relearning the Christian virtue of humility, this time at the level of the whole human community. It will mean asking the question of every procedure, as Suzuki and Knudtson suggest we do over germ cell changes, 'What does the whole of human society authorise us to do?'

This is, of course, essentially a religious question. It has no 'scientific' answer. I could wish that it did. But science does not in the end contain its own moral guidelines. Neither do social institutions, in their own right. As Durkheim saw, when we come to human institutions for moral help, we succeed only in worshipping ourselves. True health can be derived only from the Spirit that creates and sustains the universe, the Holy Spirit of the Christian creed. And the Holy Spirit is to be met in the one human institution that concerns itself with this meeting, the institution of religion. I could wish also that the Christian churches were in better shape to answer the questions that must now be put to them, and to answer them together, and to answer them in co-operation with the other world religions. For the task is nothing less than this. Nothing less than this can give us 'health' or even lead us to a determination of what 'health' might be.

4

THE MANDATE OF LOVE

(i) Patriarchy

If there is a general claim to moral order anywhere in human society then sexuality is surely the place to look. Even those who react most negatively to the notion of a natural law would agree that eating and drinking and reproduction are essential to the life of the species. Not only that, but also as social animals with possibilities of choice and with a long period of child-development, primates need a social structure of some sort to arrange their mating and nurturing activities. Human beings, with their greater capacity for choice, permanent sexual receptivity in the female and concealment of ovulation, the time in each month when a female in the fertile years can conceive a child, need these arrangements more than most. Yet add to that our apparently unique notion of 'a moral dimension' in our lives, and it would seem that the mandate of sexuality is something that we may have to invent rather than to receive directly from nature or from past social patterns. For human beings, perhaps foolishly, demand 'love' as well as 'sex'.

In spite of the notion of the 'fall', sexuality does not feature in Jewish thought as an evil. On the contrary, the goodness of sexuality, in terms of marriage and children, is part of the goodness of the original creation. Increasingly in the Old Testament the imagery of marriage is used to signify the relationship between God and Israel, culminating in Malachi's saying, 'If a man divorces or puts away his wife, says the Lord God of Israel, he overwhelms her with cruelty'.

In the New Testament the concern is rather about the relative brevity of our involvement in earthly things compared with the importance of the coming of the kingdom of God. This shift of emphasis did, nevertheless, contribute to the real problem, which was that the New Testament, with its concern for the future kingdom, did not substantially counteract the patriarchal ideas which dominated the Old Testament world.

Consequently, in spite of the radical freedom of Jesus himself towards existing rules of behaviour and in spite of the radical equality in sexuality taught by St Paul in 1 Corinthians 7.3–4, the new churches accepted the prevailing custom of the subordination of women, which enters into the New Testament itself in such passages as Ephesians 5.22 (probably not by St Paul): 'Wives, be subject to your husbands as though to the Lord; for the man is the head of the woman, just as Christ is the head of the church'. This indeed takes some explaining away, since even a moment's reflection might have convinced the author that the difference between two human beings cannot be the same as, nor even analogous to, the difference between Christ, the pre-existent Son of God present at the creation of the world, and any living creature in that world.

The basic fact about the New Testament, however, is still that, as Paul Avis puts it, 'The rehabilitation of women by Jesus remains one of the most remarkable aspects of his mission. By his fellowship with them, he enacted their incorporation into God's kingdom' (*Eros and the Sacred*, p. 106).

Nevertheless the Ephesians passage shows the early church quickly surrendering its radical potential and settling for the general social consciousness of patriarchy, as it also settles for the general social acceptance of slavery.

Historically the outstanding fact about sexuality in the western world is the prevalence of patriarchy, the 'rule of the fathers'. The particular influence of the Christian tradition has been to affirm one pattern within patriarchy, that of life-long monogamous marriage. Phillipe Ariès remarks that 'The form of marriage in which a man can repudiate his wife and remarry is undoubtedly the most widespread and normal, except in the western world' (*Western Sexuality*, p. 140). This pattern is clearly now changing, but it retains strong appeal as an ideal, not least because modern, western civilisation, perhaps uniquely in human cultural history, wishes to found the social institutions of sexuality upon the notion of 'love'.

Biologically, this aim might appear to be impossible to fulfill. There is nothing in the social structure of other animal communities which can give clear guidance on what human beings should do. There are many different arrangements for reproduction, ranging from those female spiders which eat their male partners after the sexual act, to species of birds which mate with one partner for life. No moral issue about sexuality arises in these communities. As David Attenborough remarks of the unlucky male spider, 'in terms of the success of the species as a whole, that individual disaster is of limited consequence: he lost his life after, not before he had completed his purpose' (*Life on Earth*, p. 69).

Within the order of primates there is a range of social structures which have to do not only with sexual reproduction, but also with mutual defence, co-operative food-searching and relations of power. In these complex social arrangements other forms of bonding than the sexual are fundamental to group survival. Access to sex is only one aspect of group life and may be more related to the ability to exercise power than to individual bonding. Only human beings combine the practice of exogamy – finding a marital partner outside the kin group – with the maintenance of social relationships between the kin groups that are linked by this sexual gift, so creating more complex and powerful social structures than those of other animals. This capacity to build outwards, and ultimately to create 'civilisation', gives to human personal relationships an importance that they do not acquire in other species.

The persistence of patriarchy presumably relates to its effectiveness as a form of social structure in this process of building civilisation. In many environments the human species is subjected to strong competition for resources. Our closest cousins the chimpanzees seem to lead relaxed social lives in environments which do not call for continually strenuous efforts to find warmth, shelter or food, and which do not subject them to serious predation. Human beings live more adventurously in more varied climates, more open to competition for resources and more ready for aggression, even within the species, than other animals. The human primate is the most dangerous of all animals to other animals because of its capacities for co-operation, for learning and planning and for the use of tools, but it is also the most dangerous of animals to its own kind because of its willingness to use these capacities to secure advantages within the species itself. As with all animals which present danger to themselves, questions of power relationships demand careful structuring.

The advance of human beings into rational consciousness necessarily constitutes a 'fall' into the possibility of sin. The availability of so much potential for construction and destruction sets a premium, not so much on physical power, as on knowledge and cunning in association with physical strength. Along with this must go a social system that allows cunning strength to come to the top and at the same time distributes power according to various abilities required by the community, including physical strength, emotional stability and rational judgment. A tight social structure with strong leadership, and commitment to group knowledge in the form of memory and therefore of age, linked to mating habits which ensure the protection of the young in their long period in the womb and even longer period of dependency and education out of the womb, makes for greater success against competition. So humanity has succeeded as the most competitive, brutal and intelligent of animals. The more successful humans have been among other animals and within our own species, the most we have needed to strive in order to maintain that success.

What the fall into conscious ways of living has created, therefore, is a being subject to various stresses, needing to do what no animal has ever needed to do before, namely to give a moral account of its own life and to state a formal purpose for its social structures. In the light of this the existence of human societies which apparently do not know the patriarchy, whether tribes in Papau-New Guinea or communes in California, is irrelevant to the general question of the problem of the dominance of males in human social systems. We know already that human beings are adaptable animals. What we do not know is whether there is any social structure other than patriarchy that will serve us on the same scale of civilisation as patriarchy has done.

(ii) Human Development

This situation is made more complicated by the fact that the human being has a psychological story as well as a social story. The advance of human beings into rational consciousness is a 'fall' precisely because with knowledge comes a responsibility that we are unable ever fully to achieve in practice. The psychological story is the recognition that we are lived by our needs. Erik H. Erikson tells a story about Sigmund Freud:

> Freud was once asked what he thought a normal person
> should be able to do well. The questioner probably expected
> a complicated answer. But Freud, in the curt way of his old
> days, is reported to have said: '*Lieben und arbeiten*' (to love
> and to work). It pays to ponder on this simple formula; it gets
> deeper as you think about it. For when Freud said 'love', he
> meant *genital* love, and genital *love*; when he said love *and*
> work, he meant a general work-productiveness which would
> not preoccupy the individual to the extent that he loses his
> right or capacity to be a genital and a loving being. (*Childhood
> and Society*, p. 256)

Pschoanalytic theory has frequently come under attack because it
relies more on intuitive understanding of the person than on
quantifiable experiments. Nevertheless psychoanalytic explanations
survive because they give to our experiential knowledge of ourselves
a coherence and an explanatory power which no other system of
explanation provides. Moreover from this analysis there come
pathways of change.

In the classic Freudian analysis we move in our early years
through stages of psychosexual development, beginning with an
equal interest in all our orifices and their inputs and outputs (the
'polymorphously perverse' stage of the young baby), then to an oral
stage of concern with what can be put into the mouth ('I want to eat
you') and then to a stage of concern with the anus ('I want to retain
control of me and you'). These initial stages create characteristics of
the personality which may stay with us in different degrees into
adult life, according to our success in obtaining satisfaction and in
learning to cope with frustration in these first steps of life. There
follows a 'latency period', roughly between the ages of six and eleven,
during which the child builds up other forms of development,
physical, mental and social. There are specific paths of development
for the fundamental structures of the personality concerning the
ability to love, the ability to reason, the ability to take moral
decisions and the ability for religious faith, each of which can be
tracked, though with varying degrees of confidence.

After the latency period, sexuality returns to the driving seat, as
the physical changes of puberty open up the possibilities of genital
sexuality. Here the child truly has to learn to become an adult. The
first explorations may be with the same sex, but for most the sexual

drive quickly overcomes the otherness of the opposite sex. How quickly sexual experience becomes a reality depends not only on the individual personality, but also on the way in which the particular society structures sexual experience for the individual. Following both the social and the individual pathways, successful mating closes the sexual circle with reproduction and a new generation to grow to adulthood.

To be a 'person' is consequently a considerable task of following up the sexual, emotional, cognitive, moral and spiritual pathways to become a mature human being. Personal relationships begin with the facts of birth and of being parented. It may be that we could also speak of pre-birth experiences, but at present that is a speculative matter. What we do know is that being born is a major transition, greater than anything else that happens to us except the fact of death. We come from the dark, warm, enveloping liquid into light and air and noise and above all separateness. The shock which we experience is not only physical, but also mental and moral and spiritual – it is the task of beginning an independent existence. The first months of life after birth are occupied in adjusting to the new environment and beginning the task of controlling it by assimilating it to our needs, or of accepting the necessities it imposes upon us and accommodating ourselves to them.

The centre of this initial task is the separation of the identity of the self from the identity of the mother or caring adult. From the moment of birth, babies are not passive, but in active interaction with the environment, which for the most part is the person of the mother. Only slowly does the baby realise that the environment as a whole, and the mother in particular, is not an extension of itself, as the womb may seem to be, and that the mother is in fact another person like itself.

This separateness of the mother is established at least partly by negation. The moment when the mother is not there when the baby wakes, or when she does not produce whatever relief or satisfaction the cry is meant to produce, creates a negative image, 'Not Me', which passes over into 'Bad Mother / Bad Other', just as the 'Good Mother / Good Other' image forms when satisfaction is given. Now these two images have to be united into the concept of 'Another Person', who does not exist solely for my satisfaction. None of this, of course, happens through argument or exposition; rather it happens through play and through all the activities of eating and excreting, waking and sleeping, reaching and responding which make up the baby's day.

The interaction between the mother or caring adult and the new-born child, therefore, represents a substantial task on both sides. Firstly, the interaction is intentional. It is not simply a response to biological stimulation (though that also exists), but is the result of deliberate activity by the mother towards the child and by the child towards the mother. Margaret Donaldson comments that 'We do not just sit and wait for the world to impinge on us. We try actively to interpret it, to make sense of it' (*Children's Minds*, p. 68), and she quotes research which shows this may be true even of young babies (pp. 110–13). This fact of intentionality means, however, that human behaviour can very more widely and can go wrong more disastrously than the development of other animals.

Secondly, the care of the mother for the child constitutes a gift relationship. However rewarding the child's responses and initiatives may be for the mother, mother and child are not equals in giving. We learn to love by first being loved and we have to move from the capacity to receive to the capacity to give. John Bowlby comments:

> It must never be forgotten that even the bad parent who neglects her child is nonetheless providing much for him. Except in the worst cases, she is giving him food and shelter, comforting him in distress, teaching him simple skills, and above all is providing him with that continuity of human care on which his sense of security rests. (*Child Care and the Growth of Love*, p. 76)

This process of development requires us to learn to incorporate negative experiences into a positive response to others. We become persons only through the actions towards us of other persons. Our ability to relate to other persons and our knowledge of what it is to be a person is governed largely, though not exclusively, by these experiences of the early years of childhood.

Erik Erikson has put forward a theory of eight 'ages' of human development, from birth to the acceptance of death. The analysis is of the growth that we have to make in the task of being human and in which, as we grow, we will also make mistakes. They are not chronological stages, but tasks that remain with us all our lives, in more or less unfinished states, more like stories about ourselves than psychological programmes, which nevertheless may tell the truth about ourselves.

The 'eight ages of man', as Erikson calls them, are:

Basic Trust v Basic Mistrust
Autonomy v Shame and Doubt
Initiative v Guilt
Industry v Inferiority
Identity v Role Confusion
Intimacy v Isolation
Generativity v Stagnation
Ego Integrity v Despair (*Childhood and Society*, chapter 7)

Of these 'ages', following classic Freudian theory, Erikson lays most stress on the earlier periods, up to the time of leaving the home for school. The earliest stage is occupied in coping with our basic physical needs of being held and fed and made comfortable and having our physical outputs removed in nappy-changing. This essential physical and emotional care lays the foundation for the individual to have trust in a stable and responsive human environment. We discover that we live in an ordered universe with a capacity for care. This is the beginning of the ability to love and trust other people; it is also, in the same instant, the beginning of religious trust, the ability to conceive of the universe as having purpose and meaning.

Such a foundation is never laid perfectly. When it is absent completely, the capacity for affect, for genuine feeling for others, may never be attained and the moral life may not be within that person's power. Where care is provided very inadequately, a deficit may remain that cannot be made up. For the great majority of human beings, however, sufficient care is given for a sense of community with others to be possible, however much we have still to do. The sense of community as something possible and valuable, therefore, is primarily a gift of our first carers.

The second 'age' concerns the discovery of autonomy. In the simplest ways the baby is learning to control its physical movements. Its movements become more purposeful and directed, it can hold or let go. Even at this very early stage, then, the problem of choice arises, and more than that. For the movement from choice to moral order depends also on the feedback the child receives from its efforts. In the normal course of human life some of its efforts will be frustrated. Though most responsibility still falls upon the carers, the baby also begins to have a choice of response to conflicts of interest. As Erikson says, 'Thus, to hold can become a destructive and cruel retaining or restraining, and it can become a pattern of care; to have and to hold' (p. 243). Letting-go can also be positive or negative. There is no 'innocence' in a baby, simply because everything the child undertakes is part of its eventual personality.

The third 'age' is the beginning of specifically sexual interests. From a general interest in all bodily openings and their inputs and outputs, children towards the end of early childhood begin to show signs of a more specific awareness of their own genitals and of those of others, including the differences between the sexes. While this is entirely natural, in the sense that it is proper to the child to make discoveries about its own body and the place of that body in the world of other bodies, the process of discovery also constitutes something of a threat to the child. This is because children are not yet ready for sexuality and therefore their own sexual potentiality becomes a threat. It is part of the uncomprehended power of adult life. The inner threat may also be reinforced by strong signs of disapproval and discouragement from adults of any such 'sexual' interests. Henceforth sexual initiative is always likely to be accompanied by a sense of guilt.

Consequently the child now enters into a 'latency' period, when the thought of sexual interests is put aside in favour of other sorts of activity in the world. In the fourth 'age' the child moves out into the world and concentrates on the other half of Freud's aphorism about human life, 'to love and to *work*'. Human creativity is expressed as much in working in the world as in personal relationships. The development of the capacity to organise, to plan and to acquire skills is all part of 'who we are' in the moral sense. Moreover this action in the world requires co-operation, a knowledge of others which is different from the knowledge which comes by personal love. The responsibility of the school, in which much of this learning takes place, and the importance also of pre-school experience of others, in play-groups and nursery school, cannot be emphasised enough. The learning task of the child is immense in these years. The return on such an investment, in terms of successful socialisation in adult life, means that a rationally-ordered society would make its major educational effort at this point.

The fundamental moral importance of work creates great problems for the school, because neither the school nor the adult society to which it leads can adequately meet the needs and the potentialities of every young person. Modern societies are complex, individualistic and subject to rapid and often apparently random change. In traditional societies, with a limited range of options, the developmental task is clear and holds the growing personality securely, even though it may leave much individual potential unattended to. This fundamental integration of having a secure place in a comprehensible world probably meets the human need for self-understanding better than any modern notion of 'self-fulfilment'. For self-fulfilment can come only to an already established social self.

The work of the school, in a modern society, is first of all to enable the child to understand, adapt to and contribute to the patterns that are given. Where no pattern is given that produces the rewards promised, disaster must follow. Where this happens to an individual, a sense of inferiority follows. 'The child despairs of his equipment in the tool world and in anatomy, and considers himself doomed to mediocrity or inadequacy' (p. 251). Where the child does not fail, she or he becomes the inheritor of the technological ethos of the culture – the ability to *do* in a particular way – but with a further risk of not seeing beyond technological possibilities to wider issues of human life.

If, on the other hand, the failure to provide a transition into 'industry' is a failure not only for individual children but also for a whole society or a whole segment of a society, then we may go beyond Erikson's vision and suggest that a much more dangerous alienation becomes possible. This is *anomie*, the dissatisfaction with society as a whole that leads into the breakdown of social order – crime, drug-use, disregard for all forms of love of neighbour. Such disintegration in its turn gives opportunity for totalitarian responses, for projection outwards on to real or mythical enemies, for ethnic or religious hatred and 'cleansing' of the clan. In other words, far beyond Erikson's concern for individual development, the apparently simple introduction to co-operative work and exploration in the school has profound implications for the possibilities of social order. In this respect, as Durkheim saw, modern industrial societies seem to be already well down the road of social disintegration.

Returning to the story of individual development, after the latency period of initial 'work experience' in the school, there comes at adolescence a renewed need to explore the sexual possibilities of the person. This is the stage which Erikson calls 'Identity v Role Confusion', when everything so far learned is blown apart by the new emotional turmoil of physical and emotional growth. Here the dual task must be undertaken afresh – to learn to love and to learn to work. All the work that has been done so far to create an identity, and all the failures of that work, must be brought together in a stable sense of the self. 'The sense of ego identity, then, is the accrued confidence that the inner sameness and continuity of one's meaning for others, is evidenced in the tangible promise of a "career"' (p. 253). Trust, autonomy and sexuality have to be relearned, without any security that the earlier lessons will hold.

Fortunately, the disadvantages of adolescence are also advantages. Because all has to be done again, some experiences that came out badly in the early stages may be renewed with more success as the child struggles to enter adult life. There are good adolescent experiences as well as bad ones. The security which failed earlier may be given now by new partners. The final step into adult life is to exchange the temptations of withdrawal into isolation for the dangerous self-exposure of sexual intimacy and the founding of a new family unit. The autonomy which failed to satisfy may now reappear as a real capacity to deal with the self and others.

All this is possible because of the tremendous power of the central fact of sexuality. The basic biological drive to union with another person can overcome almost all past fears and disappointments. The gift of eros, the sexual desire for one another, is that it enables life to begin again. Of course, eros leads to disappointment and to the need for new learning processes. From the dream-state of erotic fulfilment the individual, still wet behind the ears, has to enter again the moral world of work, responsibility and love – love now being not the fulfilment of erotic desire but what follows from that, the learning of the life of another person.

One might add to Erikson's story here that the Christian doctrine of marriage which regards it as a kind of licence or permission for sex has got things the wrong way round. 'Marriage' is the term for that moral order – whatever the practical arrangements involved – which gives the social structure of support to the work by which the sex-drive is led on to love and mutual support for life. It is that state in which two people can survive the process of mutual adjustment in the conditions of 'love-and-work' and achieve an integrated adult life in that society.

For, as Erikson also makes clear, there is a considerable work still to be done. Personal identity is not complete at the moment of adult sexuality. The 'Generativity' which follows is that demanded not only by the continuation of the family cycle in the new generation of children, but also the continued effort at self-affirmation through work and through intimate relationships. Being a person is not a work in which we can stand still. New challenges occur, new threats, and new defeats. Beyond all this lies the ultimate task, to cope with the threat of our own defeat in death. As a psychologist Erikson does not take us into the promise of eternal life, but sees the acceptance of death as itself the final triumph of ego-integrity. 'It is a post-narcissistic love of the human ego – not of the self– as an experience which conveys some world order and spiritual sense, no matter how dearly paid for' (p. 260). It is a reconciliation with the past as something that has been necessary and in some sense valuable. The alternative is to carry the fear of life through to the literally bitter end. But as Erikson says, 'healthy children will not fear life if their elders have integrity enough not to fear death' (p. 261).

There are, of course, problems about Erikson's analysis, including the difficulty that Freudian theory is heavily biased towards the male view of life. The psychological evaluation of child development has come a long way since 1950, as has our understanding of the psychological dynamics of the family. Erikson has, for example, nothing to say about domestic violence or child abuse. Yet the story of the 'eight ages' retains its value. We *do* change and we *do* have physical, psychological and social work to accomplish in order to become mature adults. Above all, we have to understand and accept the trajectory of our lives, from birth to death, as a single and potentially positive experience. On this there is nothing in the fundamental structure of Erikson's 'ages' that requires challenge.

(iii) The Family as a Moving Target

The late twentieth century has been a period of exceptional fluidity in the social institutions which regulate sexuality in Western Europe and North America. Betty Friedan remarked in 1981 that 'We are now on the cusp of breaking through the obsolete image of the family' (*The Second Stage*, p. 100), pointing out that 'fewer than 7 per cent of Americans are now living in that kind of family to which politicians and churchmen are always paying lip service – Daddy the breadwinner, Mother the housewife, and two children (with background bark of dog and meow of cat, and station wagon parked in the ranch-house driveway)'. In Great Britain in 1981, single persons accounted for 22 per cent of households and couples with no children a further 26 per cent; married couples with dependent children constituted less than a third of all households at 31 per cent; single parents with at least one dependent child made up 5 per cent of all households (*Social Trends 17*, Table 2.1).

The interpretation of social statistics is never easy, even in relation to the past. In relation to making predictions for the future it is perhaps a foolish exercise. Nevertheless there are now some very clear trends in the sociological account of 'the family' in Europe, which are well set out in a recent survey edited by Duncan J. Cormor, *The Relationship Revolution*. The first is a high rate of divorce, except in Catholic countries where there may be legal impediments. 'Around 40% of all marriages are likely to end in divorce in Denmark, England and Wales, Sweden and Eastern Germany, whereas in Spain and Italy fewer than 1 in 10 marriages will be ended by divorce if current rates of divorce prevail' (p. 3). The second is the separation of sexual experience from the institution of marriage. 'Today a typical woman may become sexually active at sixteen and marry, if indeed she does marry, around the time that she has her first child, on average 26 years' (p. 8). The third is the trend towards cohabitation rather than marriage. 'The decline in marriage in Sweden has been most dramatic; in 1966 the marriage rate was 7.8 marriages per thousand population, it then fell to 4.9 marriages per thousand population by 1971, a decline of 37% in five years' (p. 11). This pattern has now spread to all Western European countries. Whether or not marriage will disappear entirely is another question. As the survey concludes, 'the majority of the population in virtually all Western European countries still marry at some time in their lives, so that we must exercise caution in predicting its demise' (p. 31).

The effects of these trends on personal relationships are even more difficult to estimate. Faith Robertson Elliot quotes an American study by Wallerstein and Kelly in 1980. 'It suggests that marital break-up brings unpredictability, unreliability and insecurity into the child's world. Bewilderment, anxiety, anger, grief, shame, but above all a yearning for, and / or a sense of rejection by, the departing parent (the father in nearly all of these cases) are common responses' (*The Family*, p. 149).

Similarly, one-parent families are vulnerable in various ways, economic, social and psychological. However, Elliot comments that recent studies relate 'the vulnerability of the one-parent family not to the absence of a parent *per se* but to society's failure to endorse any family form other than the nuclear family' (p. 168). She adds, 'Many one-parent families function well. Moreover, though it has been consistently found that children growing up in one-parent families have more developmental problems than children in the unbroken nuclear family, the differences are small and do not necessarily persist into adulthood' (p. 169).

As a centre of personal relationships the family is a moving target, not only in the sense of the fluidity of the present social arrange- ments, but also in the sense of marriage – or even long-term cohabitation – not being the same experience over time. 'Marriage has often been interpreted as an institution whose essential features are static. In fact the partners and their children who live through several decades of married life find it anything but static', points out Jack Dominian (*Marriage, Faith and Love*, p. 107). There are various analysis of the family cycle, but all of them consist essentially of the fact that there is first a period of courtship and homemaking, then a period of child-rearing, then a period of dispersion of the children and then a final period of retirement and the eventual death of the partners. Divorce and remarriage complicates the pattern, but the movement from meeting through procreation to separation and death is in the end inevitable. As Dominian says at a later stage of his argument, 'We have one life and one personality to develop fully, and the fuel for this growth is love received principally from parents and spouses' (p. 275). The nature of the family cycle makes this a much more complex task than simply 'falling in love'.

Moral theologians necessarily take a positive view of the family, since they are committed to it as the primary model in human relationships. It is therefore important to recognise also that the family is an area where things can go seriously wrong. First of all the family is about power. Women still do the bulk of domestic work, even when they are in full-time employment, and men still take the more important decisions about family life. Looking at current research, Abercrombie and Warde conclude that 'Generally, the more important though less frequent decisions tend to be husband-dominated, whereas the less important though more frequent decisions are made by the wife' (*Contemporary British Society*, p. 288).

Power relations in the family are expressed more damagingly in child abuse and in physical attacks upon women, including marital rape. Now that discussion is out in the open, reported cases of sexual abuse of children by adults have increased rapidly in recent years, in Britain and elsewhere. Anthony Giddens notes that 'Statistics reported to the nation-wide data collection system in the United States charted an increase of 600 per cent in reported cases of child sexual abuse between the years 1976 and 1982 (Finkelhor, 1984)' (*Sociology*, p. 406). He adds that reported cases represent 'no more than the tip of the iceberg' and that in some surveys over one third of females and 10 per cent of males said that they had been sexually abused as children.

Domestic violence by men against women has in the past been dismissed as an inevitable part of living together and as something men might suffer from women as much as women from men. Current research has exploded these (for men) comforting myths. Dobash and Dobash note that in terms of reported offences, 'the 1982 and 1984 British Crime Survey revealed that *all* victims of domestic violence were women' (*Women, Violence and Social Change*, p. 266). For many women who suffer domestic violence the attacks are frequent and severe. Reporting in an earlier book on their own study of battered wives, Dobash and Dobash reported the following results:

A majority of the women experienced at least two attacks a week. Twenty-five per cent said that the violence usually lasted from 45 minutes to over five hours; the other 75% reported that the physical attack last 30 minutes or less. Of the latter group 22% told us that the violence usually lasted less than 5 minutes, another 25% estimated that the attacks lasted between 6 and 15 minutes, and another quarter (27%) said that it usually lasted about 30 minutes. (*Violence Against Wives*, p. 120)

Not surprisingly, much of this violence results in severe physical injury. Dobash and Dobash make it clear in their later study of the institutional context of male violence that women do not continue to live with violent men because of psychological dependency, but because of lack of real alternatives:

> The reasons for women failing to leave violent relationships have very little to do with some supposed set of unique psychological traits. Instead, an understanding of their patterns of help-seeking must be located in the nature and ferocity of male domination, coercion and violence; a moral order which places responsibilities for family problems on to women; inadequate, even condemning responses of legal, social and medical agencies; a financial and material dependence on men for the support of women and children; a wider social and economic order that makes it nearly impossible for women to leave and live on their own; the bleak prospects (well understood by most women) for single female headed households; and the lack of effective intervention in the lives of violent men and abused women. (*Women, Violence and Social Change*, pp. 232–3)

It should be added that child abuse and violence against wives are not confined to any one social class or any one country. Finally, it should be said that women also have to cope with the widespread problem of rape. Anthony Giddens notes again that the problem probably greatly exceeds the official statistics. 'A study of 1,236 women in London revealed that one in six had been raped, one in five of the remainder had fought off an attempted rape, and half of the assaults had taken place either in the woman's own house or in that of her assailant (Hall, 1965)' (*Sociology*, p. 188). Giddens lists a number of countries in which rape within marriage has now become a recognised legal offence. This multiple reality of 'the family' sets the limiting conditions for a Christian theology of marriage.

(iv) Women and Men

The basic development in terms of potential for emotional response almost certainly includes the possibility of a different experience for the male and for the female in the early years. Carol Gilligan has shown that the moral development of girls and boys differs, in so far as girls tend to look for negotiated solutions to problems based on caring attitudes, while boys tend to award the victory to one party on the basis of abstract principles, with little regard for the consequences for the persons involved:

> There seems at present to be only partial agreement between men and women about the adulthood they commonly share. In the absence of mutual understanding, relationships between the sexes continue in varying degrees of constraint, manifesting the 'paradox of egocentrism' which Piaget describes, a mystical respect for rules combined with everyone playing more or less as he pleases and paying no attention to his neighbour.... For a life-cycle understanding to address the development in adulthood of relationships characterised by co-operation, generosity, and care, that understanding must include the lives of women as well as of men. (*In a Difference Voice*, pp. 172–3)

Behind this difference in moral approaches there lies the possibility of a more fundamental differentiation between women and men which may affect all forms of relationship between the sexes. Classical Freudian theory looked more at the sexual development of boys than of girls, and arrived at the conclusion that the ancient Greek myth of Oedipus, who killed his father and unknowingly married his mother, thus provoking the wrath of the gods, represented a real experience of male sexual development. In Erikson's words, 'Psychoanalysis verifies in daily work the simple conclusion that boys attach their first genital affection to the maternal adults who have otherwise given comfort to their bodies and that they develop their first sexual rivalry against the persons who are the genital owners of these maternal persons' (*Childhood and Society*, p. 81).

On this view the neglect of female development is understandable. Girls were thought to suffer from 'penis envy' on discovering that they lacked this piece of equipment, but otherwise to have no psychological work to do at the Oedipal stage. Feminist thinking in particular has challenged this account so that 'penis envy' theory can now be seen as a male speculation about how girls might feel, not an account of female experience. Indeed, the psychological picture can now be reversed to show female experience as relatively uncomplicated and male experience as a potential source of psychological and social problems.

For the growing girl the developmental task is essentially to relate to the mother and to identify with her activities with increasing comprehension and increasing social skills. The mother as carer and nurturer provides a positive role-model which leads on naturally to commitment to wider social relationships. Attachment to another person as a role-model necessarily leads to negative as well as positive experiences, but these are containable. Indeed the negative experiences are essential to establish the separateness of the child from the mother (not-the-same-person) alongside the identification with her (good-model-to-follow).

The relationship with the father follows naturally from the relationship with the mother. Attachment to the mother directs attention to the father as a potential lover and in a healthy family this appears to be not strongly in competition with the affection of mother and father for one another. At puberty the girl's attention is directed by her sexuality towards males of her own age without seriously breaching the relationship with her father. Hudson and Jacot comment that 'She can follow the line of her mother's gaze towards her father and towards other males. The object of her desire is thus a creature inherently unfamiliar to her, even alien, but one whom she addresses from a psychologically coherent foundation' (*The Way Men Think*, p. 40). The girl therefore matures within a psychological project of the continuous enhancement of existing relationships by expanding the network of persons on the basis of already given and largely satisfactory personal models.

Consequently, for women the experience of adult sexuality is approached primarily as an affirmation of the self and of the significant other. In the words of Susan Parsons:

> Women understand embodiment not as a danger, except in the eyes of other people, but rather as opportunity, as possibility, as a continuing source of creativity. Their bodies are experienced as creative potential of a kind which can even give birth to God. Their experience of embodiment is one of togetherness, not detachment, for they know firsthand through their bodies the existence of others, and live in a

constant awareness of mutuality and relationship. ('Feminist Reflections on Embodiment and Sexuality', p. 26)

For the male, on the other hand, the difference lies in the fact that he has both to identify with the mother, in the early stages, in the same way as the female, but yet at a later stage must separate from her decisively. Whatever the degree of affection and care, the fact remains for the boy that he is not now, and is not going to become, a woman. To establish his own identity the boy must dissociate himself from the image of 'what it is to be a woman', even though the bearer of this image has been primarily responsible for his physical and emotional life so far. On the other hand the male image, 'what it is to be a man', does not seem to ease the pain of separation since the male role, even when it is strong in affection, carries different demands.

Hudson and Jacot describe the male experience of dis-identification with the mother and counter-identification with the father as 'the male wound'. They argue that this male-female difference may go back as early as experiences in the womb and that soon after birth the interactions between the mother and the child differ with the sex of the child (*The Way Men Think*, p. 41). Increasingly, as development goes on, cultural expectations will play a part in this interaction, and it would be difficult to argue exclusively that either biology creates the base for culture or culture overrides biology. What is being argued at this point is that there is biological base for the different experiences of male and female children, which is strongly reinforced by the expectations of our present culture.

In this biological–psychological–cultural situation, the male derives both costs and benefits from 'the male wound'. The cost is primarily in terms of insensitivity to feelings and so to other persons. 'Inside most males but not inside most females there must be a species of existential gulf' (*The Way Men Think*, p. 45). From this there may follow misogyny and, given the male's superior physical strength, a potential for violence against both women and children (the children perhaps being, in this context, surrogate women):

The small boy ... will find it more difficult than his sister to reciprocate affection, and his capacity for empathy will be impaired. He will tend to see those aspects of the world that are unmistakably emotional in black and white terms, either as heaven-on-earth or as unspeakably distasteful. He will be slow, too, to make sense of emotions that conflict; to detect the many shades of grey that separate black from white, and to realise that greys are often blacks and whites intricately mixed. Whatever his strengths elsewhere, in the field of intimate relations the 'male' male is bound to be at a disadvantage; even something of a cripple. His ability to experience a relationship as 'intersubjective' – as a meeting of experiential worlds – will be curtailed. (*The Way Men Think*, pp. 45–6)

The benefits of 'the male wound' are directly related to the costs. Cut off from the warmth of female emotional networks, the male is freer than the female to act as an independent agent in the world and to develop those aspects of human life which depend upon distance between the actor and the world, and which are most effectively dealt with in abstract terms. This theory then tends to explain male predominance in politics, in the professions and in the creative arts. Furthermore the wound, as a source of tension, is 'a constantly replenishing source of psychic energy' (p. 49). Hudson and Jacot comment that 'What is at issue is not ability as such, but accomplishment of the kind that only a driven need can bring about' (p. 94).

The theory of 'the male wound' is, it must be emphasised, a theory and as such must be treated with caution. Nevertheless it does provide a psychological counterpart to the social experience of maleness in our society. Men, who neither give birth nor suckle their young, carry out social roles of power and of bonding which are essential for the success of their business in the world. Consequently in child development the normal pattern is that the boy is afraid of his father, however much affection there may be on both sides, but responds to the mother with 'love' rather than 'respect'.

He responds to other males mainly as superior or inferior, but bonds with his own special tribe for particular purposes. From the age of about eight onwards the locus of his activities and self-identity is outside rather than within the home. Increasingly he needs to separate from father as well as from mother in order to establish his own power, but he does so only to take his place within other power structures which encompass all male activities in terms of hierarchy and organisation. Male on male violence occurs mainly where these structures are not yet in place or have broken down. The project of the young male, therefore, is a project of external self-assertion, which in a healthy society should be at least partly in co-operation for positive purposes.

One of the main practical problems for loosely-organised modern societies consequently is the socialisation of the young male. In the normal life-cycle the young male is in time redeemed from his externalisation of the self by the recurrence of the sexual cycle which leads him back into intimate relationships. Here 'the male wound' serves a positive purpose in that part of the attraction of the erotic is the 'otherness' of the partner of the other sex. Through sexual intimacy there is an opportunity to explore the other side of the self, the Jungian 'animus' and 'anima', the male within the female and the female within the male, which exist as potential for all of us. The different pathways of female and male need to come together so that each may be whole, though the theory of 'the male wound' may suggest that the need is greater for men than for women.

On the basis of this analysis we can see that different kinds of responses between human beings are required in different situations and at different stages of development. The world 'love' means different things at different stages of personal life. Erich Fromm, in a study called *The Art of Loving*, describes five stages of maturation in love.

The first is the infant. Infantile love is quite properly a demanding love. It says 'give me'. It recognises other people for their value in meeting demands. As Fromm remarks, with reference to the story of the fall of Eve and Adam:

> ... after man and woman have become aware of themselves and of each other, they are aware of their separateness, and of their difference, inasmuch as they belong to different sexes. But while recognising their separateness they remain strangers, because they have not yet learned to love each other (as is also made very clear by the fact that Adam defends himself by blaming Eve, rather than by trying to defend her). *The awareness of human separation, without reunion by love – is the source of shame. It is at the same time the source of guilt and anxiety.* (p. 14)

This infantile love is carried through into adult life and continues the feeling of dependence, which is a role we may all play at times.

Immature love, however, is that which does not progress beyond a desire for another person based solely on need. The problem here, according to Fromm, is an absence of sufficient self-love: 'The selfish person does not love himself too much but too little; in fact he hates himself' (p. 47). The person who has been given too little love to start with may not be able then to move to mature love: 'Infantile love follows the principle: "*I love because I am loved*". Mature love follows the principle: "*I am loved because I love*"' (p. 34).

The way out of this dilemma comes through *eros*, the sexual drive towards another person. This is first of all a physical and emotional drive which springs from basic biological needs. But it has the potential to cause me to learn about another person not only as the source of satisfactions for my needs, but also as someone whose own needs may be attended-to, so to speak, a free gift. This potential for learning about another is greatly enlarged when we come to parental love, the obverse of infantile love, for parental love says, 'I love you because you exist'. *Eros* is thus fundamental to human maturation in drawing us out of the self, into a relationship which always requires a commitment to at least one other. Criticising the western idea of love as always needing to be wholly spontaneous and totally fulfilling, Fromm remarks that 'To love somebody is not just a strong feeling – it is a decision, it is a judgment, it is a promise' (p. 44). He adds, 'Inasmuch as we are all one, we can love everybody in the same way in the sense of brotherly love. But inasmuch as we are all also different, erotic love requires certain specific, highly individual elements which exist between some people but not between all' (p. 45).

The love of the other in the more general sense of friendship or *philia*, Fromm suggests to be inseparable from the love of specific others. 'Only in the love of those who do not serve a purpose, love begins to unfold' (p. 39). Beyond these loves is the love of God, which does not necessarily imply the existence of a personal God, but a cosmic level of acceptance, rooted in self-acceptance and in the experience of oneness with others, which conveys a sense of the unity of all things in this particular human being. For Fromm himself, the human being now needs to speak of God 'only in a poetic, symbolic sense' (p. 60). His quotation from Meister Eckhart, however, suggests that there can be a Christian form of this experience:

Some people imagine that they are going to see God, that

they are going to see God as if he were standing yonder, and they here, but it is not to be so. God and I: we are one. By knowing God I take him to myself. By loving God, I penetrate him.

Fromm adds that one thing is certain about the individual's knowledge of God: 'the nature of his love for God corresponds to the nature of his love of man ...' (p. 61). This love for others, however, depends on the experience of relations in the family, which themselves depend on what the structure of society allows.

(v) Homosexual Relationships

The most controversial aspect of sexual relationships today, within Christian morality, is the claim that relationships between freely-consenting adults of the same sex may be sufficiently loving and committed to justify physical sex. Clearly there are two possible forms of argument here.

One says simply that wherever the Bible addresses the subject of homosexual relations it condemns them, particularly in Romans 1.18–31. After this nothing more needs to be said, except in terms of the pastoral care necessary for those who have this orientation. On this subject most of the major churches have a common view that the orientation itself is not sinful, that such persons should be accepted into the life of the church, that possibly the church and certainly society as a whole should acknowledge considerable guilt for discrimination and even the incitement of hatred against homo-sexuals in the past, but that none of this is a reason for giving permission for physical relationships. This is the view of 'objective morality', that the act itself is forbidden by God, without respect to the surrounding conditions.

The other form of argument begins from the claim of situation ethics that what God requires of us is to love our fellow human beings and that deep love can and should be expressed physically, unless it can be shown that some specific harm arises from it. There is no form of this argument, however, which justifies sexual promis-cuity without the hope of a long-term relationship. On this view it is the quality of a relationship, the degree of love and care and willingness to sacrifice something of the self for the other, that justifies physical sex precisely because this physical self-giving helps to create the love that binds two into one.

Clearly no mediation is possible between these two arguments as moral positions, but some things can be said by way of preliminary considerations about the origin and nature of homosexuality.

The first fact is that there is no clear cause of homosexuality. On the one hand the term 'homosexuality' covers a range of behaviours, not all of which are likely to be of the same origin. Leaving aside trans-sexualism (the desire to be a person of the opposite sex), transvestitism (the desire to dress and behave, from time to time, as a member of the opposite sex) and paedophilia (the desire for sexual relationships with children of either sex), adult same-sex behaviour covers the same sort of range as adult heterosexual behaviour, which also does not have a single 'cause'.

Here it has to be noted that each of us has different layers of 'sexuality', which relate to different causes. First comes the purely physical, which is gender, the possession of female or male sexual organs. For 'objective morality', this is all we need to know. Charles Curran notes that until recently in the Catholic Church, 'magisterial pronouncements frequently spoke of the primary and secondary ends of marriage'. Here 'primary' meant intercourse for the purpose of reproduction, which was common to all animals and 'secondary' meant intercourse in order to express love, which was thought to be found only in human beings ('Natural Law', in *Directions in Fundamental Moral Theology*, pp. 131–2).

A situational ethic, on the other hand, might wish to call the unitive aim primary and let the reproductive aim place itself within this love.

After physical gender comes sexual orientation. This is the desire which we have for another person as a sexual partner, a desire which then defines our own sexuality. Like many basic features of the human psyche, including the acquisition of language, our basic sexual orientation seems to be fixed at an early age, possibly between four and six years old. This statement is complicated, however, by the fact that relatively few people are oriented exclusively to one sex or the other. Most of us are somewhere on a scale between exclusively heterosexual and exclusively homosexual, with at least some possibility of attraction to members of our own sex and of the opposite sex. This helps to account for 'opportunist' homosexuality, under conditions where no member of the opposite sex is available, but has to be distinguished from rape, which under all conditions is an attempt to exercise power, often with implications of fear and hatred of the sexual object.

After sexual orientation comes sexual lifestyle. This is the way in which I choose to live, which may be in opposition to gender or to orientation. A homosexual lifestyle is in opposition to gender, but not necessarily to orientation, which is also a 'given' part of a person's nature. On the other hand, a homosexual person who marries and has a family is following gender in opposition to orientation, a move which is probably ill-advised and likely to bring grief to all involved. Lifestyle choices, however, are heavily influenced by what is possible within a given society.

For this reason it is important that homosexuals should 'come out' and be open about their orientation wherever possible, so that each human being may have the free choice of understanding their own nature. Where freedom is given, homosexual persons are not substantially different from their fellow citizens, except in sexual orientation. The information which we now have from social research such as that of Kinsey, and later of Bell and Weinberg, should set many fears at rest on this score – homosexual people are really not a threat to anyone, except perhaps those who are so crippled by 'morality' that they fear to look at what is in themselves.

This brings us back to the question of causation. For it must be recognised that human homosexuality is different from homosexual behaviour in other animals. In other animals it is understandable as an alternative activity for males who lose out in the competition for oestrous females. In humans it seems to serve no biological purpose, nor to be caused by lack of access to females. Though some research suggests possible genetic bases for sexual orientation, it is necessary to be cautious in accepting the present limited research as a general explanation of such widespread and diverse forms of behaviour. Indeed, it may be that no specific explanation is necessary, and that human homosexuality is simply part of the flexibility of behaviour that comes with our wider consciousness.

The debate between 'nature' and 'nurture' is unlikely to be settled by any amount of observation or research on creatures as complex as ourselves, but one suggestion about nurture is of interest, at least to those who accept the general principles of Freudian psychology. Elizabeth Moberly has argued that same-sex attractions have their origin in a deficit of same-sex affection and affirmation in early childhood, which homosexual people try to replace through same-sex experiences in adult life. If this is so, says Moberly, they may be looking in the one place where they cannot find what they want. For since the parent or carer of the same sex is the source of the disappointment, every person of that sex will be approached not only with hope, but also with resentment and a desire to punish the source of the loss of esteem. If the real need of every human being is to progress to mature heterosexual relationships, then it is impossible to come to rest securely in the previous, immature stage. Moberly does not argue that same-sex affection has no value; on the contrary she sees it as at least a serious attempt to relate, but adds that 'What is improper is the eroticisation of the friendship' (*Homosexuality*, p. 20).

Moberly's argument in part depends on the answer to a practical question, Do homosexual people succeed in creating long-term relationships at a level analogous to those of heterosexual people? Allowing for the problems which arise for homosexuals because their relationships do not have the kind of social support given to heterosexual relationships, there does not seem good reason to suppose that homosexual people in general cannot form long-term relationships. Moberly in fact recognises that for some a resolution of their problems can occur within same-sex relationships and adds that it 'may well have done so more often than is known' (p. 19). It also needs to be noted that Moberly's conclusions may to some extent be influenced by her evangelical Christian commitment to keeping people out of active same-sex relationships, in which field she is a campaigner.

The moral issue, then, cannot be settled on the basis of biology or clinical psychology or social research. It requires a decision, whether on the basis of 'objective morality' or on the basis of observation and allowing people to speak for themselves, that homosexual relations are or are not harmful.

Here the Bible is not directly helpful, simply because nothing in the Bible addresses the issue of loving same-sex commitment. The action which brings destruction to Sodom and Gomorrah in Genesis 19 is rape. The same-sex activity which Paul condemns in Romans 1 has, according to the argument of the letter, been inflicted on the people as a punishment of idolatry. The terms used in the First Letter to the Corinthians (6.9) and the First Letter to Timothy (1.10) appear to refer to sexual perversion, which has to be read in the context of the concern in the classical world about an adult male taking what was thought to be a female role. Indeed the whole Biblical and classical world is so far away from us in its understanding of sexuality that it is very difficult to draw any conclusions from it about sexuality today. William Countryman has pointed out in *Dirt, Greed and Sex* that in the Old Testament all sexual references have to be read in the context of concerns about ritual purity and about property rights, not about 'relationships' in the modern sense. No one in the ancient world gave primacy to feeling and commitment over property and legal rights, in the way that this is done in a modern document such as the Quaker working party report, *Towards a Quaker View of Sex*, which began the debate on 'quality of commitment' in Britain in 1963.

(vi) Christian Marriage

What does have to be taken from the New Testament is the fact that lifelong commitment in marriage is the way of preparation for the life of the kingdom of God which is most freely open to most human beings. Gender gives it a physical basis, reproduction gives it a biological purpose, and the potential for love, between woman and man and between parents and children, creates the moral opportunity for growth to the maturity of human relating. Historically celibacy has also been accepted as a calling, and sometimes given a higher value than marriage, but marriage remains the norm in the sense of being the path that most can take. At the same time it has to be recognised that the moral demand of lifelong marriage is not one that can be automatically fulfilled.

This central Christian thesis on personal relationships has been clearly set out by the Second Vatican Council of the Roman Catholic Church in the 'Pastoral Constitution on the Church in Today's World' (*Gaudium et Spes*) in 1965. 'The intimate community character of married life and love, established by the Creator and deriving its structure from his laws, is based on the conjugal pact, an irrevocable personal consent. From this human act by which the parties give and receive each other there arises an institution which by divine ordinance is stable, even in the eyes of society' (Article 48). In the encyclical letter *Humanae Vitae*, issued in 1968, Pope Paul VI said that married love is 'fully *human*', as an act of freewill by which the partners give themselves to one another, it is 'a love which is *total*', in which nothing is held back out of self-interest; it is '*faithful* and *exclusive* of all other, and this until death'; and it is a love which is '*creative of life*', since it brings new life into being through children (Article 9).

This central conviction of Christian ethics has to be given substance in the practical human realities of pairing and failing to pair. Helen Oppenheimer remarks that 'Faith is not keeping pointless rules but holding on loyally to the idea that there really is a point which will appear in due course' (*Marriage*, p. 6). Rather than going on about rules, we need to look at ways of keeping faith, through emphasis upon such qualities as integrity, which is 'moving in one piece'; transparency about who we are and what we are doing; and accepting responsibility for maintaining momentum in relationships, recognising that marriage is not just a legal act. 'It is to make a plunge, not a prediction' (p. 26).

Christian moral theory also has to recognise that the practicalities of family life may be a very long way from the theological ideal, and that God has given us an autonomy which parallels the autonomy which parents ought to give to children. 'Why should we suppose', asks Oppenheimer, 'that our heavenly Father is an overprotective parent who values nothing but obedience?' (p. 90). This very autonomy means that marriages must sometimes fail. Without freedom to fail we would not be moral beings. Consequently, as Oppenheimer says again, 'We need to be able to say that marriage and the family are excellent but not absolute' (p. 113).

Christian realism about what we are and what we can be means that Christian moral theology has to accept the possibility both of remarriage after divorce and of same-sex love and sexual relationships. The point about divorce is now widely admitted. Because it takes two to make the marital relationship, some marriages are bound to fail. Because the new relationship is a new start, it cannot be impeded absolutely by the previous existence of the old one, nor can it be predicted in advance to fail. There is every reason in terms of personal development for continuing to urge the central Christian teaching of lifelong commitment as the primary ideal. It offers the greatest opportunity for growth in the knowledge of the self and of the other, the greatest potential for moral change, and the greatest security for children. But in the face of the realities of 'the family', it cannot be made into an absolute moral rule. Our society has difficulty enough in 'placing' the widowed and the divorced and those attracted to the same sex – it cannot be the business of Christians to exclude them also from the church.

Who we are, in the context of sexuality, depends not only on our physical make-up or gender, but also on the direction imposed upon our psychological development by early experiences which create sexual identity, and on the opportunities which are created by the social roles that are available in the local community. Consequently femaleness and maleness and heterosexuality and homosexuality are questions not simply of physical nature, but also of personal and social definition in a specific society. These definitions are mediated through the notion of 'the family', but this also is subject to social definition. What any society needs for its own survival is a structure that provides stable conditions for reproduction, for child nurture and for the socialisation of the young into adult roles. But this means that the family must also deal competently with feelings as well as with social rules.

Both children and parents need emotional security and a chance to enlarge their self-understanding and their possibilities of relating to other persons. Birth, growth, courtship, pair-bonding, reproduction and child-rearing are developmental experiences, but so are old age and death. Human beings need not only feeling but also faith, the capacity to envisage the world as a whole and to act in unity with that whole. Dependence on and trust in parents leads to independence and the ability to give to others; dependence on and trust in God, which parallels the relation to parents, leads to independence in the sense of being able to exercise responsibility in the interests of the whole creation.

The creation story of Genesis chapter 1 gives the human beings the task of acting 'as God' on earth and of filling the earth with their own species. The much earlier story in Genesis chapter 2 sees the man and the woman as created for each other and in chapter 3 sets out the story of their moral and spiritual fall and expulsion from Eden, which is the rationale for the experiences of the pain of childbirth and the heavy weight of labour.

These stories are reflections upon the basic conditions of human existence. They recognise the unavoidable necessities of human life: reproduction, pain and labour. The prologue to the long drama of the book of Genesis sets out something more. In chapter 1 Genesis contains a promise that the drama of creation is a moral act, giving to human beings the dynamic to become the true representatives of God on earth.

> God created human beings in his own image; in the image of God he created them; male and female he created them. (Genesis 1.27)

The Hebrew Bible sees this first of all as an evolutionary task: 'be fruitful and increase, fill the earth and subdue it' (Genesis 1.28). Yet from the beginning, with the concept of companionship, something more is promised: 'The man gave names to all cattle, to the birds of the air, and to every wild animal; but for the man himself no suitable partner was found' (Genesis 2.20). From the fact of duality comes the idea of mutual need, love and completion. The image of God requires two human beings in mutuality, sharing in the power to create life as a conscious act of choice.

This ability for conscious choice in the human beings also constitutes a problem. The Old Testament makes the union of woman and man, by which they constitute the 'image of God', into a picture of the relationship between God and the people of Israel (Isaiah 49.14–21; Hosea 1.2 – 3.5). But this is in the context of the continuing failure of the people to keep to the faithfulness that ought to persist between Israel and God. In Malachi, at the end of the Old Testament, there is a clear denunciation of divorce at the human level, indicating that the demand for faithfulness covers both the human and the divine loves. The Jewish teaching of the goodness of sexuality becomes both a base and a reference point for teaching about the goodness of love, and mutual trust between the people and God. Sexuality is therefore a potent and a positive force in human life. It is the first place where human beings can undertake their calling to 'image' God on earth.

With the New Testament a further teaching appears. The rich imagery of woman and man as together forming the image of God, with their potential to rule the earth rightly, is extended to take in a new promise, that of a future which is rooted in earthly life, but eventually takes over as a new creation, with a new humanity given now in Jesus Christ. 'He is the image of the invisible God, his is the primacy over all creation' (Colossians 1.15). The 'image' is now the measure of the immense spiritual power given to those who place their future wholly in God. That this future is still rooted in the reality of human life, even human sexual life, in the same way as in the Old Testament, is shown by the teaching against divorce in the Gospels of Matthew and Mark (Matthew 19.3–9; Mark 10.1–12). The moral demand for faithful mutual love cannot be separated from the requirement for social justice which is also a New Testament commandment, but equally there can be no justice in social structures without a foundation of mutual personal love.

The mandate of sexuality is therefore a commitment to the moral ordering of everything that finds its origin in human love.

> Awake, north wind, and come, south
>   wind!
> Blow upon my garden, to spread its
>   spices abroad
> that my beloved may come to his
>   garden
> and enjoy the choice fruit
> (Song of Songs 4.16)

This where we all begin, but the moral possibilities of the mandate are enormously varied, held together only by the single commitment to love in our personal lives for the good of the creation as a whole.

5

THE MANDATE OF JUSTICE

(i) Poverty

'Poverty blights the lives of a fifth of Britain's population and around a quarter of its children' (Carey Oppenheim, *Poverty: The Facts*, p. 136). The brute fact that must dominate any discussion of justice is the existence of poverty. Now 'poverty' is a relative term between nations and within nations. But even at the crude level recognised by government responses in Britain, poverty is not something that is going to go away:

> Since 1979 the number of people in Britain living at or below the Supplementary Benefit level – that is to say the state's own assessment of the income required to sustain the lowest living standard at which any member of society should be expected to live – has increased dramatically, from 6.1 to 8.9 million persons; from 11.5% to 16.6% of the population. Although there has been a slight fall in pensioner poverty since 1979, the incidence remains high; 3.0 million people of whom 2.0 live alone. This means that a third of all pensioners live in poverty. (Duncan B. Forrester and Danus Skene, *Just Sharing*, p. 33)

At the same time, as a result of deliberate government policy, the balance of justice has been tipped against the poor:

> Between 1979 and 1987, the richest fifth of society saw their share of total household income (after taxes and cash benefits) *rise* from 40% to 45%; the poorest saw theirs *fall* from 6.1% to 5.1%. For the first time since the Second World War the poorest half of the population have found that their share of total income is dropping. (Oppenheim, *Poverty: The Facts*, p. 1)

124

Poverty is an experience of exclusion. Unless poverty is defined as absolute poverty, when people starve or freeze to death, the notion of poverty demands an assessment of what is proper to human life in a given society. Poverty in rich countries consists of a list of things a family – or a single person, or some members, particularly the mother, within a family – is not able to do. 'Relative poverty is about social exclusion imposed by an inadequate income. It is not only about having to go short of food or clothing, it is also about not being able to join a local sports club, or send your children on a school trip, or go out with friends, or have a Christmas dinner ...' (Oppenheim, p. 7).

In poor countries it may mean the difference between life and death, in all countries it may mean the difference between long and short expectations of life, lower or higher child mortality, lower or higher experience of illness, higher or lower chances of work, higher or lower quality of life, including living conditions, personal safety and the chance of children being exposed to drugs and the associated violence.

The notion of poverty is separate from the notion of an 'underclass'. This is a term coined in the USA for a culture of dependency created by leaving people to depend on social benefits or 'handouts', so depriving them of the initiative to find work and create their own lives. The 'underclass' theory has this much to be said for it, that leaving people to depend on handouts instead of creating conditions in which they can form their own lives is not the most desirable response to poverty. Indeed we have fallen into the habit of stupidly paying people to do nothing while many useful jobs wait to be done, from janitorial services offering protection to people in high-rise buildings to renewal of the infrastructure of roads, bridges, railways, water supplies and sewerage. The inability of capitalist society to put money into socially useful projects is one of its greatest failures.

This problem of organisational ineptitude in the notion of what constitutes 'benefits' should not, however, be used to conceal another set of facts about the creation of poverty. For domestic poverty is not simply an economic fact and it is certainly not just an economic accident. On the contrary, it is the product of specific systems – rules about social benefits, laws about part-time work, laws about the rights of employers and employees, the effective use of the right of association to form trade unions and to form employers associations and the control of the markets for labour and for products. In this sense poverty is always a systems failure – or more accurately the deliberate product of systems, rather than a personal fault.

Robert Chote comments on the abolition of Wages Councils, the bodies which set minimum rates for the lowest-paid workers in Britain, 'last November a greengrocer advertised in his local Job Centre for an assistant, offering £65 for a 37 hour week. Two months earlier it would have been illegal for the greengrocer to pay less than £119 a week for the same job.' The protection offered by the Wages Councils covered the sort of jobs open to the weakest members of the labour market, such as single parents. Rather than giving flexibility to the labour market, the abolition of the Councils is likely to make the poor still poorer. 'The cuts of 30p or more in hourly wage rates typically seen since the abolition of the Wages Councils may seem trivial. But economists at Cambridge University Microsimulation Unit estimate that this is enough on average to cut the incomes after taxes and benefits of the poorest tenth of the population by nearly 7 per cent.' Chote concludes that 'the real impact of the Wages Councils appears not to have been to damage employment, but to cut profits and to redistribute income from low-paying employers to low-paid employees'. He adds that 'The Government may well think that this is reason enough to be rid of them, but it should at least be honest about its rationale' (*The Independent*, 21 February 1994, p. 29).

In all of this governments are not neutral and churches ought not to be neutral either. The churches in Britain have for a long time been aware of poverty as a problem which is a necessary part of their agenda. Some action has been taken on a small scale: for example, the Church of England report *Faith in the City* in 1985 led to effective action to raise money for projects in urban priority areas. Other Christian bodies have taken other initiatives. The problem with economic justice has not been one of goodwill but of the complexity of the systems to be addressed. Christian goodwill cannot make a dent on economic systems unless there is a serious attempt at the analysis of possible alternatives. But one place that Christians can start is by insisting that alternatives do exist, in world trade, in the approach to ecosystems, in intermediate technology, and in the assumptions we make in the rich countries about the importance of produces and services and about the nature of 'wealth'.

For behind every system lies an ideology. British economic and social policy since 1979 has been running on an ideology which says that nothing matters except the financial control of expenditure to reduce expense in all areas of public action, while all areas of private action should go free of challenge and regulation of any sort. This has been a covert way of saying that it is desirable to help those who already have advantages and to increase the disadvantages of those who already have little. Quite explicitly recent British and American governments have argued that the rich must be rewarded in order to encourage them to work, while the poor must be whipped in order to get the same result. This is a dark and greedy view of human nature which Christian faith refuses to follow.

Alongside the questions about domestic poverty there is another set of questions, about international aid and trading relationships. On Friday, 10 December 1993 *The Guardian* carried the following text on the front of its second section, introducing an article on the American investment bank, Goldman Sachs:

Q. What's the difference between Tanzania and Goldman Sachs?

A. One is an African country that makes $2.2 billion a year and shares it among 24 million people. The other is an investment bank that makes $2.4 billion ... and shares most of it between 161 people.

FAIR ENOUGH?

The disparity between the resources available in rich countries and in poor countries today is very striking and is not becoming noticeably less as time goes on. Some – a very small proportion – of 'Third World' countries have done well through economic development, but most have become relatively poorer, and some absolutely poorer.

The people who have really done well out of the poverty of the Third World and the development programmes and loans that have followed from it have been the bankers and manufacturers, particularly the armaments manufacturers, of the 'First World'. As Susan George points out, all that bankers really require is that their loans be serviced, that is, that the interest due to them continues to be paid, even if there is no serious prospect of the capital of the loan ever being repaid. For this purpose, as development programmes have failed to 'get off the ground' in terms of enabling the less developed nations to earn their own way in international trade, First World banks have made new loans to their debtors for the simple purpose of paying the interest due on earlier loans. Some of this rush to lend arose from the fact that the banks had so much money that they needed to handle, as a result of the funds that became available to them after the oil price increases in 1973–74 and 1979–80, that almost any scheme would do to place the money. So sovereign states, being regarded as the ultimate safe borrowers, unable to get out of their obligations by going bankrupt, were urged to take the short-term view by borrowing to cover their international interest deficits, rather than to invest in wealth creation. Now, however, comes the crunch, when the circle of investment and repayment closes in on itself. 'Many Third World countries are now so deeply in hock that all their new loans are devoted entirely to servicing old ones' (Susan George, *A Fate Worst Than Debt*, p. 13).

The effect of this policy by First World lenders has been to reward governments that keep interest payments flowing back to the First World, rather than governments that use money sensibly to improve wealth creation and the underlying services that wealth creation requires, including communication, education and health among their own people:

> The debt problem is not really a banking crisis. It is a development crisis. Huge debt repayments not only reduce spending on needed human services. They also prevent essential capital investment that could provide new jobs and new income in the future. Unless there is major change, the future is bleak. Poor debtor economies will continue to shrink, essential social services will be cut even more, and millions of people will be submerged in even greater poverty. (Ronald Sider, *Rich Christians in an Age of Hunger*, pp. 143–4)

In this way 'development aid' has often not helped the Third World, but has increased its misery. Alongside the rash lending policies of the commercial banks has gone the demand for 'financial rectitude' laid down by the International Monetary Fund for governmental international aid. Clearly it is desirable that all governments should observe the rules of prudent finance, including many lending countries which do not always have good records in this respect, but in practice the IMF rules have demanded that the people of the debtor countries first be made poorer, before aid can be given to, hopefully, help them to become richer. 'The July issue of *World Bank News* noted that in Zambia, where IMF wage caps had been imposed, incomes in 1986 were less than 60 per cent of their 1974 level. In Chile, the real minimum wage in 1985 had dropped below the 1981 level' (Sider, *Rich Christians in an Age of Hunger*, p. 143).

Sometimes these policies work in the long run, sometimes they do not. In the short run, however, they give a distinct stimulus to the tendency of the ruling élites of poor countries to look for solutions to the problem of poverty in the area of repression rather than the area of justice. Heavy investment in military hardware is character-istic of the 'national security state':

> It is precisely the poorest countries, especially those in Africa with large debts to service, that tend to spend most heavily on national security. Ethiopia, which has been waging a pro-tracted war against liberation struggles in its northern prov-inces (Eritrea and Tigré), is at the bottom of the African poverty barrel. Its GNP is $4.3 billion, which works out to about $110 per Ethiopian, the lowest per capita GNP anywhere in the world, according to World Bank figures. This does not prevent Ethiopia from spending $13 per head and per year on its military, but only $7 on health and education combined. (George, *A Fate Worse Than Debt*, p. 22)

Ethiopia has now, at least temporarily, solved its internal security problem by a change of regime, but the general point remains true, that military response to the tensions set up by extreme poverty, or by extreme disparities between rich and poor is the easy option. Both by way of internal use of force and by way of distraction through boosting external threats or interests, such as the Argentinian attack on the British-held Falkland Islands (Las Malvinas) in the early

1980s, 'national security' has been an attractive reply for many governments of economically struggling countries to any sort of opposition. State use of violence has never attracted condemnation from the financial authorities of the First World, even where torture and murder are involved.

Alongside this moral blindness in the international financial system there has been another, equally damaging to the interest of the peoples of the less-developed countries. This is the acceptance by the bankers of the financial corruption of the ruling élites. Imelda Marcos' collection of shoes became an international joke after the fall of the Marcos presidency in the Philippines, but it is no joke when seen as a symbol of the combination of bribery, profiteering and capital flight which prevent poor peoples benefiting from what attempts at development *do* come their way. Susan George reports that the Bank for International Settlements estimates that $55 billion moved northwards from Latin America in 1977–83, and that capital flight (sometimes taking money away in suitcases) could have amounted to 70 per cent of all new loans to Latin America from 1983 to 1985 (George, *A Fate Worse Than Debt*, p. 20).

Finally, there is the question of trade. How did poor countries become 'poor', so to speak? Why do they not help themselves? The answer is twofold. In the first place many less-developed countries were held as colonial territories by metropolitan powers such as Spain, France, Germany, Britain and the USA, which did not want these territories to develop in ways that threatened their own economic interests. Mahatma Gandhi's famous campaign in the 1930s to persuade Indians to burn British-made cloth and replace it with what they could weave themselves thus had a sound economic basis. The lack of commitment to the economic development of colonial territories paralleled the lack of commitment to their democratic development. This has, for example, left Britain with egg on its face in trying to make Hong Kong 'democratic' in the last years before it is handed back to China.

The other reason for underdevelopment has been the technique adopted by the metropolitan powers, as the colonial links were broken, of replacing direct control by the control of the terms of trade through tariffs and other means. As Ronald Sider notes, 'In fact, the World Bank indicates that the trade barriers imposed by rich nations on goods from poor nations cost poor nations $50–$100 billion a year' (*Rich Christians in an Age of Hunger*, p. 135).

Alongside this has been the fact that on the whole the less-developed nations depend more on primary products for their export earnings and less on 'value-added manufactured goods' than do the First World countries. Primary products, from copper to sugar cane, tend to vary widely in price, with crises of overproduction (less easily controlled than with manufactured goods). In general primary producers have less 'clout' in the market than the rich countries, with their ability to stockpile, to subsidise their own producers and to find alternative sources of supply. In other words, for a variety of reasons the odds in international trade are stacked against the poorer countries, partly because they *are* poor and have fewer options. As the Brandt report summarises it:

> Many defects and imperfections have constrained the operation of commodity markets. The developing countries have had little opportunity to participate in the processing, transportation, marketing and distribution of their commodities. Many have also faced volatile prices; tariff and non-tariff barriers against exports, especially of processed products; declining prices in real terms for long periods; inadequate investment and uncertainties in mineral exploration and development; a tendency towards market concentration among importers and hence unequal bargaining power. (*North–South: A Programme for Survival*, p. 141)

The practical results of these structural economic issues can be seen on the ground in the lives of particular peoples. Of peasants in Bolivia, Susan George writes:

> Life for the peasants is particularly brutal: four out of every ten of their children will not see their fifth birthday; half the rural population cannot read or write (not surprisingly, four out of every five of these illiterates are women); and most will live out their short lives (under fifty years on average) without ever seeing a doctor, since there is only one for every 20,000 rural people. Sanitary facilities, permanent housing, pure drinking water supply and so on are poor to non-existent. (*A Fate Worse Than Debt*, p. 148)

In the particular case of Bolivia these circumstances rebound straight back on to the rich world. Since there is one crop that always brings good prices, a supply of cocaine is assured for our cities, from Washington to Manchester, for the indefinite future.

The saddest thing about all this is that the Third World debt problem is not enormous, in world financial terms (as the Goldman Sachs example also indicates). Susan George gives estimates which put total Third World debt at about 10 per cent of the world's annual economic turnover (*A Fate Worse Than Debt*, p. 12). This is a problem that *can* be managed, given goodwill and a new approach to the ideology of economic systems. The change of thought that will be required, however, is very large.

Ronald Sider suggests that what we need is not new or more techniques of 'development', but a new model of what is 'economic'. Industrial development on the current model, plus rising expectations of consumption, plus a rapidly growing world population makes a pattern that cannot be sustained indefinitely. Lifestyles and expectations in the rich world, and in the aspiring to be rich world, have to change drastically. This will be painful and disruptive, particularly in the rich world. 'Even if we reached the biblical norm of distributional justice, we would have to ask ourselves the next question: should we once again pursue the same sort of economic growth we formerly did? The obvious answer is no' (*Rich Christians in an Age of Hunger*, p. 246).

So the problems of domestic poverty and affluence in the rich world and of the poverty of the 'Two-thirds' world can in the end not be separated. The fundamental immorality of the world financial system – immoral in its lack of attention to morality – is the same thing as the attempt to deny the value of moral analysis of the fate of the poor in the 'Fourth World', the underworld of the rich countries. Both come from the same dangerous misconception, that we do not belong together in one vessel, the 'oikumene' which is the whole inhabited earth, created by God but committed definitively into our care. The price of this ignorance will be nothing else than the destruction of all our values. Truly we 'cannot serve God and Mammon'. We cannot even serve Mammon and our own moral natures. For Christians, as Forrester and Skene conclude, there are immediate responses of lifestyle:

> We have argued that the only credible response must be on three related fronts;

our personal lifestyle – how do we deal with our possessions and open ourselves to the need around us?

the life of the church – how may each congregation be an experiment in community and sharing, and the whole church provide a foretaste of the just sharing and fellowship of the Kingdom?

and *in national policy* – how may the nation best express its respect for the dignity and value of each person and establish structures of just sharing? This last is particularly contentious ground, but Christians and citizens of a democracy cannot responsibly refuse to enter it. (*Just Sharing*, p. 124)

Lifestyle and the way of life of the church are within our own control, as individuals and as faithful congregations – but what about national and international policies? Here some major difficulties of analysis arise.

(ii) Equality

The surprising discovery of the twentieth century is that economic justice may in principle not be possible. This would have been no surprise to people in the ancient world, who were aware of randomness as the primary quality of matter, but since the eighteenth century we have come to expect that the world can be made subject to human rationality and to increasing possibilities of equality in one sense or another. The Jewish and Christian tradition, however, has differed from both of these in seeing the world as based on an order that is neither entirely natural nor exclusively based on human rationality, but centred on a notion of justice which is proposed by God and defined by spiritual ends, yet still worked-out through the material creation. This religious sense of order is not concerned with equality but with ontology, the giving to each part of creation its proper place, according to the manner and purpose of its creation.

The idea of equality is attractive, though not Biblical, because it is the simplest form of distribution laying claim to justice. So long as we are concerned only with the elementary necessities of life there is much to be said for it. Food, water, clothing and shelter are the beginning-points of human life. They exist because the world exists and because the simplest forms of human labour – collecting and building – are applied to the world in the search for fulfilment.

Even so, a modification has to be introduced, even at the beginning, to the brutal simplicity of an equality of need to survive by eating, drinking and keeping warm or cool. For even these necessities involve differences of need. The baby at the breast, the nursing mother, the growing child and the hunting and gathering adult, all have the same necessity to survive but different needs by which they are able to do so. A steelworker has different needs of food and drink and clothing from an office worker, and so do those who live in the tropics from those who live within the Arctic Circle.

This simple concept of need is relatively easy to deal with when economic life is at a low level and when population is small in relation to resources. By introducing the steel worker and the office worker, however, another complication is revealed. At an early stage of human civilisation the organisation of labour and the nature of the product of labour rises above the provision of the barest necessities. After food, clothing and shelter come weapons of war, agricultural implements and cultural objects in the realms of religion and of art. Religion and art are at first inextricably inter-mixed. Indeed, for all we know, story and song may be as necessary to human existence as food and shelter. Yet the existence of religion and art implies a surplus of energy and attention above the simplest gathering and building to survive. Where there is a surplus there come choices. With choices there come moral and religious questions.

Increasingly, as a civilisation becomes more complex, these choices are freed from the determination imposed by the simple necessity of survival. Need can no longer be defined as that without which a human being will not be able to exist or to perform the simplest labour. Now two new considerations take prominence. These are wants and abilities. What guides the choices of individuals and of groups beyond the need for bare necessities? Is there any way to mediate between conflicting desires? What effect in terms of distribution should we give to different abilities? Is there a moral imperative to distribute justly but unequally because different people do different things well or badly?

Of these two considerations, 'wants' and 'abilities', the question of wants is undoubtedly the more difficult. For in a material world, all wants cannot be satisfied. Some wants are impossible in principle to satisfy, such as to fly to the moon without a spacecraft. Some wants can be satisfied only if no one else, even with an equal claim, is allowed the same satisfaction, such as the desire to holiday in Torremolinos but still keep it as a small, 'unspoiled' Spanish fishing village. Some wants, if satisfied, give pleasure to some but not to others, such as holidaying in Torremolinos as a major resort, or alternatively backpacking through Nepal.

At first sight this last point does not seem an enormous difficulty. Some can go to Torremolinos and some to Nepal. Not every choice is constricted by the limits of resources. Even in Britain we have both great cities and remaining areas of wilderness. Yet the non-interchangeability of personal satisfactions is the biggest problem of distributive justice, for it means that we cannot even in principle set out to achieve equality of satisfactions. Such a term has no meaning. The limitation of physical resources is a serious matter – not everybody can have everything they want – but it could be dealt with in theory by lowering the standard of welfare for everyone. The inability to compare satisfactions between individuals and groups means that we do not even know what 'welfare' should be. Giving everyone the same size of shoe would clearly be inequitable, but would it be inequitable to give them the same colour or the same design?

Of course the fact that something is impossible to do perfectly in principle does not mean that we should not attempt it in practice. Rough and ready approximations will often serve well enough in social policy. If a total of production is to be shared out one way or another, and if the limits of physical reality mean that we cannot fulfil everybody's wants, dreams and fantasies, can we nevertheless shape a system of distribution that would give the greatest number of satisfactions to the greatest number of people, and would such a system be in some sense equitable? This staple question of utilitarian thought does not avoid the problem of interpersonal comparisons of satisfactions, but it might well function on the basis of people's declared wants and satisfactions, assuming some necessary degree of rationality in the population.

The difficulties then seem to be twofold. In the first place, the current discussion of welfare economics suggests that the kind of games that can be played to produce different outcomes do not conclusively offer a single, universal outcome that can be accepted

by everyone as rational and equitable. The utilitarian hope is simply
not a practical proposition. Even an amateur look at such practical
issues as the problem of what is 'fair' in world trade, or what is 'just'
in social security payments might suggest this conclusion. The more
technical the analysis, however, the more difficult the notion of
'justice' becomes. Equally, the experience of the 'command' economies of the former Communist bloc of Eastern Europe and of
South-East Asia suggests that rational planning for the satisfaction
of human needs is more difficult than was hoped in the first heady
days of the soviet revolution.

This practical intractability of justice in economic matters
points us to the other difficulty, which is that all these practical
efforts are based upon an assumption of human rationality
which is defined in purely economic terms. But human individuals are not simply bundles of economic self-interests. We may or
may not see our own economic interests clearly, which is one
problem, but it is another problem that we also have other
interests and responsibilities, for which our own economic self-
interest may play a secondary role. As Amartya Sen suggests, 'A
person who chooses on the basis of a systematic preference
ordering that takes note of self-interest as well as other objectives
may well possess an integrated personality, but his or her behaviour would not typically coincide with one of self-interest
maximisation' ('Beneconfusion', in Meeks, *Thoughtful Economic
Man*, p. 14).

Nor is this multiplicity of interests within the human person the
only complication. For many of our choices arise not out of
individual decisions, but out of relationships and out of group
decisions. Even the decision about what constitutes 'food' is a group
decision, as may be discovered by the naive Anglo-Saxon confronted
with baked snails, or the unwary southerner facing tripe, black
pudding or pigs' trotters in Lancashire. As Michael Walzer comments, 'Goods in the world have shared meanings because conception and creation are social processes' (*Spheres of Justice*, p. 7). Justice
in distribution therefore cannot be dealt with solely on the basis of
a calculation of individual wants or needs, but has to relate also to
the much broader concept of the place of the individual in their
network of relationships. Individual wants and needs can be understood only in the context of social arrangements and therefore of
structures of power.

Over against this social vision there is a position which says quite simply that human affairs run best when private property is protected, without any question of 'justice' in the distribution of property. On this view there is no higher right than the possession of private property. Only in defence of the state can claims be made upon property by way of taxation, and then only by the general assent of those involved. It is notoriously difficult to account for the existing distribution of property, in any society, by a theory of justice, since it can, for example, never seem 'right' to those who are not possessors when the possessors use their wealth for luxuries while the 'have-nots' lack food, shelter, medicine or education. The modern defence of property, since it cannot be based on current use, relies on the single argument that historical property rights are the least harmful basis for distribution.

Like the argument for democracy, that however unsatisfactory it may be, it is better in practice than any alternative, this is a serious point. Any distribution undertaken in the name of a current sense of justice, which is arbitrary in relation to historical rights, will itself in time become a historical right, to be attacked by a new form of principled distribution. Moreover, any principled redistribution will begin to fail after a generation or so, either because new forms of enterprise shift the balance of advantage, or because in-built rigidities begin to leave wealth in the hands of those who do not deserve it on the original principle of distribution.

Faced with these long-term problems, a system of beginning from historical property rights and relying on the working of free markets in a clear legal framework to carry on the business of distribution begins to make sense. As we have seen in the world currency markets in 1992, the results of market action do not always satisfy all the parties involved – in this case the banks were satisfied but the national governments were not. The libertarian argument, however, is not about maximum satisfaction for all parties, but about arriving at the 'least worse' result. Raymond Plant quotes from Fred Hirsch the phrase 'in principle unprincipled' as a description of market operations, to illustrate the argument of Friedrich von Hayek that the greatest moral advantage of markets is the fact that they do not act on principle at all (*Modern Political Thought*, p. 88). Markets do not seek out individuals to do them good or to do them harm and their outcomes are the result not of social engineering but of thousands of decisions beyond the control of particular individuals, corporations or governments.

The work of Hayek, among other economists, and of Karl Popper, among other philosophers, gave clear warning, long before the economic and political collapse of the communist states, of the danger of linking ideology with practical economic and political programmes, even for what were initially humane ends. Plant summarises Hayek's view in the comparison that 'Socialism based upon social justice has the prospect of restoring the idea of a substantive political community, but this is not comparable with the freedom and diversity of liberal society' (*Modern Political Thought*, p. 87). So far the argument is primarily about political liberty and its dependence on economic liberty. When nobody in a bureaucracy can give orders to markets or dispose of the property of individuals and institutions by administrative *fiat*, political liberties are also protected and pluralism and diversity can flourish.

The other part of the argument is that a free market system in fact produces more wealth for everybody than does a centrally controlled and ideologically directed system. That capitalism has been better than communism at innovation, at increasing productivity and in the combination of mass output with responsiveness to consumer demand is clear. This is one reason why communism has never succeeded in taking power in an industrialised nation except by the use of force. This does give capitalism a substantial moral advantage in the argument between liberty and direction. Even a socialist thinker such as Michael Harrington recognises that 'Between 1945 and (roughly) 1975, advanced capitalism went through an unparalleled period of economic growth and rising living standards for the mass of the people' (*Socialism, Past and Future*, pp. 102–3). It was this growth which made possible the welfare state in the social democracies of Western Europe; as Harrington notes, 'the expansion of the welfare state was largely financed out of economic growth, not through redistribution' (p. 104). It is the end of this period of growth which is now causing tensions in these same services, across both Western Europe and the United States.

This period of prosperity, extending for many well beyond 1975, has given plausibility to the economic side of the case put forward by the libertarians, that under capitalism, even though the relative distance between rich and poor remains the same, everybody benefits. Raymond Plant summarises the argument as put forward by Hayek:

> Hayek holds to what is variously known as the 'echelon advance' or 'trickle down' theory of economic growth. He takes the view that a dynamic economy requires inequalities if it is to be innovative. Innovation requires rich people to provide demand for new products, but once produced these products do not remain the preserve of the rich ... What the rich consume today will be consumed by more and more people tomorrow. (*Modern Political Thought*, p. 89)

The fact that the enjoyment of goods trickles down unevenly, according to some combination of individual work and individual good fortune (such as good health) does not matter so long as the market is not discriminating deliberately against individuals. The difficulty about this, as Plant points out, is that while markets do not, in general, discriminate against individuals, they may well do so against groups, even though still not intentionally:

> We cannot predict in a free market what the economic outcome will be for an individual. However, this is not the only judgment we might want to make. We might, for example, want to consider the economic consequences not for an individual but for a group – in this case the position of those who, given the existing inequalities, enter the market with the least resources. Now it might well be the case that we can foresee that for this group as a whole, those who enter the market with least, are likely to end up with least. (*Modern Political Thought*, p. 91)

What is too easily forgotten by libertarians, furthermore, is the admitted fact that few, if any, markets are 'free' in Adam Smith's original sense of being easily entered or quitted at any time by both buyers and sellers. Western capitalist markets are certainly freer than those of, say, communist markets in the former Soviet Russia, but they contain nevertheless substantial imperfections. These are in practice sufficient to raise serious doubts about the 'justice' of such a system. Older economists such as Marshall and Pigou, doughty defenders of capitalism though they were, nonetheless were also aware of the need to subject markets to constant scrutiny. In terms of the consequences of their outputs in practical and not just in ideological terms, whether the ideology be of the left or of the right, markets cannot in a humane society be left to run themselves entirely.

Because 'market forces' are only one part of the structures that form human society, they also cannot guarantee to us liberty or anything else. Capitalism has co-operated freely and profitably with regimes that have been the clear enemies of political liberty, from Nazi Germany, through Greece under the colonels, to many Latin American and Asian countries in the present time. Michael Novak, a leading prophet of modern capitalism from a Catholic perspective, attacks the socialism of Jürgen Moltman and of those Latin American Christians who are concerned with the fight against poverty and oppression in their own countries. 'In Latin America, however, Christian socialism is rather more aggressive, rather less democratic, and rather more clerical' (*The Spirit of Democratic Capitalism*, p. 270). In a recent reference to modern martyrdom Moltmann notes that 'In the last ten years, more than 850 Catholic priests were murdered in Latin America, not to speak of unnumbered Christian laymen and lay women; and the people who murdered them consider themselves to be Christians' (*The Way of Jesus Christ*, p. 198).

One good reason why 'liberation theology' has been developed by the Catholic clergy, many of them missionaries from North America or Europe, is that in countries where property is defended with this degree of ferocity, political liberty and the sanctity of life have largely disappeared. Political statements that are part of the much admired 'diversity' of the USA may bring death when uttered further south. Throughout the world we are not, and we cannot be, concerned solely with abstract economic indicators, without looking at the human effects of these indicators and adding that into the account. The deflecting of attention from the realities of political and economic power is not simply an expression of philosophical principles. It also in practice, whether intentionally or not, serves political agendas concerned with keeping things as they are, which is in favour of those who already possess. The historical capitalist connivance with a list of vile regimes matches precisely what some libertarian theorists regard as their greatest treasure, the principled refusal to consider the human consequences of economic acts.

So what is there still that we can do about economic morality?

John Rawls has produced the most influential modern philosophical theory on the possibility of defining social justice. He begins from 'the traditional theory of the social contract as represented by Locke, Rousseau and Kant' (*A Theory of Justice*, p. viii), namely that society is to be understood as if it were the result of an original contract or agreement among people coming together to form an organised community for the first time. This does not mean that one has to suppose that such an original agreement in fact took place, only that we are to proceed *as if* such an original agreement had taken place. 'It is understood as a purely hypothetical situation characterised so as to lead to a certain conception of justice' (p. 12). The requirement is not for a historical original situation, but for a type of agreement into which any citizen may suppose themself to have entered at any time.

The assumption is then made that the social rules should be those which we would choose if we did not know what our own position in the society to be formed would be. This 'veil of ignorance' ensures that every contracting person will desire 'fairness', the best possible practical deal for every member of the society. Justice under these circumstances is not a blanket equality in everything, rather it is the practical outcome of the application of two principles, which are the principle of equality and the difference principle.

This first principle of justice as fairness is a requirement for a basic equality of distribution of major social goods: 'the general conception of justice as fairness requires that all primary social goods be distributed equally unless an unequal distribution would be to everyone's advantage' (p. 150). The social goods which are to be thus equally distributed concern rights and opportunities as much as possessions. 'The primary social goods, to give them in broad categories, are rights and liberties, opportunities and powers, income and wealth' (p. 92). Rawls adds that 'A very important primary good is a sense of one's own worth'.

The second principle of justice as fairness relates to situations in which it may be necessary or desirable to move away from strict equality of primary goods. As Rawls puts it at the beginning of his exposition of the theory of justice, 'the second holds that social and economic inequalities, for example inequalities of wealth and authority, are just only if they result in compensating benefits for everyone, and in particular for the least advantaged members of society' (pp. 14–15).

In relation to authority it is clear that in any constitutional arrangement for a large-scale society, some must govern while others obey – there will always have to be politicians – but this is 'just' only if the process of political rule conveys benefits for all, greater than would be enjoyed without the benefits of this particular arrangement for civil order. (What is true on the large scale can also be true for the small scale. In the 1970s there were some experiments in Britain with worker co-operatives, but in the successful firms an early radicalism of equality of power was soon tempered by the rediscovered need for firm decision-making, leading to the reinvention of managerial authority.)

The 'difference' principle also suggests in the area of wealth that there may be situations in which the greater wealth of some creates benefits for all. On the one hand the capacity of the rich to sustain research and investment may lead to greater wealth production for all; or to the production of kinds of social benefits not otherwise available, such as museums or grand opera. On the other hand, as Clement of Alexandria argued in the third century, the actual existence of poverty (which people might fall into through illness or other incapacity) requires relief to be given by those who have a surplus – no surplus, no poor relief! The application of the difference principle here depends on a practical assessment of the way a society works. Does wealth in fact trickle down from the spending and investment of the rich to the poor? Or is it the existence of the rich that in fact creates the poverty of the poor?

Rawls takes the view that in a democratic society in which all citizens accept the need for a general sense of justice, the two principles will work together to show the 'possessors' that they need to earn the moral co-operation of the less well endowed in order to act justly in society:

> The intuitive idea is that since everyone's well-being depends upon a scheme of co-operation without which no one could have a satisfactory life, the division of advantages should be such as to draw forth the willing co-operation of everyone taking part in it, including those less well situated. Yet this can be expected only if reasonable terms are proposed. The two principles mentioned seem to be a fair agreement on the

basis of which those better endowed, or more fortunate in their social position, neither of which we can be said to deserve, could expect the willing co-operation of others when some workable scheme is a necessary condition of the welfare of all. (p. 15)

Rawls does not put forward his principles of justice as necessary truths but as ones that those seeking justice do in fact accept or might reasonably be persuaded to do so. The notion of the original contract under the 'veil of ignorance' is really a metaphor, a device to enable us to look at a collection of intuitions and arguments which can be worked out in some detail as a prescription for a just society. These intuitions exist only in the context of the general moral assumptions of a liberal democratic society. This is both the strength and the weakness of the theory. The theory has a strength because it greatly clarifies the discourse in liberal democratic societies about the nature of equality and of justice. It has a weakness because outside the canons of modern western liberal democratic societies – which are not *necessary* truths – it may not carry much conviction. This is important because even those of us who now have these privileges may not be living in such societies for very much longer.

That proper self-interest may require some sharing, some attention to a concept of general welfare, is an important philosophical argument. It does not differ vastly in practice from the Christian concept that in a God-created world there is a demand arising directly from the mandate of human dignity that created sources should be available to all according to their need. What both viewpoints have in common at this point, however, is the difficulty of seeing just how well any form of distributive justice can be made to work.

(iii) The Power to Act

If 'equality' is not a viable concept in practice, it may be possible, argues Amartya Sen, to base a concern for social justice on the notion of 'capabilities'. This would say that each should have the right to develop her or his capacities to the greatest measure permitted by the total available resources. This would be much nearer to the concept of 'equality of opportunity' than to simple 'equality'.

Such an aim would have to be measured against another and apparently equally valid measure, which is to give a reward for 'work done'. It is difficult in practice to separate reward for work done from reward for social advantages such as education and access to social contacts. It is also part of the initial problem that we are trying to define what might be a 'proper' reward on any basis chosen. Nevertheless the simplest form of justice in rewards for labour would be one that aimed, not at equality or at meeting needs, or at maintaining a historically given situation, but one that matched what is put into work with the reward received.

Where abilities are scarce and an open market for them exists, this is a good practical system. The rewards given to opera singers, soccer players or romantic novelists are not really a problem. When we move on to more ordinary occupations, however, the complication appears that there is not a 'market' for ability in the same sense. Institutions such as schools or hospitals cannot behave in the same way as manufacturers of jeans or canners of herrings, at least not without grave damage to their primary objectives of care for education or care for health. There are good practical reasons for adopting criteria of stability, job satisfaction and delivery of care alongside management considerations of financial efficiency and smooth flow of work. The loss to school of teacher commitment to pupils or to hospitals of nurses' commitment to patients cannot be quantified in financial terms.

The notion of 'reward' is complex because it involves the whole range of social values across the whole range of social institutions. The rewards paid to various occupations indicate not only 'market value' but also the social value the community attributes to this particular work. Work 'places' us within the community quite as firmly as birth or education and is an important part of our sense of communal, and therefore self, worth. The rewarding of abilities is much more complex than establishing a market value and the health of communities depends on our observing and respecting this complexity. 'Reward' cannot be a matter simply of individual effort.

Amartya Sen suggests that a form of distribution based on 'rights', which specifies the rules of distribution and ownership irrespective of the outcomes of the procedure, is 'fundamentally defective' because some outcomes, even though based on clear property rights, are too terrible to be accepted, as in a famine where people starve because they do not have the money to exercise effective demand for the food which exists in sufficient quantities. He comments that as over against those who see rights as based solely on the past history of ownership, 'Consequent states of affairs may not be the *only* things that matter, but they can nevertheless matter' (*Resources, Values and Development*, p. 313).

Sen suggests that the weakness of the libertarian view is that it is concerned only with a negative – that someone else should not stop me from doing something – and asks, 'Why is it important that I should not be stopped from doing something and – at the same time – unimportant whether or not I can in fact do that thing?' (*Resources, Values and Development*, p. 313). Once consequences are allowed to count at all, even though only in extreme circumstances, the question of a positive evaluation of moral consequences cannot be avoided. This leads Sen to move from the consideration of ownership to the consideration of capabilities, so transferring attention from goods to persons. This, he argues, is indeed a question of freedom. 'In fact, the natural interpretation of the traditional view of positive freedoms is in terms of capabilities to function. They specify what a person can or cannot do, *or* can or cannot be' (*Resources, Values and Development*, p. 316).

'The freedom to hold what I possess' versus 'The freedom to become what I have the potential to be' is the centre of the problem of distributive justice. It cannot be settled by any method of working out rights and entitlements in detail, not only because of the fallibility of all such attempts, but also because the tension between the two claims is grounded in differences of moral perception which are not reconcilable. What can be said, very briefly, is that nowhere in Christian doctrine of creation can property rights be held to be absolute.

In a discussion of the problems of socialism published in 1984 before the fall of Communism in Eastern Europe, Alan Ryan makes the point that ownership of property, in the sense in which this was a lively question for socialists, is not the chief issue. Rather the chief issue is or should be that of access to power. He remarks:

> Marx, though not Mill, tended to think that the reason why states existed, and why they developed bureaucracies, elaborate legal systems and the power of police and army to enforce their provisions, was because the owners of property needed to be defended against the propertiless.

It seemed to follow that once private ownership of industry had been abolished, there would be no need for political domination. But once it is admitted that men may have an interest in domination, for other than material reasons, and once it is admitted that they can satisfy their material interests without actually *owning* anything, it becomes clear that socialism is wholly consistent with tyranny, with inequality of welfare on the grand scale. (*Property and Political Theory*, p. 188)

The question of justice is therefore a question about where real power lies.

Real power, in a society operating with large-scale technology, lies with those who control the processes of production, including today the production of services, and whose moral interest lies in technological virtue, or efficiency. This power of the managerial bureaucracy has been as great under socialism as under capitalism, though with less resulting efficiency in socialism because of the absence of the control provided by the relatively competitive markets of capitalism worldwide. The search for efficiency through managerialism may now be coming to an end, not only, as both Geoffrey Hawthorn and Alasdair MacIntyre have suggested, through a kind of disillusionment with the system, but also because there are at least some signs that the system itself may be coming to an end. For large-scale industrial capitalism, including the financial and other services which also depend on it, can no longer avoid or overcome the inter-linked problems of the inevitable environmental damage of industrial production, of the end of the era of cheap energy of the past 200 years, and perhaps of the end of the much briefer reign of the period of free trade. None of this indicates that we are about to enter into the age of utopia, but quite the reverse, that for a long time to come western society will be even more unjust and dysfunctional than it is now.

To return, however, to Ryan's argument, it is clear from what has already happened that there is a common problem across both capitalism and the old communist states that empowering all citizens to act fully and freely in a society is not something that we know how to do, either in practice in terms of processes and structures or in theory through political thought. Ryan puts the problem like this:

Property rights are still important, because it is still true that what you own, how much you own, and what you can do with it makes a lot of difference to your well-being and security – and not only in capitalist societies; owning a car in the Soviet Union is plainly a matter of some consequence for your happiness and self-esteem. But property rights are nowadays important because they are *rights* rather than because they are *property* rights. (*Property and Political Theory*, p. 192)

He adds, 'Marx and Mill and a lot of nineteenth-century writers may have been wrong about the way industrial society would develop – overestimating the pressure of hardship or moral autonomy or solidarity; but they were not wrong about the importance of the subjects with which they were dealing' (p. 192).

The questions which the nineteenth century raised have not been solved in the twentieth century. We know only that the practical side of justice, as both economic and political power, is more difficult and less creative of hope than most nineteenth century theorists supposed. The true 'Dismal Science' is perhaps not political economy, as Carlyle thought, but sociology, that twentieth-century invention which began, in the work of Weber and Durkheim, with grave misgivings about the quality of human existence in industrial society, and which brings us to the end of the century with those same misgivings largely reinforced.

(iv) A World Needing Renewal

The difficulty which follows is that our morality of work and our abundance of production have not given rise to a form of society which can satisfy the human need to be more than a servant of technology. Neither the pursuit of equality as the twentieth-century dream, nor the pursuit of liberty, the dream of the eighteenth century which has returned to haunt us again now, has a capacity to solve the problem of *anomie*. No abstract justice and no abstract freedom can actually place us in a communal world where our being is discovered and affirmed through the harmonious relationships of persons working for co-operative ends.

The early Christian dream of unity without ownership was

expressed in the description of what follows the ideal 'first day' of the church, the Day of Pentecost, which matches the primal innocence of creation. 'All the believers agreed to hold everything in common: they began to sell their property and possessions and distribute to everyone according to his need' (Acts 2.44–45).

This vision has been repeated throughout history by small groups for short periods – perhaps the Christians in first-century Jerusalem, certainly the early monastic movement in the deserts of Syria and Judea, the first flowering of the Franciscan movement and the nineteenth-century industrial or agricultural communes such as Robert Owen's New Lanark or the Shakers in the USA. It is perhaps the same dream which has now turned westerners to eastern cults. Shadowy as it is, this dream sets the ultimate standard of justice for Christian faith, the hope in Christ of the fulfilment of that great social promise which surely *ought* to be true, 'From each according to his ability, to each according to his needs'.

Jacques Ellul wrote in 1969 that 'A transformation in the lived morality is taking place under our eyes' (*To Will and to Do*, p. 185). The Christian morality of the early modern period suited the development of the bourgeois world of capitalism, giving protection to property and encouraging hard work by the individual. The new technology of the nineteenth and twentieth centuries required a new morality, concerned solely with external acts. 'The situation calls for a behaviour on man's part which is exact, precise, in harmony with the working of all the categories of techniques which are proliferating in our society. And this behaviour should be fixed, not on the basis of moral principles, but in terms of precise technological rules – psychological and sociological' (*To Will and to Do*, p. 188).

The emphasis of this technological morality is on success, measured by external factors, which means primarily material gain, though Ellul also noted the 'confidence in the future' of this technology, its 'assurance in hope which is astonishing in troubled time' (*To Will and to Do*, p. 197). Zygmunt Bauman similarly notes that 'The unconstrained rule of technology means that causal determination is substituted for purpose and choice'. He adds, 'Indeed, no intellectual or moral reference point seems to be conceivable from which to assess, evaluate and criticise the directions technology may take except for the sober evaluation of possibilities technology itself has created. The reason of means is at its most triumphant when ends finally peter out in the quicksand of problem-solving' (*Modernity and the Holocaust*, p. 220).

In a very definite sense twentieth-century civilisation has now come to an end, not because the century has run out of years, but because the ideological fuel on which it has been running, both Marxist and capitalist, has been used up. The notion of the 'post-modern' is an attempt at an intellectual response to this situation, but there is, it seems, nothing beyond the modern to which to go. The temper of this end-of-the-century decade is to look back. Post-modern architecture covers the conceptual emptiness of large frame buildings with pseudo-classical decoration. Post-modern politicians cover the conceptual emptiness of consumerist greed with appeals for a return to 'basic values'. In intellectual life, deconstruction can aim only at its own deconstruction. Indeed the leading intellectual temper is now to look back in a return to Aristotelian concepts of 'the good', a much better purpose, perhaps, than most in the period since we quit the world of German Idealism at the beginning of the century. In religion also the great temptation is to go backwards into the ghetto of crude fundamentalism allied to ethnic nationalism.

This temptation of religion, in the face of the despairing modern world, would write off the world and concentrate on 'faith' as a personal spiritual act. But no such response is possible for Christian faith. As Charles Elliott says:

> The Kingdom is not some kind of extraterrestrial entity that will be superimposed on this world. Nor is it a process of 'spiritual' or 'internal' change that will leave the outer realities looking much the same. It is the liberation of the world we live in, know, touch, smell, suffer, from all that corrupts and destroys it. (*Praying the Kingdom*, p. 1)

Christian faith can be exercised only in specific contexts, the affairs of the world which give specific meaning to 'love' and 'hope' and 'faith'. As Jan Milic Lochman has pointed out, the Hussite slogan at the time of the Reformation was *status mundi renovabitur*, 'the nature of the world is that is to be made new'. This promise and command of grace is the primary Christian input into every form of social order.* Only to the extent to which this is meaningful in the

*In a lecture on 'After Socialism: Christianity and Marxism – Yesterday and Today', given in the School of Divinity in St Andrews on 22 February 1994.

barrio and tenement, in the homes of the poor where it gives hope, and in the homes of the rich to move them to take action for the poor, can Christian faith claim to be 'true'.

The central concern of Christian ethics in the twentieth century has rightly been the relationship between political power and justice. Because Christian social thinking is founded not on academic exercises alone, but also on the lived experience of millions of people in the parishes and presbyteries and dioceses and conferences of the churches throughout the whole world, the knowledge of human needs comes from the grassroots and works upwards to church officials and academics. So the churches have been forced to respond, in practice and in theological analysis, to the real state of the world in which the kingdom comes.

Figures in this area are 'guesstimates', but Leonardo and Clodovis Boff suggest as conservative estimates that there are, world-wide,

> five-hundred million persons starving;
> one billion, six-hundred million persons whose life expectancy is less than sixty years (when a person in one of the developed countries reaches the age of forty five, he or she is reaching middle age; in most of Africa or Latin America, a person has little hope of living to that age);
> one billion persons living in absolute poverty;
> one billion, five-hundred million persons with no access to the most basic medical care;
> five-hundred million persons with no work or only occasional work and a per capita income of less than $150 a year;
> eight-hundred-fourteen million who are illiterate;
> two billion with no regular, dependable water supply. (*Introducing Liberation Theology*, p. 2)

What this situation suggests (and it is probably getting worse rather than better) is that 'justice' must include some concept of access to the world's goods for the most basic necessities of life for all the world's people.

In Protestant thinking, concern about this kind of justice began with the response to the evils of industrial capitalism, in the United States particularly in the 'Social Gospel' movement of the late nineteenth century. The simple optimism about the possibilities of social improvement in the thought of Walter Rauschenbusch and others was very attractive, but it did not survive the First World War and the economic and political problems which followed. Reinhold Niebuhr, who like Rauschenbusch and like Karl Barth and Dietrich Bonhoeffer in Europe, had his roots in parish ministry and in personal experience of the lives of the Christian lay people, nevertheless took a more balanced view of the possibilities, arguing both for the necessity of a religious vision of what society might become and for the equal necessity of a very cautious expectation of what might be produced in practice as a result of social change.

Protestant thought did not move substantially away from Niebuhr's position in the years after the end of the Second World War in 1945. Catholic theology, which had similarly been developing a social concern as a result of industrial experience in Europe, as expressed in the social encyclicals from *Rerum Novarum* in 1891 onwards, was given a new impetus by the Second Vatican Council which met at intervals from 1962 to 1965. This Council expressed the world-wide concern of the church's bishops and clergy about poverty, oppression, and the need for development of both economic opportunities and human rights in its last major document, which was 'The Pastoral Constitution on the Church in Today's World' (*Gaudium et Spes*).

This thinking at the highest level of the church's teaching authority gave encouragement to those working in conditions of desperate poverty to press ahead with the analysis that came to be called 'liberation theology' or more accurately 'contextual theology'. The cry of the world's poor is simple and easy to understand. The term 'contextual theology' means that wherever the Gospel is preached, this cry must be the first to be heard. When people have not enough food, no clean water, little or no access to medical care or to education, in a society in which it is possible to provide these things for all at a basic level, then this must be the first problem for a Christian conscience. The words of judgment given in Matthew's Gospel cannot be evaded:

> For when I was hungry, you gave me food; when thirsty, you gave me drink; when I was a stranger, you took me into your home; when naked, you clothed me; when I was ill, you came to my help; when in prison, you visited me. (Matthew 25.35, 36)

This is the Christian social charter, and there is nothing in it about the grateful poor, or about being the right colour or being of the

right religion, or being of the right ideology, or any other discrimination we can think of. It is simply about the needs of human beings.

It has to be acknowledged that the New Testament does not go
into a detailed consideration of economic and political structures,
nor would such an analysis be much use in the changed conditions
of a society which exists nearly 2,000 years later. What is made
abundantly clear, however, in the whole of the Bible, is that 'the
authorities' have the power either to do God's work or to be
demonic in exceeding their calling. In this sense the link between
justice and political power is clear. Whenever power is used to
defend economic inequalities which cause some to fall below the
basic conditions of human existence, that power is demonic and
needs to be unmasked and opposed, even though the costs of doing
this may be very high. The one great ethical lesson of the twentieth
century has been that *all* structures are more than merely neutral,
they work either with the Gospel or against the Word of God, not
only in whether or not they support religion, but also in whether or
not they support the humanness of all human beings.

As the Pastoral Constitution on the Church in Today's World
states, 'Even in social and economic life the dignity of the human
person and the integrity of his vocation, along with the good of
society as a whole, are to be recognised and furthered' (*Gaudium et
Spes,* Section 64). In these opening words from the chapter on
'Social-Economic Life' the Council sets out the teaching that the
kingdom of God is not a purely spiritual matter, nor something to
be dealt with only by prayer, but a commitment to serious concern
about everything that happens to human beings, at work and in the
market place, as well as in home, school or church.

The Pastoral Constitution goes on to welcome economic enterprise and technical progress, so long as these are within the context
of human wholeness: 'the basic purpose of production is not mere
increase of goods, nor gain, nor domination, but the service of man
– of man in his entirety, with attention to his material needs and his
intellectual, moral and spiritual demands in the proper order; the
needs of any man, let us add, any group of men, any race or region'
(Section 64). It is not only that human needs have to be met, but that
work itself, the work of every human being, has the highest value.
'Indeed we hold that by offering his labour to God man is associated
with the redemptive work of Christ' (Section 67). It is our labour
that contributes to the fulfilling of the creation of God on earth,

which in Paul Tillich's words is 'the overcoming of non-being by
being'.

What is not fully expressed in the Pastoral Constitution is the
degree of tension that such a principle must generate in practice.
Since the Second Vatican Council the attention of Christian moral
theologians has turned increasingly to what Gustavo Gutiérrez has
called 'the irruption of the poor' into history (*A Theology of
Liberation*, p. xx). The Council certainly led the way in this, quoting
the ancient saying, 'Feed a man who is dying from hunger – if you
have not fed him you have killed him' (*Gaudium et Spes*, Section 69).
Yet the demand in the same Article that the world economy should
be 'regulated by justice and accompanied by charity' does not
commit Christian faith fully to the position envisaged by contextual
theology. Later Catholic thinking, including papal encyclicals, has
moved on to the phrase 'the preferential option for the poor' to
indicate that Christians must now take on a more active role to
redress the balance of the creation of wealth and the spending of it.

The 'base ecclesial communities' of the church in Latin America,
which are pastoral action-reflection groups, centred on local needs,
point one direction in which the church can go in carrying out its
prophetic calling. This is not a matter of the simplistic imitation of
a given model, but rather of showing a profound respect for the life
of the people to whom the Gospel is addressed. These communities
are meetings in which ordinary people, groups of neighbours, begin
to assess their own reality in the light of the Bible and of the
eucharist, in order to see truly what their life is now and what it
might become. The threefold process, SEE – JUDGE – ACT,
means that the community sees for the first time what is its reality,
judges that the reality has specific causes, some of which can be
changed, and selects targets for immediate action to change that
reality where it can be changed and to alleviate the effects where the
situation cannot basically be changed.

The means may be of the simplest: literacy programmes, the
teaching of basic domestic skills, pressure on local government for
necessities of life such as clean water and adequate treatment of
sewage, finding accommodation for the homeless, taking up questions of workers' rights and the application of laws to protect labour,
such as legislation on minimum wages or the right to organise trade
unions. This process has a threefold significance. In the first place
it restores self-respect to the members of the communities, who see

themselves at last as people able to act in the world for effective change. Secondly, the existence of the groups as elements of the church commits the church itself to action and reflection for change, so that 'theology' is no longer an abstract subject, but a practical commitment to a new understanding both of 'society' and of 'church'. Thirdly, since in many parts of the world such simple changes menace the political order, the church as a whole becomes committed to that defence of human dignity which may involve life itself.

'Liberation Theology' has come under severe criticism from people ranging from Latin American dictators, who fear political change, to the CIA and American and European business leaders, who fear interruption of markets or the loss of cheap labour. It has also created theological fear about loss of control, particularly in church bureaucracies. The fact is that liberation theology exists and creates fear simply because it draws attention to the actual existence of the poor. In 1968 the Latin American Episcopal Conference of the Catholic Church held its second conference at Medellín in Columbia. Penny Lernoux records Bishop Padim from Brazil as recalling:

> Only when we had assembled at Medellín and spent a week in discussions, with slide presentations illustrating the statistics of poverty, did we begin to have a global vision. For many of those attending ... it was an eye-opening experience as well as cause for fright, because the situation was much worse than they had expected. So the delegates were prepared to make a commitment. ('The Long Path to Puebla', in John Eagleson and Philip Scharper, *Puebla and Beyond*, p. 11)

The attempt by Latin American and Vatican conservatives to suppress liberation theology at the third conference of the Latin American bishops at Puebla in 1979 failed because once again the facts were incontrovertible. As the Puebla report says, 'So we brand the situation of inhuman poverty in which millions of Latin Americans live as the most devastating and humiliating kind of scourge' ('Evangelization in Latin America's Present and Future', Section 29, in *Puebla and Beyond*, p. 128). Evangelisation, the furthering of the work of Jesus Christ for the world, cannot be separated from this knowledge. Even Pope John Paul II, deeply suspicious of any suggestion of Marxist analysis in the situation, was confronted by and recognised the necessity of responding to the cry of the hungry and the oppressed. His address to the Indians of Oxaca and Chiapas on 29 January 1979, was full of concern for the down-trodden state of his hearers and their right to justice (*Puebla and Beyond*, pp. 81–3). As Robert McAffee Brown comments:

> The pope learned a number of things during his trip. His first speeches had little reference to the poor. But by the end of his trip, having mingled with the poor, he was speaking in ringing tones about the need for basic social change and the need for the Church to work with the poor and not only on behalf of them. Who taught him? The people themselves. ('The Significance of Puebla for the Protestant Churches in North America', in *Puebla and Beyond*, p. 344)

More recent teaching, particularly by Pope John Paul II, has been considerably more reserved about aspects of the work of the theology of liberation in Latin America, particularly as this has attacked some church institutions themselves as part of the structures of oppression. Nevertheless the central theme has not been denied, but has remained a deep concern of papal teaching. Leonardo and Clodovis Boff themselves quote the Vatican Instruction, 'Some Aspects of Liberation Theology' (6 August 1984), as saying, 'It is not possible for a single instant to forget the situations of dramatic poverty from which the challenge set to theologians springs – the challenge to work out a genuine theology of liberation' (*Introducing Liberation Theology*, p. 3).

Alongside the teaching of the Second Vatican Council there have been three other influences which have helped to create a more radical Christian vision of society, and which certainly already influenced some of the people taking part in the Council itself.

The first has been the rediscovery of the Biblical teaching of the church as the people of God, being led to justice as God first led the people of Israel out of Egypt and through the wilderness into the promised land. This was partly the work of the 'Biblical theology' movement of the 1940s and partly the work of the German theologians on the 'theology of hope' after 1945, deriving from the philosophy of Ernst Bloch and expressed first in Jürgen Moltmann's classic *The Theology of Hope*.

The second influence has been the personal experience of pastors and theologians working among those in Latin America and Asia from whom hope has been almost entirely taken away. This has been powerfully explored by C. S. Song in *The Tears of Lady Meng*, in a meditation on a Chinese folk tale, 'The Faithful Lady Meng', whose tears dissolved the foundations of the great defensive wall under which her husband had been buried by the emperor as a human sacrifice made to keep the wall from falling down. Song comments:

> Pain alone does not bring sense to life. Pain alone does not reveal the meaning of history. Pain alone does not ennoble humanity. And pain alone does not make the present worth living. There must be, besides pain, hope. There must be, besides the present, a future. There must be, besides one dreadful destruction after another, one joyful construction after another. Life is a race against pain. History is a never-ending process of construction on the ruins of destruction. It is this kind of political theology that we find in some of the finest folk literature, folk songs, folk dance, and folk dramas. This is the political theology of the people or the *minjung*, as Korean Christians like to call it. In these 'folkthings', we Christians may perceive reflections of the cross. In them we may also gain a glimpse of the resurrection. (pp. 19–30)

He adds, 'This in fact was the political theology of Jesus Christ – the theology of living with people'.

The third influence has been the life of the eucharistic community. Tissa Balasuriya, writing in Sri Lanka, says of the connection between the eucharist and justice, 'The eucharist is spiritual food insofar as it leads to greater love, self-unity and communion among persons and groups. Today this requires love among persons and an effective action for justice' (*The Eucharist and Human Liberation*, p. 22).

From Latin America, in one of the first books to put forward 'liberation theology', Gustavo Gutiérrez has reminded us that the eucharist is the primary work of the church. 'The place of the mission of the Church is where the celebration of the Lord's supper and the creation of human fellowship are indissolubly joined. This is what it means in an active and concrete way to be the sacrament of the salvation of the world' (*A Theology of Liberation*, p. 148). He goes on, 'The first task of the Church is to celebrate with joy the gift of the salvific action of God in humanity, accomplished through the death and resurrection of Christ. This is the Eucharist: a memorial and a thanksgiving' (p. 148). The power of the celebration of the Lord's supper to change our view of the world lies in the fact that it takes up the theme of liberation from the Jewish Passover and adds to it the Christian liberation from death to life, from sin to grace, in the risen life of Jesus Christ. 'Liberation from sin is at the very root of political liberation. The former reveals what is really involved in the latter. But on the other hand, communion with God and others presupposes the abolition of all injustice and exploitation. This is expressed by the very fact that the Eucharist was instituted during a meal' (p. 149).

From this revolution in theology – which is really a return to Biblical roots – there has come a new perception of history for Christians. Instead of a division into spiritual history (the history of salvation) and material history (which is doomed to disappear without trace), there is now a recognition that even for theology there is only one history, only one realm where salvation is played out. This is not the Marxist belief that only material history is real, nor is it a complete rejection of St Augustine's theology of the two cities. Rather it is a recognition that the loyalty of the heavenly city is real only if it takes the earthly city with great seriousness as the place where salvation is carried out in practice. Faith in the heavenly city is the faith that Christ is lord also of the earthly city.

This does not mean that Christians have a specific blueprint for economic enterprise and political rule. Quite the contrary, in fact – Christians more than anyone have cause to be sceptical about the ultimate value of any particular proposals. Reinhold Niebuhr's definition of original sin as our tendency to overreach ourselves and over-estimate our own abilities still holds good. But it does mean that Christians have absolute confidence in putting to every such scheme a moral demand, the demand put so succinctly by the Pastoral Constitution. 'God intended the earth and all it contains for the use of all men and peoples, so created goods should flow fairly to all' (*Gaudium et Spes*, Section 69).

(v) The Integrity of Creation

During the 1970s, discussion in the World Council of Churches developed around a lengthening phrase, which eventually became 'a just, participatory and sustainable society'. Like the deposit of fossils which shows the gradual evolution of species, this final phrase records the perception of a series of problems which stand in the way of the achievement of justice. In the 1980s the phrase 'the integrity of creation' was added to the discussion and placed a new question mark against the possibility of justice. By the end of the decade the phrase had become 'justice, peace and the integrity of creation' which is rather like being in favour of motherhood and apple pie, but at least has the advantage of stressing the interrelationships of what we most desire.

The notion of 'justice' was, as Ronald Preston points out, inherent in the very first stance of the World Council of Churches on issues of social ethics, the demand for all societies to accept that they could be held to be morally responsible for their actions. 'The concept of The Responsible Society provided a criterion which could be brought to bear on any social order and it was used in practice to express challenges to both sides in the cold war, to the capitalist economies of the West and the centralised Soviet economy of the USSR and its satellites' (*The Future of Christian Ethics*, p. 75).

The notion of responsibility became a more specific demand for justice when the newly-independent former colonies of the First World began to demand their full status in the world. This debate revolved around the word 'development', both how to define it and how to achieve it. Here the blame was put upon the First World for the exploitative attitudes that, as we have seen at the beginning of this chapter, still continue today.

In the 1960s, however, it was still possible to suppose that structures of international trade and aid could be adjusted in such a way that all the less-developed countries could achieve lift off. The theory was that beyond a certain point the injection of capital would become self-sustaining as enough profit was made by enterprises within a country to provide new enterprise capital for further investment. Once this takeoff point was reached the country would simply join the international capitalist system in its own right, though at a lower level than some of the older players.

Towards the end of the 1960s questions began to be asked about aspects of this policy. For one thing, it was becoming clear that the model was not working for many countries. When the World Council of Churches held an international consultation on development issues at Montreux in 1970, it was already possible to see the debt-crisis – the increase in borrowing beyond any possibility of repayment – taking shape. As Samuel Parmar said:

> From the experience of the sixties it can be concluded that international economic co-operation has not helped in leading developing nations towards self-reliance ... The burden of debt repayments has increased to the point where nearly half of the current external assistance is used up by developing nations for debt repayments. At this rate by 1980 some developing countries will have to earmark all their aid for repayments, so that the net inflow of resources will be zero.
> (*Fetters of Injustice*, p. 52)

Consequently 'aid' was already beginning to look more like another form of 'exploitation'. What had certainly begun as a generous gesture, on the lines of the 'Marshall Plan' of aid from the USA which speeded the restoration of normal life in Europe after the disasters of the Second World War, now turned out to be a long-term form of new colonialism. Some of the causes certainly lay in corruption in the receiving countries, some lay in a failure to shift effectively from dependence on the export of primary products to the export of high-value manufactured products.

What was gradually identified as the chief cause, however, was the choice of inappropriate forms of development: high-prestige, large-scale projects such as dams where low-scale projects of boreholes and simple pumps might be better; high-technology imports, from factories to tractors, which reduced the demand for labour, where simpler, 'intermediate' technology might have served local purposes and kept people gainfully employed; and the introduction of advanced services in capital cities, such as major hospitals doing advanced surgery, rather than simpler medical programmes curing basic diseases in rural areas. The problem with this indictment, of course, is that none, or few, of these projects were bad in themselves. But sometimes they were not the best choices in view of limited resources and particular local conditions.

Two pressures were creating this distortion of responses to real need. The first was that development projects were being selected by the donors of the aid according to their own desire to export high-technology goods and skills. Many donors were in fact insisting that their aid come straight back to them in the form of orders for their own products. The other pressure was that this game suited those members of the managing class in receiving countries who could profit by these choices. So the less-developed countries were at least sometimes at risk of having their interests damaged by a collusion of greed and short-sightedness between the donors and their own rulers.

So the word 'participatory' entered the ecumenical debate. As Ronald Preston says, 'Participation was added later, largely through the insistence of the WCC Churches' Commission on Participation in Development which reflected the strong feelings of Christians in the Third World that they were excluded from power-sharing in economic matters by the affluent countries, and that many of their own governments were run by corrupt political élites' (*The Future of Christian Ethics*, p. 261, note 3). The concern about participation was not confined to the Third World. In the 1960s a study by a working group of the French Protestant Church, 'The Church and the Powers', discussed the relationship of economic change, increasingly-complex technologies and concentration of industrial power into the hands of fewer international companies. They concluded that these trends could threaten the political basis of democratic society even in the apparently stable First World countries. On the one hand the ideology of 'free markets' was being proclaimed with increasing stridency, on the other hand some markets were becoming less free, such as atomic energy, which required high security because of the dangerous nature of its materials. 'Security' could easily become an excuse for reducing the freedom of information which is essential to democracy. Equally, the sheer technical complexity of many operations could prevent a proper democratic understanding of what was going on. All of this was long before the accidents at Three Mile Island in the USA and Chernobyl in the USSR alerted the general public to the reality of the 'need to know' about the atomic energy industry in every country. 'Participation' needs to be a constant demand in every kind of society.

In the 1960s the Vatican also registered concern about the nature of 'development'. The encyclical letter *Populorum Progressio*, 'On Fostering the Development of Peoples', of Pope Paul VI in 1967 expressed the wish that development should be a fulfilling of the whole nature of human beings, economic, spiritual and moral. 'Development cannot be limited to mere economic growth. In order to be authentic, it must be complete, integral; that is, it has to promote the good of every man and of the whole man' (Section 14).

Pope Paul VI clearly saw that justice, in its original sense in this debate of a fairer share of the world's resources for all the world's people, was a fundamental requirement for the other meanings of development to be fulfilled. It was in this letter that recognition was given to the fact that structural forces in society, the arrangements of institutions rather than individual wills, could gravely impede the development process. Even, this letter admits, the use of force by the oppressed in some circumstances is understandable, though only as a last resort and with grave doubts about the possible results. 'When whole populations destitute of necessities live in a state of dependence barring them from all initiative and responsibility, and all opportunity to advance culturally and share in social and political life, recourse to violence, as a means to right these wrongs to human dignity, is a grave temptation' (Section 30). However, the letter also warned that violence, except in the most extreme conditions, could also lead to new injustices and disasters. 'A real evil should not be fought at the cost of greater misery' (Section 31).

At the Montreux consultation in 1970 Dom Helder Camara, Archbishop of Recife in North East Brazil, commented:

> Our responsibility as Christians makes us tremble. The Northern hemisphere, the developed area of the world, the 20% who possess 80% of the world's resources, are of Christian origin ... The 20% who let 80% stagnate in a situation which is often subhuman – what right have they to allege that Communism crushes the human person? (*Fetters of Injustice*, p. 62)

He said also that after *Populorum Progressio* Christians did not require any more documents on the theory of development. 'The problem that we now have to tackle is that of putting our fine theories into practice' (p. 63).

It was *Populorum Progressio* also which recognised that the path to peace for the whole world lay through painful processes of change which could empower whole peoples to begin to make choices for themselves. As Paulo Freire, building on the kind of thinking emerging in and since the Second Vatican Council, argued in *Pedagogy of the Oppressed*, the 'marginalised' people of his own

continent of Latin America were those who did not yet have a
history, who did not yet know themselves as makers of the world.
For the oppressed the way to both peace and justice lies through
'conscientization', a coming to consciousness about the nature of
their own lives and the facts of the oppression that determines those
lives. There could be no justice, Freire said, without the full
participation in society of its poorest, weakest members, those who
could not conceive of themselves as actors at all.

So the 1970s became the decade of liberation theology, in which
both Catholic and Protestant communities in Latin America saw a
congruence between the Christian demand for justice and various
kinds of analysis of the nature of power in society. For some, such
as the Columbian priest Camillo Torres, this became an invitation
to participate in armed struggle. For others, notably Archbishop
Helder Camara, violence was always a source of further violence,
even though the pattern began with the violence of the state and of
the possessors against the poor.

For all who recognised the centrality of the question of justice to
Christian faith, the nature of power and the nature of possessions
became crucial practical issues. The 'preferential option for the
poor' now meant not only kindness, but hard political and economic analysis of why things were so – a task undertaken with great
seriousness by the Catholic bishops of Latin America at their
conference at Medellín in 1968.

Unfortunately for the hopes of justice, another debate was under
way at the same time which threatened the very basis of the concept
of sharing. This was not immediately apparent, because it was not
immediately clear how serious the situation was. Nevertheless the
introduction of the word 'sustainable' into ecumenical debate at a
consultation on science and technology in Bucharest in 1974
marked the emergence of a theme that was already of concern to
some economists and ecologists, the possibility that human economic activity was becoming too destructive for the biological
world, the 'biosphere', to sustain it indefinitely without destroying
human life itself.

For it became clear during the 1970s that the original model of
development might fail on a crucial point, the impossibility of all
countries industrialising to the levels already known in the First
World countries. The pressure such an increase in activity would
put upon world resources of energy and raw materials could not be

sustained indefinitely. A report to the US government in 1969 estimated that (guessing at future discoveries) world oil reserves would be effectively depleted, in relation to present rates of extraction, by the end of next century:

> For the purposes of the present study, the principal result of the foregoing estimates of the approximate magnitudes of both the United States' and the world's supply of the fossil fuels are the following:

> If these substances continue to be used principally for their energy contents, and if they continue to supply the bulk of the world's energy requirements, the time required to exhaust the middle 80 per cent of the ultimate resources of the members of the petroleum family – crude oil, natural gas, and natural-gas liquids, tar-sand oil, and shale oil – will probably be only about a century. (*Resources and Man*, p. 205)

The committee added that on the time scale of the whole history of human civilisation, the 'epoch of the fossil fuels can only be a transitory and ephemeral event – an event, nonetheless, which has exercised the most drastic influence experienced by the human species during its entire biological history'.

Even though the figures in such calculations are always open to some challenge, the new fact which had appeared on the world economic horizon was that human industrial activity was now on such a large scale that possible physical limits were beginning to appear and had to be included in any calculation of development and of justice.

As well as oil, forests were being cleared at rates which were well beyond those at which trees could be replanted and come to maturity and other resources were under similar 'kamikaze' attack. Moreover the clearing of forests was leading to erosion and flooding and possibly even to climatic change. Agriculture was being pushed to new limits, with possibly destructive effects on the composition of the soil and again with risks of erosion, and in large areas of Africa 'desertification' was removing increasing areas from production altogether.

The world 'sustainable' now began to mean that there could be no concept of 'justice' in the long-term that was not adjusted to the

sort of expectation of consumption that was realistic for the world
as a whole. In other words, justice now meant that everybody had
to lower their expectations, not that every country could be brought
up to the levels of consumption enjoyed and expected in the First
World. Since, as Barabara Ward pointed out, the citizens of the First
World use vastly more of the world's resources than the citizens of
the Third World, the population policies of the First World must
be put into question. Apart from war and famine,

> If we prefer, as a species, to employ somewhat less brutal and
> indiscriminate methods of birth control, then we have to
> relate population to what the planet can support. It therefore
> follows that an American baby, who will require a million
> calories of food and thirteen tons of coal a year during an
> average lifetime of sixty five years, is going to run through the
> biosphere's available supplies at least 500 times faster than an
> Indian baby looking forward to fifty years with an annual
> consumption of perhaps half a million calories and almost no
> energy save what he will himself produce from those calories.
> The sheer increase in the numbers of Indian babies does, of
> course, change the calculation. But if our concern is to take
> unsupportable strains off the biosphere, the goals underlying
> population policy must include, for high-consumption soci-
> eties, a family size at which their populations become stable.
> (*Only One Earth*, p. 176)

Today a final factor has emerged, that our industrialising use of
resources threatens not only the supply of the resources themselves,
but also the way in which the biosphere works to enable life to be
sustained. Even rainfall can no longer be regarded as an unlimited
resource of fresh water. Even the oceans can no longer be regarded
as an unlimited resource, either for a supply of food or as a place to
dump waste. Even the atmosphere can no longer be regarded as an
unlimited resource, either of fresh air or of protection against the
sun's ultraviolet light which damages both human beings and
plants. Too many chemicals have already gone unnoticed into the
atmosphere, destroying the ozone layer which protects us against
ultraviolet light, and increasing the carbon dioxide which reflects
our own heat sources back to us on the planet's surface.
The fact that we cannot yet securely put figures on these changes

or predict accurately what may follow from them does not mean that we are not right to be deeply alarmed now. The fact is that our destruction of the environment is already in some ways beyond our control both because of our lack of knowledge and because of the time-lags involved in stopping the processes once we have identified dangers and agreed on political action.

Moreover the action required very often looks like stopping the poorer countries from enjoying the benefits of increased industrial production just at the point when they are beginning to see some possibilities of higher consumption and better living standards. As Gamani Corea of the Institute for Policy Studies in Colombo, Ceylon, argued at the 'Earth Summit' in Rio in 1992, no solution based on two different levels of living will be acceptable. 'The real quest has to be for a style of living which can be adopted by all countries, rich and poor, and consistent with the environment and the planet' (quoted in Granberg-Michaelson, *Redeeming the Creation*, p. 15).

So the ecumenical debate has moved finally to the term 'the integrity of creation', which recognises that justice now must be a concern for the capacity to survive of all species, including our own. It recognises the fact that human survival on the planet earth can no longer be an exclusive demand, because human beings cannot survive by themselves on the planet and because we do not know fully what the conditions may be by which we can survive. We do not know what our interdependence is, not only with lions and tigers and butterflies and whales, but also with micro-organisms in the soil and in the oceans, and with the interactions of the sun and the winds and the waves. For all the things that we do, from making chemicals to driving motor vehicles down green rides or across arctic wastes, to the things that we do not even notice that we are doing, create effects that can make or break our chances of survival.

Human beings are now therefore called to an accounting on a world scale, in a way that we have never attempted before. We have to notice the most minute of our actions. We have to weigh the real interests of particular human beings – fisherfolk, miners, consumers of fuel for heating, air-conditioning or refrigeration, supersonic travellers, military air movements, slash-and-burn farmers, keepers of goats – to see what their actions mean in a global context. No one has 'rights' any more, in terms of actions which have an impact on the environment, except by general human permission. The individual right to consume is no longer sacrosanct. There is no human activity that cannot be challenged, until all the accounting has been done.

Above all, we have to acquire the foresight, the willingness even in advance of the ability, to look ahead to see the meaning of our actions for the next generation and for the ones beyond that. We can no longer rely on technology to save us, for technology has become a large part of the problem. We can no longer rely on increased consumption by all to give us justice, for increased consumption will be death to human life. We can no longer assume that 'standards' must rise, for clearly the future is that standards must fall, until we have, all over the globe, a standard of life that will not take us one step further towards disaster.

The world has finally begun to take action on these problems. The United Nations Conference on the Human Environment at Stockholm in 1972 led to the setting up of the United Nations Environmental Programme, which produced the report *Our Common Future* (the Brundtland report) in 1987. This report certainly recognised the gravity of the problems, but has been criticised for continuing to discuss 'sustainability' in the context of a commitment to continued economic growth. Jonathon Porritt of the British Green movement charged the authors with 'lack of intellectual rigour' and described the attempt to combine concern for the environment with commitment to continued growth as 'a deliberate, politically-expedient cop-out' (*Green Christians*, February / April 1990, p. 9, quoted in David Gosling, *A New Earth*, pp. 81–2).

Twenty years after the Stockholm Conference the United Nations made a major effort to involve national parliaments, non-governmental organisations and world public opinion in a debate over what were now considered to be extremely urgent environmental issues. The Rio Earth Summit of 1992 on the Environment and Development marked a sea-change in the international perception of the ecological crisis. Wesley Granberg-Michaelson summarises the result: 'Historically the Earth Summit will come to mark the time when the world realised that development as traditionally understood has failed', (*Redeeming the Creation*, p. 1). As Boutros Boutros-Ghali, Secretary-General of the United Nations put it, 'The time of the finite world has come' (*Redeeming the Creation*, p. 6).

This poses particular problems for the Third World. On the one hand it is now recognised that poverty is a cause of environmental degradation, as well as a result of it. Being poor causes people to strip the earth, but stripping the earth causes people to be very poor in a permanent way. On the other hand, as we have seen, there is no morally acceptable solution to be found in freezing economic production and distribution patterns in the form that they take in a particular historical moment. Gamani Corea's warning about two different lifestyles identifies a potent source of future tension.

The achievements of the Earth Summit are not yet clear. Certainly there was much immediate publicity and many expressions of right thinking and goodwill, as in the Rio Declaration on Environment and Development, with its 17 Principles about rights and duties on environmental issues. The two binding international Conventions on Biodiversity and on Climate commit the nations to some practical actions, as in a less binding way does the Declaration of Principles on Forestry Management. All this, however, depends on individual nations now meeting these international obligations in practice, particularly where it causes economic pain.

The religious implications of all this are not easy to see. Clearly for Christians there is an impetus towards placing emphasis on the theology of creation by God's Word. Indeed this will be a recovery of a very old knowledge, which we are now rediscovering in Britain through the return to Celtic roots. Esther de Waal quotes a seventeenth-century Welsh writer, still in that living tradition, who says 'The Trinity abides with us exactly the same as the ore in the earth, or a man in his house, or a child in the womb, or a fire in the stove, or the sea in a well or as the soul is in the eye' (*A World Made Whole*, p. 134).

There is also the new debate, moving in the opposite direction, as to whether the species *Homo sapiens* is indeed the crown of the whole creation, or only one species claiming consideration among many others. There is the new shape given to the old doctrine of 'original sin', our apparent inability to get things right whatever we do, by goodwill as much as by ill-will, not least in the failure of a political consensus to form around specific ecological issues and objectives. The failure to plan seriously for changes of lifestyle, on such matters as energy use, seems in the time-scale which we now have in which to save the earth, evidence of our irremediable failure to see and to accept responsibility where it is necessary to do so. 'The good which I want to do, I fail to do; but what I do is the wrong which is against my will' (Romans 7.19).

There is, above all, now a new problem about 'justice'. It is no longer possible to assume that the questions about justice, nationally or internationally, can be solved or even partly solved by greater economic growth. Is 'justice' as an aim now therefore to be abandoned, so that we can concentrate on justice for other species, on biodiversity and the care of physical and biological systems? Does 'the integrity of creation' now mean that justice among human beings is a thing of the past? Surely not. Certainly we have to rethink justice within the more general concept of lifestyle, but no lifestyle that does not produce what can widely be recognised as justice (not equality) in terms of access to the basic goods of land, water, food, shelter, employment and at least some medicine and education can be in any way acceptable to the Christian conscience, however hard the practical programme which this implies may be to bring about.

The Four Horsemen of the Apocalypse – the agents of war, famine, plague and pestilence – are no doubt waiting in the wings to come forward and solve our problems in their own way. Meanwhile the clear responsibility of those human beings who have religious convictions is to show the way in abandoning consumerism without abandoning justice. Above all what is needed is a work of religious imagination to help us to envisage our possible acceptable futures. This future, is after all, going to be one with a great deal of pain in it. For attitudes and expectations cannot be changed overnight, and there is a great deal of interdependence in our lifestyles which cannot be changed at the flick of a magician's wand.

Christian faith is not, and never has been, simply about private satisfactions, though many people have tried to use it so. In the Bible, faith is about simplicity of life, about justice for all, about the full participation of every human being in the work of the kingdom and about hope that a full human life is possible. The adoption of the theme 'The Integrity of Creation' as a basis for ecumenical study is in itself a most necessary recognition of our primary problem, but it is only the beginning of a long and hard process of thought and action. As David Gosling writes of the process of 'Covenanting for Justice, Peace and the Integrity of Creation', the theological basis for this thought and action is the word *shalom*, peace:

The wholeness towards which God's creative spirit draws the universe is not achievable in this life. It is located in the future, where the biblical word for peace, *shalom*, best describes its character, and in the life of Jesus Christ, who is the sign of that future hope ... The duty of the Church is to be a sign of the world's coming into being, inviting people to participate in God's creative activity, which encompasses the whole of creation. God's future kingdom of peace is being realised in many ways by many different types of people; what makes the Church distinctive in this respect is not that it does this better, but that it can *interpret* what is happening. (*A New Earth*, p. 9)

6

THE MANDATE OF THE CHURCH

(i) The Work of Prophecy

Writing in *The Observer* about an incident in which a woman who reprimanded some children for stealing flowers from a park was subsequently subjected to attack by their families and told by the police that 'it would have been better not to have got involved', Katherine Whitehorn reflected on the problem that respect for general morality, as opposed to family or tribal loyalties, does not seem to come naturally to us. The potentiality for the kind of aggression described in the article exists in all of us, though women 'have managed to submerge their aggression better than men'. Nevertheless, she wondered, since the instincts are in us all, how do we control them? 'Religion?' Maybe; but the ones currently gaining ground aren't encouraging, as seen in Iran or the likes of Waco' (*The Observer*, 1 May 1994).

It is characteristic of social critics at this moment in our civilisation that religion is to be disposed of as quickly as possible, preferably by relating it to distant and bizarre examples. That which is immediately at hand is assumed to be already dead, or too near dead to be of any account. If any journalist had gone in search of the nearest Anglican or Methodist or Catholic or United Reformed Church, or better still the nearest Black church, they would have found some very ordinary people attempting precisely the task which Katherine Whitehorn saw as so necessary and so difficult to find – the task of making morality, our common commitment to one another, central in their daily lives.

For it is in the church and nowhere else that the social institution is found which commits us to care for one another, to accept a communal loyalty above that of self or family or tribe, which tells us that we define ourselves by our attitudes to other people and that this

170

act of self-construction holds good not just now but for eternity. It is the church, and only the church, which provides the social power to hold together the always fragile structure of civilisation, which provides us with a reason for being social selves and with the hope for a greater community to come.

The church can be derided and indeed it is and has been all the things which people conceive it to be – small-minded, too concerned with its own ways and its own past, unsure of its own purposes and always too eager to control others for the sake of the greater good.

Yet this same body is the place also where slowly and painfully we become transformed, becoming part of the community of the eucharistic bread and wine, the community of the confession of sins and amendment of life, the community of care about the world, not for our own good but because it is, now and always, God's world. It is this transformation of ordinary people into those who will dare anything for the scarcely-to-be-comprehended God-created world – 'the saints who are in Corinth' – or Rome or Jerusalem or Liverpool – that constitutes the existence of the church, so that those who despair should become those who dare to hope for the power of God in their lives and who dare to pray for the transforming power of God in the lives of others.

This is not a dramatic fact, it does not shine forth greatly in the world, it accomplishes no visible miracles, it is never complete. Yet the slow and painful pushing forward of the people who constitute the church day by day creates the ground of all the possibilities that we can hope for of social justice and of mutual love. When the church is derided or opposed or ignored, then we have no more hope of love or justice. Then moral discrimination fails and the power to make moral choices fails and the vision that moral choice is possible disappears.

Only when it is already too late, when the direction of life has been decided, when the moral offer *has* been refused or not understood, when nothing has been passed on to the next generation, then indeed the passing of traditional morality and Christian practice may be regretted. Then the words 'If only …' may be heard. What past generations built up, by faith and by painful experience, will then finally have been let go. Then it will be too late for regrets. The moral structures into which earlier generations were born did not grow naturally or appear accidentally. They were struggled-for and bought at a price. We who have asked for moral freedom are already finding, and will find much more in the future, that what we have lost will not easily be brought back. When we reject the church we reject not only pews and hymns and ministers but the disciplined knowledge of the self and of others under God which all the outward life of the church exists to shelter and nourish, from the mightiest cathedral to the humblest chapel or upper room. Starting such a faith again is not a matter of a simple wish.

Since the days of the 'Enlightenment' of the eighteenth century, many have supposed that without the church there would be freedom and the reign of reason and even, perhaps, love. Without the *deformed* church, the church of censorship and arrogant power, there is indeed greater freedom. The acceptance of religious pluralism is a great gain of modern times, compared with either mediaeval 'Christendom' or modern fundamentalisms from the Moral Majority to the resurgent fundamentalisms of Hinduism and Islam. Without religion at all, however, there is not freedom but anarchy, not reason but fear, not love but the selfish tribalisms which now begin to frighten us in real earnest.

For the true function of the church (and perhaps of the ecclesial communities of other great religions) is, among other things, to prophesy; not only to pronounce judgment but also to discriminate where judgment is needed, not only to show godly reverence but also to show God-given courage to oppose injustice and ignorance, not only to practise the conservation of ancient custom but also to practise the proclamation of radical love. The voice of the church is a prophetic voice and without the church there is not a new prophecy, but no prophecy at all.

Franz Jägerstätter, a Catholic layman executed by the Nazi government in Austria for his opposition to National Socialism, told this story about the power of evil to disguise itself as something attractive and morally true, even in the sight of church authorities:

> Once, when the Social Democrats were in power in Austria, the Church said it was impossible for a Social Democrat to be a Catholic too – and now? Let me begin by describing an experience I had one summer night in 1938. At first, I lay awake in my bed until almost midnight, unable to sleep, although I was not sick; I must have fallen asleep anyway. All of a sudden, I saw a beautiful shining railroad train that

circled around a mountain. Streams of children – and adults as well – rushed toward the train and could not be held back. I would rather not say how many adults did not join the ride. Then I heard a voice say to me, 'This train is going to hell'. Immediately it seemed as if someone took me by the hand and the same voice said, 'Now we will go to purgatory'. And oh! so frightful was the suffering I saw and felt, I could have thought I was in hell itself if the voice had not told me we were going to purgatory. Probably no more than a few seconds passed while I saw this. Then I heard a sigh and saw a light – and all was gone. (Gordon Zahn, *In Solitary Witness: The Life and Death of Franz Jägerstätter*, quoted in *The Catholic Worker* [New York], September 1993, p. 5)

The vision of the train was a symbol for the evil underlying the surface attractiveness of the National Socialist ideology. That evil was creeping into all aspects of the national life of Austria, so that the question, not yet recognised by his own church authorities, 'Should I be a National Socialist or a Catholic?' was also a choice between heaven and hell.

The mandate of the church is this work of prophecy, of 'discerning the spirits', of knowing the real nature of the choice between heaven and hell. As Dominique Barbé says, 'The mystic is a person who is conscious of the *real* human tragedy – a religious tragedy – that is much more serious than a political or economic tragedy' (*A Theology of Conflict*, p. 172). This means that we have to take the human world more rather than less seriously. This prophetic task of the church is a task of education, of discernment, of judgment and of method. In the first place it is about the understanding of human growth as a task of education or nurture, and in the second place it is about understanding the world as a realm of tension between sin and the achievement of right action. In the third place it is about seeing the point at which justice can 'break through' the present situation into something new and creative; and finally it is about the way in which all this is to be done, by adopting the path of non-violence wherever this can justly be used. For at the end of the day the whole task of prophecy is about the proper use of power: how we perceive power, how we apply power, how we experience power. In all these ways, Christian prophecy is about the transfer of power over the self and over others to God, in order to have power given back to us to use in a new way. To do this, we have first to understand our own human nature as bearing both power and hope.

(a) Empowerment

Education is about 'empowerment', the process by which we come to know and extend our own capacities and potential powers. In the early years of this century John Dewey wrote of the need in education to give every individual the opportunity to exercise what he called 'experimental intelligence'. The immaturity of the young was not an absence of power. On the contrary, 'Taken absolutely, instead of comparatively, immaturity designates a positive force or ability, the *power* to grow. We do not have to draw out or educe positive activities from a child, as some educational doctrines would have it. Where there is life, there are already eager and impassioned activities' (*Democracy and Education*, p. 42). Dewey sees the human being as essentially an exploring animal, using intelligence to reflect upon experience and devising activities or experiments to test the insights of intelligence upon fresh experience. This stance is strongly supported by modern studies of the psychology of young children, which show them to be much more interactive in educational processes than was once supposed.

The function of education, says Dewey, is to be 'the enterprise of supplying the conditions which ensure growth, or adequacy of life, irrespective of age' (p. 51). The teacher is the person who has knowledge of the subject ahead of the pupil, and whose speciality is to know what the pupil is capable of doing at the present moment with the subject. 'The problem of teaching is to keep the experience of the student moving in the direction of what the expert already knows' (p. 184).

This task cannot be understood without knowledge also of the social environment of learning. This is the environment of the school, and it is also the environment of the wider community in which the school is situated. These communities both make demands upon the learning process and also set limits upon it.

The process of education is 'prophetic', within certain limits, because it is about extending the powers of the child in a context which raises issues about the self and the community. There is inevitably both co-operation and tension between education and religion, because both are concerned with the self-understanding of the individual in society. What the Christian faith has to understand is that part of its prophetic function is precisely to engage with and advance the function of education both as a matter of respect for individual capacities and as the provision of opportunities for every human being to engage in the business of exploration of the self and the world.

The world-changing potential of education is, of course, a cause of concern to many, who would like it either suppressed or brought under tight political control of one sort or another. The churches, because of their own fears of losing control over social patterns, can easily be made co-conspirators in such suppression. Such a stance is made easier by the fact that philosophers of education have tended to see religion as a force for suppressing free enquiry, which indeed it can be. True prophecy, however, has always been about breaking through established orders and extending human potential. True prophecy and true education stand on the same ground.

The educational task in the schools extends, as Dewey saw, into the whole of human life. So Paulo Freire, as we noted in the previous chapter, writing from a philosophical basis which combines Catholic Christian belief and Marxist social criticism, defines the point of prophecy as the 'conscientization' of the oppressed to the facts of their domination and the possibility of the overthrow of the oppressor, wherever oppression is to be found. In practice oppression is easy enough to find when we apply to our living reality the Gospel concern for the poor, the orphan, the widow, the prisoner and the powerless. Freire's particular point is about those who are so deeply oppressed, so 'marginal' to the centres of power in society, that they are unable to envisage for themselves the possibility of change.

For these poor, deprived of the most fundamental right of self-perception as a being who can initiate change, an educational act is needed as a prophetic break-through. Something must stir the consciousness of the person to say, 'I am a human being, a maker in the world in community with other makers'. For Freire, the education which brings this dawning of consciousness and leads to change is a revolutionary act, but it is also a Christian act. As he says in the preface to *Pedagogy of the Oppressed*, 'From these pages I hope at least the following will endure: my trust in the people, and my faith in the creation of a world in which it will be easier to love' (p. 19).

Freire's approach to education developed through his work in promoting adult literacy campaigns in Brazil after the Second

World War. Rather than follow a simple process of alphabetisation, using reading books full of such interesting sentences as 'Eva saw the grape' and 'John takes care of the trees' (*Cultural Action for Freedom*, p. 24), he looked for ways of breaking through not merely the inability to read but the inability to think of oneself as a person in history. He realised from his own childhood experience that to be one of the poor is to live in what he calls a 'culture of silence'. The ignorance and lethargy of the poor are produced by the whole situation of economic, social and political domination of their society by the possessors – landlords, politicians, educators and church leaders. The poor do not need to be taught how to read 'Eva saw the grape'; they need to be taught how to overcome the reality of their situation, how to cease to be 'marginalised', how to become liberated human beings and take charge of their own destiny – what Freire refers to as 'learning to name the world':

> The difference between animals – who (because their activity does not constitute limit-acts) cannot create products detached from themselves – and men – who through their action upon the world create the realm of culture and history – is that only the latter are beings of the praxis. Only men *are* praxis – the praxis which, as the reflection and action which truly transform reality, is the source of knowledge and creation. Animal activity, which occurs without a praxis, is not creative; man's transforming activity is. (*Pedagogy of the Oppressed*, p. 73)

Before the person learning to read can begin to 'name the world', she or he must first begin to *see* the world. The poor know that they have a number of separate problems – lack of medical help, not enough food, a difficult landowner – but do not always see this as a unified problem in terms of a need for and a possibility of social change. Particularly in rural areas, but also for the poor of towns, fatalism prevents the possibility of conceptualising change.

To learn to read, therefore, as a process of 'naming the world', as Adam did in the older creation story (Genesis 2.18–20), involves a change of consciousness about the nature of the actual world. What Freire calls the 'problem-posing' or 'dialogical' approach to adult literacy concentrates on words which are of existential importance to the students and enters into dialogue with them about this reality.

So they discuss, not 'the cat sat on the mat', but 'shanty town' and 'hunger' and 'drugs' and 'violence'.

In 'banking' education, which is the opposite of the dialogical approach, education is used to contradict reality. Freire quotes an adult reading primer:

> Peter did not know how to read. Peter was ashamed. One day, Peter went to school and registered for a night course. Peter's teacher was very good. Peter knows how to read now. Look at Peter's face. [These lessons are generally illustrated]. Peter is smiling. He is a happy man. He already has a good job. Everyone ought to follow his example. (*Cultural Action for Freedom*, p. 25)

'Normal' education is always political in sense that it aims to conserve the present structures, even though in North East Brazil – or Brixton in London, or Toxteth in Birmingham, or Pilton in Edinburgh – the level of unemployment might make it very unlikely that any 'Peter' or 'Eva' would get 'a good job'.

In this sense all education is inescapably 'political'. The task of the churches, among other social institutions, is therefore to see *how* education is political and not to cease to comment upon it, including the education done in their own way of training ministers and lay people in the Christian faith.

There are four criteria for a humanising education that emerge from Freire's work. The first is the fundamental belief that it is human beings who create culture. The world is not something given, to which we have to conform, but the world is that of which we have to become conscious in order to transform it and ourselves. The second criterion is that fully human living is a combination of action and reflection. These two must not be separated; we reflect in order to take action to transform the world, and each action creates a new situation which requires fresh reflection; we have to discover continually the new situation that we are in and new limits that we have to overcome. The third criterion is that education is a process of working with people, not of 'teaching' them. Obviously there are skills and knowledge which educators have as resources available to the students, and the more technical the subject, the more important this resource. Such resources nevertheless are always gifts to be given when the students require them, not tasks to

be imposed. The fourth criterion follows on from this, that education, like revolution, is an act of love; 'Dialogue cannot exist,
however, in the absence of a profound love for the world and for
men. The naming of the world, which is an act of creation and
recreation, is not possible if it is not infused with love' (*Pedagogy of
the Oppressed*, p. 62).

As experience has shown in many countries, the attempt to bring
change to the lives of the poorest is always seen as a revolutionary act
by those who hold power, and bloodshed has followed prophecy
many times, including the assassination of church and community
leaders, such as Archbishop Romero in El Salvador and Martin
Luther King in the USA. The fear of Freire's 'conscientization',
which is another name for Dewey's 'experimental intelligence', is a
testimony to its power, but also a sign that true prophecy, which
seeks the empowerment of the down-trodden and oppressed, will
always meet strong resistance.

(b) The Discernment of Sin

The problem raised by this analysis is not about its prophetic force,
but about the simplicity of its hope for the world. The Christian
commitment about the nature of our reality is that the world is the
place where Christ's action is already going on. Consequently, in
Christ change is to be both expected and desired. To leave all change
until the end of the world is to be defeated as Christians before we
have even started. But the Christian hope of change is also marked
by a profound realisation that we live in the world of sin. Rather than
a simple hope of progress on earth, Christians live in a more
paradoxical hope of good coming out of evil. We recognise the
world as being in the condition which Dietrich Bonhoeffer called
'the penultimate', the time before the fullness of the kingdom of
God.

This means that in the present world the prophetic task of the
church is the discernment of sin, fuelled by the hope of the victory
of Jesus Christ over all manifestations of sin. Bonhoeffer wrote in his
book *Ethics* of the Christian struggle in the world at the personal and
social levels as a process of 'conformation', by which Jesus Christ
gradually takes over both ourselves and the world. Bonhoeffer's
fundamental perspective was formed by the conviction of the
absolute victory of Christ in the present and in the future over all the
problems of the world, based on the confidence that victory over the

negative powers in the world has already been achieved. 'The world is not divided between Christ and the devil, but, whether it recognises it or not, it is solely and entirely the world of Christ' ('Thinking in Terms of Two Spheres,' in *Ethics*, p. 176).

Now the world has to be seen primarily as the place where this ultimate victory is being worked out within history. History for Bonhoeffer is the 'penultimate', the arena where the encounter between the ultimate victory and the present power of evil takes place. The penultimate is not the absolute good of the final condition of existence with God, but it is good in itself as the time when good and evil co-exist to work out their purposes. Many things which will not have reality for us in the future have a necessity and even a value for us now as part of our conformation to Christ.

Until the human being 'crosses the frontier of death, even though he has already risen again with Christ, he remains in the world of the penultimate, the world into which Jesus entered and the world in which the cross stands' ('The Ultimate and the Penultimate', in *Ethics*, pp. 109–10). This means that we should neither despise the present as irrelevant, nor overvalue it as being all that there is, but rather treat it seriously as a time of unmasking, recognition, change and growth, which will bring us to our own place in the kingdom of love.

This affirmation of the victory of Jesus Christ over all the randomness of history does not mean that 'sin' is being taken lightly. Quite the contrary, for sin is that which stands in the way of victory. Sin is not a matter of our annoying God by not keeping certain rules, but a matter of destroying the potential to grow, in others and in ourselves. It is easy enough to destroy the human body – dictators take control of the bodies of their subjects, soldiers threaten death, murderers kill. To control the human spirit is more difficult. At the social level it requires the organisation of terror and the great lie persistently and on a large scale; at the domestic level also it requires violence and persistence in the denial of reality. These are great evils in themselves.

One thing alone finally destroys the human spirit, however, and that is to walk away from the light. By our own choice we can walk away from the light that is in us and so destroy our own spirit. There are many ways of doing this, but anything which concentrates on the self at the expense of the other, or denies the reality of the other, is a form of self-destruction. Everything which denies the other is also a denial of God. For this reason Christian thought can never abandon the doctrine of hell, for 'hell' is the image of the ultimate misunderstanding of freedom as being the continual enlargement of the self, rather than the freeing of others from what binds them against their true possibilities. Christian freedom is always 'for others', never 'for myself alone'. Since the possibility really exists of refusing this path, in the name of 'free will', it follows that the possibility of real self-destruction also exists. It is indeed possible for us to destroy ourselves for ever. Not to teach this would be a grave failure of responsibility.

(c) The Pursuit of Creative Justice

All of this can be summed up in the argument of Paul Tillich, that human life is not a simple following of rules, but a great moral struggle between the force of 'being' and the force of 'non-being', in which being slowly overcomes non-being, but always at a cost and always with the risk of falling back into non-being again. Tillich, who escaped from National Socialism in Germany to the freedom of the USA in 1933, described the human situation in more buoyant terms than Bonhoeffer. In *Love, Power and Justice* he described human life as a struggle between 'being' and 'non-being' in which the function of being was to overcome non-being, but the function of non-being was, as it were, to provoke being into action. While Tillich's thought clearly has its roots in existentialism, it also has its roots in the Protestant work ethic in a way that Bonhoeffer's thought does not. For Tillich, through grace, we are indeed responsible for our own salvation, and for the salvation of the world.

Tillich saw work as part of the fundamental nature of the creation itself, not as a punishment for sin but as the self-expression of everything that lives. The purpose of all being is self-expression. Tillich suggests that the work of being alive is structured by a 'trinity' of love, power and justice. 'Power' is not meant here simply as a sociological term, though the sociology of institutions is relevant to its use. 'Sociological power, namely the chance to carry through one's will against social resistance, is not the content of the will to power. The latter is the drive of everything to realise itself with increasing intensity and extensity' (*Love, Power and Justice*, p. 36).

Here Nietzsche's 'will to power' becomes a work to be done. For Tillich all work fundamentally is an act of love. All work which is good for human beings brings about what he calls 'the reunion of the separated'. In a very simple form this means that everything which derives from the initial act of creation belongs together, even though presently separated by necessary differentiations. As we work we change, we specialise, we separate, yet we belong together. It is a reversal of the story of the tower of Babel (Genesis 11.1–9) in which God destroyed the self-building ambitions of humankind and punished them with the division of languages. The great tower was an attempt by humans to storm heaven; now we may recognise our calling to become one through that which exists already in unity, namely God.

This work of reuniting the separated is not first of all a matter of overcoming sociological barriers, though that is included in it. The work exists first at an ontological level, that is, at the level of the nature of God. For it is the task of all being, including the being of God, to overcome non-being. Here we enter an area of some complexity. 'Non-being' is not the same as 'nothing', not a mere absence of any particular content. On the contrary, non-being is what at present prevents us from living as we have the potential to live. 'The will to power is not the will of men to attain power over men, but it is the self-affirmation of life in its self-transcending dynamics, overcoming internal and external resistance' (*Love, Power and Justice*, p. 37).

It should be made clear at this point that Tillich is not trying to prove anything by deductive argument. He is rather pointing to human experience, the experience of having to 'overcome' in order to 'be', and suggesting that this experience is true even of the being of God in creating a world. Moreover Tillich is clear that all such language is not descriptive in the sense of being fully set out in human descriptions as a series of 'facts', but is descriptive in the sense of being metaphorical, saying 'I think it must be something like this'.

With all the problems that are caused by the use of speculative language, it is worthwhile paying attention to Tillich's argument, because it does carry one very large benefit: it enables us to see the human experience of 'overcoming' as not merely an accidental feature of our existence in a material universe, but as a fundamental moral commitment, which is present in a simple form in the existence of any living creature, but comes to consciousness as a moral commitment only, so far as we know, for human beings themselves.

Professor J. Z. Young, FRS, in a letter to a London newspaper, commented that the sociobiologists' analogy of 'the selfish gene' is too narrow. 'A broader view shows that all living things have been striving creatively for three billion years to perform the wonderful task of weaving living matter out of dead atoms.' Professor Young went on to say that 'Human beings, like the rest, have the instincts from their DNA to press on with the task' and suggested that in this way science provides a basis for 'a philosophy of life' (*The Independent*, 14 May 1992). Professor Young did not, of course, go on from this to make any reference to God. On the contrary, his purpose was to suggest the sufficiency of science as a basis for a wider concept of morality and of mutual commitment than can be derived from the concept of the 'selfish gene' as concerned only to reproduce itself. Nevertheless his point is worth making because the metaphor of living creatures 'performing a wonderful task' is undoubtedly part of what Tillich is arguing in his metaphor of being overcoming non-being. It is that to live is a *moral* task derived from the fact of creation itself.

To return then to Tillich's own language, we may say that non-being is properly seen as an experience that is a necessary part of the positive experience of being. Non-being exists in order to over-come, both internally and externally; being grows by overcoming and incorporating non-being. This growth comes by the choice of a possibility which is actualised. The actualising does not destroy the fact that other possibilities have existed or continue to exist. Simply the choice gives finite form to being, makes it 'this' and not 'that'. Every choice consequently becomes embedded in time and place. The making of choices restricts being in this sense, but the further possibilities which develop out of each new situation remain endless. 'Human power is the possibility of man to overcome non-being infinitely' (*Love, Power and Justice*, p. 40).

This theory of being has strong implications for the nature of justice. If being is a process of overcoming, in which nothing is guaranteed in advance, if 'life is tentative', as Tillich says (*Love, Power and Justice*, p. 41), then justice cannot be a fixed system of rewards, nor indeed of punishments. Justice is first of all to be found in structure. Unless there is form of some sort, a dynamic process is simply anarchy. 'Everything wants to grow', says Tillich, but 'That which has no form has no being' (*Love, Power and Justice*, p. 54). Within any given form the growth which is necessary for being alive creates risks. The attempt to transcend the self opens the self to the risk of destruction as well as creation. Even God took a risk in creating, that the creation might choose self-destruction.

Consequently, justice may also involve taking risks. The requirements of justice are, firstly, the adequacy of form to content; secondly 'equality before the law' in the sense of openness to the potentiality of being to actualise itself in every human being; thirdly, freedom for the person to choose for themselves the actualisation that will take place; and finally the recognition of solidarity or unity as the ultimate goal. These tasks of justice exist because God is both the beginning and the end of the process by which being overcomes and incorporates non-being. A process which does not recognise God as source and goal has no possibility of achieving justice.

Every human event therefore has one of two characteristics. Either it is an acceptance of the moral work of creation or it is a refusal of it; either it is a recognition of God's presence in the finite or it is a refusal of it. That which is unjust is that which destroys the potential to actualise in the other or in the self. Proportional justice is that which deals with human beings according to their present form, the actualisation already achieved. Creative justice is that which – at times – acts according to a future possibility rather than a present achievement, positive or negative. Tillich suggests that in some cases we can and do give up proportional justice for the sake of creative justice. 'What is the criterion of creative justice? In order to answer this question one must ask which is the ultimate intrinsic claim for justice in a being? The answer is: Fulfilment within the unity of universal fulfilment.' But he adds, 'The religious symbol for this is the kingdom of God' (*Love, Power and Justice*, p. 65).

Tillich's modernisation of 'the Protestant ethic' (for such it is) is well worth having. The creative energy to make something of the world is a gift both of creation and of the new creation in Christ. The New Testament has too short a timescale for the coming of the kingdom to consider the nature of work in the interim period. In the longer timescale which now rules, work has to be considered both a blessing and a curse: a blessing because it is a co-operation in and with the creation to bring about good for creatures, but a curse because the material world is not easily made amenable to human interests, and even more because we cannot easily define the 'good' that we would produce.

What Tillich suggests is that this ambiguity is inseparable from our situation of being finite creatures in a material universe, but that the very ambiguity is what offers us the opportunity and the risk of transcendence. It is not only we, but also God who is involved in the ambiguity. Charles Hartshorne, discussing Tillich's earlier work, argues that God's infinitude can be true only in respect of what is not already actualised. 'It is the pure "power of being" which is only one aspect of God (if language is used clearly), that is, sheer potency, without actuality. This ultimate *power to be* anything at all is strictly infinite. No actual limits exist where there is no actuality at all.' This means that 'God is finite, but not simply as we are' ('Tillich's Doctrine of God', in Kegley and Bretall, *The Theology of Paul Tillich*, pp. 180–1). God as infinite includes all possible actualisations, God as finite includes those which are actualised and so fixed in time and place. Tillich's theology of being thus places an enormously high valuation on human acts, not only as the self-actualisation of human beings but also as the self-actualisation of God in the world.

(d) The Priority of Non-Violence

The most important part of the self-actualisation of human beings as those who know the Being of God is the work of non-violence. For the discerning of spirits, the central work of prophecy, is only half-done unless it leads to an alternative vision, a sense of what the kingdom of God can be in the here and now. Despite all the difficulties, the pursuit of the Christian faith is the pursuit of one great social vision, a vision of a world which is without fear because it is without the violent use of force to secure selfish ends. It is the vision of a society in which power is always exercised in proportion to moral ends.

Within the Christian faith the central story is about an act of non-violent resistance. Jesus chose to allow himself to be taken to the cross. He had other choices: there were also the options of giving way to the authorities' notion of peace by saying nothing that could be construed as opposition, or leading a political revolt by armed resistance, such as the nation showed itself ready for a generation later. To maintain the claim of the kingdom of God, however, was to make a stand against both the religious and the political authorities. It led inevitably to Jesus' death. Yet the New Testament makes it clear that Jesus did not go to his death without objection before God and a sense of dismay about what was to come (Luke 22.42; Mark 15.34). The resistance was not accomplished without cost.

Even the inner resources of the resister could not prevent that cost being felt.

This paradigm of resistance through a commitment to non-violence is not a teaching in the New Testament along with other teaching: it is the central pattern of the Christian faith. This is what the whole story is about, and without that non-violent but still active resistance, there would have been no 'atonement', no reconciliation between God and sinful human beings. At the same time Jesus' death is not an invitation to passivity. In the first place, it was a deliberately willed public act of defiance in the face of those who preferred order before truth. In the second place, it was done with the utmost confidence that God would provide a positive response. Whether Jesus foresaw his own resurrection is not clear; what is clear is that he expected in some sense to be 'vindicated', to be proved right in his whole approach to his mission on behalf of God.

What was necessary public action for one who thought himself to be God's messenger at a critical moment in the life of the holy people does not translate directly into a model for general action by all people everywhere. There is, in my view, no rule arising out of this which says 'Never offer resistance by force'. Jürgen Moltmann, discussing the commitment to peacemaking in the Sermon on the Mount, says 'the centre of the Sermon on the Mount is the liberation from violence; enmity is to be surmounted through the creation of peace. The presupposition here is that humanity's real sin is the violence that leads to death; and that consequently humanity's salvation is to be found in the peace that serves our common life' (*The Way of Jesus Christ*, p. 127).

Moltmann comments that even the passage about not offering resistance to one who is evil (Matthew 2.39–42) has as its premise, not the renunciation of violence but the existence of 'a sovereign power over violence and counter-violence' (*The Way of Jesus Christ*, p. 129). His conclusion is that the renunciation of false force is not the renunciation of all social use of power. '"Freedom from vio-lence" does not mean de-politicisation. Nor does it mean the renunciation of power; for our language distinguishes very clearly between violence and power. We give the name of power to the just use of force' (*The Way of Jesus Christ*, pp. 129–30). The Christian function is to criticise violence in order to rob it of its claim to legitimacy, not to give up entirely the possibility of exercising restraint upon those who seek to do harm.

The Christian concern here is the promotion of 'peace' rather than the choice of non-violence as the answer to every situation. As Oh Jae Shik emphasises, peace is a question of non-violent change, but sometimes it must be the change that has the highest priority, not the non-violence:

> In many cases, reconciliation has meant the weaker surrendering to the stronger for survival. Furthermore, can trust be built without correcting the wrongs committed in past relations? So the issue is whether there is a stronger power or moral authority over and above the conflicting parties to reconcile them in such a way that justice is realised.
>
> The same applies to the violence-non-violence debate. The matter is more complicated than the way it is presented in academic discussions. Quite often people are drawn into violence. They do not subscribe to violence under normal circumstances. Also, in most cases, violence is a response to previous violence. It is provoked. ('Justice in Peace: From Whose Perspective?' in Niles, *Between the Flood and the Rainbow*, pp. 160–1)

Oh Jae Shik writes here from his own experience of people's movements for peace in Asia. As in Pope Paul VI's letter *Populorum Progressio*, it is not possible entirely to deny to the poor a right to self-defence against the state and other aggressors. As Oh Jae Shik also warns, the use of force must be carefully calculated in relation to its possible results:

> In terms of strategy, violent action must lead to positive results. To resort to violence in sheer anger or in reaction to preceding violence cannot be justified in terms of strategy. The premature use of violence will provide a good excuse of the opponent to use even more violent means. Also, the use of violence tends to create a vicious cycle of violence ... But, there are historical precedents, although rare, where violence has been effective and therefore justified. In summary, I am not prepared to denounce all use of violence on religious grounds. (p. 161)

This puts the ball sharply back into our own court. The nature of human freedom is such that we cannot be assured of salvation ethically by sticking to clear and simple rules. The decision about what is 'violence' and what is 'proper restraint' rests always and only with us.

The practice of non-violence is a spiritual commitment, but a spiritual commitment to change, not to inaction. It is the lesson of the whole history of the modern experience of non-violent resistance, from the work of Frederick Douglass among American Black people in the nineteenth century, through Mohandas Gandhi drawing on Hindu spirituality in working for human rights in South Africa and India in the early twentieth century, to the testimony of Martin Luther King and others in the Civil Rights Movement in the United States in the second half of this century, that spiritual commitment, faith in the truth within the self and the gift of the loss of fear is the root of the power of non-violent resistance.

In the mass demonstrations for civil rights in Birmingham, Alabama in April and May 1963, the volunteers were asked to sign a pledge which included the commitments to:

1. *Meditate* daily on the teachings and life of Jesus.

2. *Remember* always that the non-violent movement in Birmingham seeks justice and reconciliation – not victory.

3. *Walk* and *Talk* in the manner of love for God is love.

4. *Pray* daily to be used by God, in order that all men might be free.

(Lerone Bennett, *What Manner of Man*, p. 135)

Writing of the struggle for human rights in Brazil, Dominique Barbé summarises the discipline required for non-violent action:

The purity of our means, the intelligent selection of symbolic actions calculated to move the noblest part of the popular conscience, the careful construction of a network of ever broader and broader struggle (campaigns of disobedience), and the clarity of the political objectives we seek, are the four essential conditions for the credibility of the non-violent alternative in the coming years. (*A Theology of Conflict*, p. 81)

Later, discussing a particular campaign, in favour of the legally-required but not practised payment of a minimum wage, in which an army unit was faced-down by peaceful mass non-aggression, he comments that 'each situation demands a non-violent response appropriate to it. What worked on 1 May 1980, might not work on 1 May 1981'. He adds:

> Active non-violence requires a shrewdness that will not be spoon-fed with fairytales. Non-violence has always had to defend itself against charges of being a naive sentimentality or a beautiful, irresponsible idealism. 'Be as harmless as doves but as wise as serpents,' Jesus tells us (Matt. 10.16). If goodness is all one has, one will be plucked like a pear. If one is merely prudent, one will also be cruel. (*A Theology of Conflict*, p. 123)

What the New Testament story tells us is that there is at all times only one proper purpose for the use of force, and that is to disarm the use of force. It tells us also that the disarming of improper force, robbing naked power of its pretension to legitimacy, is not 'an' ethical aim, but the central purpose of the Gospel, at every level from the personal to the global community. It tells us also that, whatever the odds, we must not give up the hope that robbing violence of its power is possible, even at the global level. As an institutional practice it needs many frustrating hours and days of such matters as United Nations peacekeeping forces and negotiations with people in conflicts. But it is an aim that can never be given up entirely.

Finally, as Moltmann again says, 'Love of our enemies is not recompensing love, that returns what it has received. It is *creative* love. Anyone who repays evil with good has stopped just reacting. He is creating something new' (*The Way of Jesus Christ*, p. 131).

(ii) The Vision of God

The roots of modern democracy lie in the Protestant Reformation with its insistence on the Old Testament doctrines of the priesthood of all believers (Exodus 19.6; cf. 1 Peter 2.5) and the supremacy of the individual conscience (Jeremiah 31.32–34), coupled with the affirmation of the ontological equality of all believers (Galatians

3.28), which is in effect a New Testament summary of these teachings. Though the Reformers were by no means setting out to create electoral democracy through universal suffrage, their affirmation of human dignity and of the human potential for change which is implicit in these ideas, together with the concomitant demand for religious liberty, made possible the eighteenth-century break-through into the notions of the 'rights of man' and the unalienable right to 'Life, Liberty and the pursuit of Happiness' of the American Declaration of Independence.

The only problem was that without the ultimate and cosmic definition of rights as part of the stewardship which we receive from God, it became less and less clear whether they meant anything other than a subjective demand for personal satisfactions. The Freudian revolution clarified much about our psycho-sexual development, but it had the unfortunate side-effect of confirming the wrong direction of our notions of human dignity into an elevation of the inner self as the measure of all things.

The Christian vision of 'glory', on the other hand, establishes the creation of the cosmos as the context for human happiness and human dignity. The Westminster *Shorter Catechism* of 1648 begins:

Q.1. *What is the chief end of man?*
A.   Man's chief end is to glorify God and to enjoy Him for ever.

All human activity in the world is to be seen as a search for true knowledge of God. Only so can we have true knowledge of ourselves and only so can we have true knowledge of one another. The most focused form of this search is 'spirituality', the knowledge of God through prayer. There is a very serious sense in which Christian ethics can be seen as a subdivision of Christian spirituality, a part of the discipline which governs the way by which we come to see God.

Indeed it could be said with some justice that the reason why we find Christian ethics difficult today, both to perceive and to follow, is that we have lost the habit of prayer, and even the sense of the necessity of prayer for fullness of life. This sense of uncertainty can be seen in the way in which our spirituality today is fragmented into feminist spirituality, ecological spirituality, ethnic spirituality of all sorts, including the British search for 'Celtic' roots, and even a recovery of traditional spiritual paths, such as the 'exercises' of St Ignatius of Loyola.

Of the three great formative periods in the development of the tradition of Christian spirituality, it was the first, that of the Greek theologians, which gave us the most daring thought of all, that it is possible to enter into the presence of God and be transfigured by divine light:

> 'I've already told you,' said Father Seraphim 'that it's very simple. I've talked at length about the state of those who are in the Spirit of God; I've also explained to you how we can recognise this presence in ourselves ... What more is necessary, my friend?'
>
> 'I must understand better everything that you have said to me.'
>
> 'My friend, we are both at this moment in the Spirit of God ... Why won't you look at me?'
>
> 'I can't look at you, Father – I replied – your eyes shine like lightening; your face has become more dazzling than the sun, and it hurts my eyes to look at you.'
>
> 'Don't be afraid,' said he, 'at this very moment you've become as bright as I have. You are also at present in the fullness of the Spirit of God; otherwise you wouldn't be able to see me as you do see me.' (Vladimir Lossky, *The Mystical Theology of the Eastern Church*, pp. 227–8)

Lossky's account of the dialogue of the nineteenth-century Russian *starets* or holy man, St Seraphim of Sarov, with his disciple, underlines how literally the Orthodox Church understands the nature of divine light. Human beings can have direct access, not to God's essence, but to the energies of God, the divine radiance which forms the world and keeps it in being. In this light is freedom, the power to move ever onwards in the path of the light, without end and without fear. God is the unlimited possibility of change for ever. It is this change which is 'perfection', not some static condition of rest after labour. Even perfection is to be 'on the move'. For this reason the universe for Orthodox theology is represented by a moving pattern or dance (*perichoresis*), which also represents the life of the Holy Trinity. The celebration of the dance of the Trinity is indeed the central motif of Orthodox thought and life.

The second great period of development in spirituality was that of mediaeval Europe from which we have a host of magnificent writings, from the life of St Francis of Assisi to the reflections of the lady Julian of Norwich and the anguish of St John of the Cross in the 'dark night of the soul', which he describes as the final stage of cleansing before the union of the soul with God. Nevertheless, it was this period which marked western spirituality with the characteristics of individualism, of concentration on sin and the cross rather than on the holy Trinity, and of the adoration of the human character and suffering of Jesus, the *devotio moderna* or 'new devotion' of 'the imitation of Christ', which now to some extent we have to strive to undo. The mediaeval tradition in the west is enormously rich, and repays every effort at study of it a thousand-fold, but much of it is now opaque to modern thought, in part because the theologians of the Reformation rejected it so decisively as being part of that monasticism which they rightly thought to bear the blame for many of the ills of the mediaeval western church.

After the Reformation both the Protestant and the Catholic churches shifted their emphasis to the instruction of the laity, through better theological education for both clergy and laity. In Britain the most important influence was the puritan concern with holiness, well represented by the Anglican divine Jeremy Taylor whose books on *Holy Living* (1650) and *Holy Dying* (1651) remain classics of the genre. The same emphasis on the moral and spiritual instruction of the whole church can be found in Methodism, in the structure of discipline of the Church of Scotland, and throughout Protestant Europe and the new North American communities of settlers. It appeared equally strongly among Catholics in the instructional works of St Francis of Sales and later among the Quietists of the Port Royale. There was a general Western European assumption that the spiritual way was a way of discipline, of charity and of personal restraint.

This has never been better expressed than by George Herbert in the poems in *The Temple*, such as 'Trinity Sunday':

> Lord, who has form'd me out of mud
>   And hast redeem'd me through thy blood,
>   And sanctifi'd me to do good;
>
> Purge all my sins done heretofore;

> For I confess my heavy score,
> And I will strive to sin no more.

> Enrich my heart, mouth, hands in me,
>   With faith, with hope, with charity;
>   That I may run, rise, rest with thee.

In 'Prayer (I)' Herbert defines prayer in the lovely phrase 'Heaven in ordinarie' meaning that in prayer we encounter heaven itself, but in the dress of ordinary, daily life. There is in this tradition a profound acceptance of ordinary life as the place where God is found:

> Prayer, the church's banquet, angel's age,
>   God's breath in man returning to his birth,
>   The soul in paraphrase, heart in pilgrimage,
> The Christian plummet sounding heav'n and earth:

> Engine against th' Almightie, sinner's towre,
>   Reversed thunder, Christ-side-piercing spear,
>   The six daies' world transposing in an houre,
> A kinde of tune, which all things heare and fear;

> Softnesse, and peace, and joy, and love, and blisse,
>   Exalted manna, gladnesse of the best,
>   Heaven in ordinarie, man well drest,
> The milkie way, the bird of Paradise,

>   Church-bels beyond the stars heard, the soul's bloud,
>   The land of spices, something understood.

Herbert sees prayer as both the natural response of the created human being, giving back to God the breath which formed the life of Adam, and also as a kind of impetus of the human being against God, waging warfare in order to be heard. Yet this warfare has fulfilment in a peace which is both exotic and strange, 'the land of spices', and at the same time is heaven brought down to earth, 'heaven in ordinarie'. And at the last, this 'engine against the Almighty', this 'sound beyond the stars', is no more than a little knowledge of God, 'something understood'.

So prayer is both something natural to us and something strange, something comforting and something that tells us in the end about our finitude. Rarely has so complete a teaching about prayer been compressed into so little a space. It is a moment equalled only by Herbert's definition of the atonement in a single line of 'The Reprisal': 'For by the death I die for thee'.

The distance between this and any merely romanticising view of the world can be illustrated by a story told by Thomas Merton, a twentieth-century American monastic. In *The Sign of Jonas* he tells how one day he saw a hawk strike into a flock of starlings. 'It was a terrible and yet beautiful thing, that lightning flight, straight as an arrow, that killed the slowest starling.' A strong opponent of nuclear weapons and of the then raging war in Vietnam, he reflects on 'the terrible fact that some men love war'. Then he adds, 'But in the end, I think that hawk is to be studied by saints and contemplatives; because he knows his business. I wish I knew my business as well as he does his' (p. 268).

Alongside this major tradition there can also be traced a minor but contrasting tradition of what may be called 'dialectical' spirituality. This is not so much concerned with the unity and continuity of experience as with the doubt and tension that exist within the spiritual life. This is essentially a modern, post-Reformation consciousness, but its roots can be traced through Eckhart back to the notion of the divine darkness that plays so strong a part in the spirituality of the Orthodox Church. In its modern form, however, it is the child of that watershed in western thought which we call 'the Enlightenment'.

In spirituality its beginning is marked by William Blake, who wrote a century and a half after George Herbert. Blake more than anybody else was aware of the contradictions and tensions which had to be held together in the new industrial society. In one of his best-loved poems, 'The Tyger', he expressed the continuity and the discontinuity between nature and the equally harsh industrial world:

What the hammer? what the chain?
In what furnace was thy brain?
What the anvil? what dread grasp
Dare its deadly terrors clasp?
(*Blake*, p. 50)

Here he poses the moral question which it is the task of spirituality rather than moral theory to answer: 'Did he who made the Lamb make thee?'

The nineteenth century was increasingly disturbed by this question, in one form or another, from Thomas Arnold's doubts to Nietzsche's declaration of the death of God, and the answer became increasingly turned in upon the self, until with the existentialists of the twentieth century there seemed to be nothing left to base life on but the isolated human consciousness. For a long time organised religion simply resisted asking the question. Blake was regarded as very much an outsider, and indeed the question was seen as one for outsiders, such as Simone Weil, rather than one for the church itself to attempt to answer.

Now, however, the question is well inside the church's own door and the answer is seen to lie not in the denial of the problem but in the recognition of the existence of the abyss. The Welsh priest and poet R. S. Thomas expressed the tensions of human life in an early poem, 'Song for Gwydion':

> When I was a child and the soft flesh was forming
> Quietly as snow on the bare boughs of bone,
> My father brought me trout from the green river
> From whose chill lips the water song had flown.
>
> Dull grew their eyes, the beautiful, blithe garland
> Of stipples faded, as light shocked the brain;
> They were the first sweet sacrifice I tasted,
> A young god, ignorant of the blood's stain.
> (*Selected Poems 1946–1968*, p. 14)

Here there is both the destructive chill of winter, and the warm glow of life in the child's pleasure, the pagan recognition that life comes through the death of others. Because it is the experience of a child, no other resolution is required.

By the end of his life Thomas was exploring more forcefully the absence of God and in a late poem, 'Threshold', he points to the fact that we cannot expect to hold on to what we have, yet do not know what will be there when we let go:

> I emerge from the mind's
> cave into the worse darkness
> outside, where things pass and
> the Lord is in none of them.

I have heard the still, small voice
and it was that of the bacteria
demolishing my cosmos. I
have lingered too long on

this threshold, but where can I go?
To look back is to lose the soul
I was leading upward towards
the light. To look forward? Ah,

what balance is needed at
the edges of such an abyss.
I am alone on the surface
of a turning planet. What

to do but, like Michelangelo's
Adam, put my hand
out into unknown space,
hoping for the reciprocating touch?
(*Later Poems 1972–1982*, p. 155)

This is a peculiarly modern sensibility. When St John of the Cross at the end of the sixteenth century wrote of the deeper penetration of the ascetic by contemplation into God as a penetration into 'nothing', he did not mean that he did not know what was there, rather that the reality of God could not be expressed, could scarcely be intellectually understood and could hardly be spiritually borne. The 'nothing' was the term for the reality of God which overwhelmed all human resources. Thomas's abyss, on the other hand, seems to be the name for a real sense of letting-go without knowing where we shall fall.

This 'dialectical' spirituality asserts a need to reach out in the face of uncertainty. It is the product of the particular world in which we live, so shaped by science and technology that God has in effect been privatised. The lack of balance in our individually-separated, operationally-orientated world has created an insecurity about the human future, in which hope has become a desperate act. All previous Christian spirituality – although it has sometimes been the product of an élite – has claimed the human centre ground, the ability to provide the final explanation of all human affairs.

This is not to say that there has been no room for doubt and fear in Christian spirituality. The end of Mark's Gospel is indeed one of the most dramatic literary devices in the Bible: 'Then they went out and ran away from the tomb, trembling with amazement. They said nothing to anyone, for they were afraid' (16.8). Certainly it seems to have been too dramatic for the later editors who were unable to leave it as the last word, and no doubt the author of Mark knew also that it was being addressed to a church which already knew itself to be the continuation of the story.

Nevertheless the emphasis is important: fear and trembling are a real part of the spiritual experience. The Orthodox Church describes this as *apophatic* or negative theology, the necessity to admit that all our knowledge of God is in the end non-knowledge. Only in and through this darkness do we come to a full knowledge of the light, the state that T. S. Eliot describes as

> A condition of complete simplicity
> (Costing not less than everything)
> ('Little Gidding', in *Four Quartets*, p. 44)

Yet all doubt and all fear come to an end in the eucharist, the feast of the presence of God on earth in the midst of the community called together in the name of Jesus, the man from Nazareth. The church in all its forms is the community called into existence by the simple action of Jesus at the Last Supper:

> During supper he took bread, and having said the blessing he broke it and gave it to them, with the words: 'Take this; this is my body.' Then he took a cup, and having offered thanks to God he gave it to them; and they all drank from it. And he said to them, 'This is my blood, the blood of the covenant, shed for many. Truly, I tell you: never again shall I drink from the fruit of the vine until that day when I drink it new in the kingdom of God.' (Mark 14.22–25)

From that moment, those who confess Jesus as lord, who share the bread and the cup and who attempt to love their fellow human beings have been what the world calls 'Christians'.

It took the church a while to work out what this was all about. Paul, whose account was the earliest record to be written down, adds, 'For every time you eat this bread and drink the cup, you proclaim the death of the Lord, until he comes (1 Corinthians 11.26). He also says, 'Because there is one loaf, we, though many, are one body' (1 Corinthians 10.17). These themes of death, resurrection and unity are the themes of the eucharist, the sacrament of thanksgiving.

In the eucharist the Christian community looks to the past, the present and the future. To the past because, as Paul says, all Christian life looks back to the death and resurrection of Jesus. Towards the end of the First Letter to the Corinthians Paul has an extended treatment of death. It begins with the assertion of resurrection. 'But the truth is, Christ was raised to life – the firstfruits of the harvest of the dead' (15.20).

The letter goes on to teach that the new life begins in the old life but is not the same thing. 'The seed you sow does not come to life unless it has first died ... So it is with the resurrection of the dead: what is sown as a perishable thing is raised imperishable' (15.36, 42). The letter ends with the assertion of the necessity of this transformation for every human being. 'What I mean, my friends, is this: flesh and blood can never possess the kingdom of God, the perishable cannot possess the imperishable' (15.50). What began in history is to be completed beyond history, not denying the reality of the past but asserting the necessity of going beyond it, so that what is good in the past carries forward and what is evil is swept away. Then comes the cry of triumph, 'Death is swallowed up, victory is won' (15.54).

So the Christians moved from being Jews celebrating the yearly Passover, the anniversary of the escape from Egypt, to being a community celebrating at the beginning of every new week the death and resurrection of Jesus, through the life of Jesus present among them. Any and every meal could be a 'thanksgiving', as was Paul's meal with the people on the vessel in danger of shipwreck in the Adriatic:

> Shortly before daybreak Paul urged them all to take some food. 'For the last fourteen days,' he said, 'you have lived in suspense and gone hungry; you have eaten nothing. So have something to eat, I beg you; your lives depend on it. Remember, not a hair of your heads will be lost.' With these words, he took bread, gave thanks to God in front of them all, broke it, and began eating. Then they plucked up courage, and began to take food themselves. (Acts 27.33–36)

It would be difficult to claim that this was not 'eucharist'. As C. K. Barrett remarks, in our understanding of the present life of the church we need to take the New Testament seriously enough to believe that the same reality happens now. He asks 'whether we believe that every member of the church is in some sense a minister and in every sense a priest ... whether every meal we take, especially every meal the church takes together, is transformed by the fact of the real presence; whether we honestly believe that it is better to give than to receive, to serve than to be served' (*Church, Ministry and Sacraments*, p. 101).

The presence of Jesus for which the church gives thanks is that which is revealed by the actual fact of service in the world. The enacted, sacramental presence of Jesus is not a magical rite which automatically guarantees salvation. It is rather the symbolic or sacramental presentation of an ethical fact. The ethic of the sacrament lies in our commitment to one another as the community of the church (is there really care for one another?) and in our commitment as the church to the world (is there really care for the human community in its setting in the created earth?). The thanksgiving in the present, therefore, is a thanksgiving not only for grace and for achievement in the past, but also for the potential to be fulfilled in the future.

Because the church is in process, is on the way to a destination at which it has not yet arrived, the eucharist is also a thanksgiving in anticipation. The celebration of the present-day community is a foretaste of the celebration that will come when all the harvest is gathered in. This future celebration, however, is not only a hope, but also a present reality. There is a sense in which the present celebration *is* the future reality. The eucharist is the present form of that future reality. In the words of the 'Cherubic Hymn' of the Liturgy of St John Chrysostom,

> We that in a figure answer to the Cherubim, and join with them in singing the Thrice-holy hymn to the life-giving Trinity, let us lay aside all the cares of this life:
>
> For we are now to receive the King of all, invisibly escorted by the ranks of angels. Alleluia, alleluia, alleluia.

In every eucharist the church enters into its future because it enters into the risen presence of Christ. But, as Alexander Schmemann says, 'this is not an "other" world, different from the one God has created and given to us. It is our same world, *already* perfected in Christ, but *not yet* in us' (*For the Life of the World*, p. 42).

In Orthodox theology the place where the darkness of God becomes visible light for all is the divine liturgy. The church at the time of the liturgy is the gate of heaven standing open on the earth. Here the human being truly fulfils the human calling to be 'the priest of creation', foreshadowed in the task of Eve and Adam in the garden, but made fully visible in Christ, the first and the last of human beings, present at the creation and signifying now the future victory already present and living in our lives. For we cannot remain in the tension of the 'Threshold', even though we sometimes experience it. Rather we have to move on, to the Biblical promise of 'the End Time'. In this future, all tensions become harmony, all needs can be fulfilled. In the words of the book of Isaiah,

> Then the wolf will live with the lamb,
> and the leopard lie down with the kid.
> (Isaiah 11.6)

There will no longer be competition, because there will no longer be scarcity of resources.

> Come for water, all who are thirsty;
> though you have no money, come,
>   buy grain and eat;
> come, buy wine and milk,
> not for money, not for a price.
> (Isaiah 55.1)

The eucharistic community is the place where these visions of the first and second Isaiah are taken seriously. Only in the eucharistic community is there both a hope that the vision has future meaning and a commitment to begin to turn that meaning into reality today. As a meal the eucharist is the symbol and expression of our embodiment, because in it the fruits of the earth are first received from God and then offered back in thanksgiving, as a sign of our common ownership of earth. As a common meal the eucharist is a sign of justice, because no one may be turned away, rich or poor, white or black, male or female, slave or free. As a meal the eucharist is the expression of the sacred community, because it is always the sign of hope for the future of the whole of creation. So the world itself is the sign and sacrament held up for our hope in the eucharistic offering.

This means that there can be no true spirituality of creation without some sense of 'church', of being a people called to worship for the renewing of the world. As the Orthodox theologian K. M. George says, 'The church's task is to transfigure the whole creation so that all that is created is restored from its distortions and made the body of Christ. The material creation is called back through Christ the God-Man to the original transparency, the capacity to receive and reflect the glory of God' ('Towards a Eucharistic Ecology', in Gennadios Limouris, *Justice, Peace and the Integrity of Creation*, p. 53). All of this calls for a new theology of sacredness. Indeed, K. M. George's phrase 'called back' might be better expressed as 'called forward', into a new state that the creation has not experienced before.

(iii) The Unity of the Cosmos in Christ

When Robert Burns wrote his 'Second Epistle to J. Lapraik' in 1785, he was looking at a world which could be understood and managed by the 'social, friendly, honest man, Whate'er he be'. As we survey the vast emptiness of space, the burgeoning populations of earth, the puny efforts of our authorities to understand and to manage our lives, we may well be excused for wondering whether such a thing as a 'royal mandate' for life on this earth could possibly exist. The Christian hope, shared with all the great religions of human kind, is that it can and it does. The mandate lies, not in details of dogma or worship or ethics, but in the acceptance of our common life on earth, our common ownership of the earth, and our common responsibility, one to another and to every living creature.

Thomas Berry says of the Christian ceremony of baptism that while it brings the child or the adult who is baptised into relationship with the earthly community of the church and with the divine community of God, it fails to bring these persons explicitly into the natural community of which the water is also a sign and a part:

> We use the water, but we do not exactly relate to the water.
> We use it as a symbol of purification. We still do not

appreciate the water itself. In the blessing of the water during the Easter vigil, however, there is a rather wonderful invocation regarding the water as it is taken into the world of the sacred. But there is still the problem of leaving out the natural world in its primary role. (*Befriending the Earth*, p. 48)

He contrasts this with the ceremony of the Omaha Indians in which the new-born child is presented to the earth and to the sky in a series of invocations of help for the new life: 'Oh ye clouds, winds, rains, all ye powers that move across the atmosphere, I bid you hear us. Into your midst has come a new life. Consent ye, we implore, make its path smooth.'

Here the new life is recognised in its dependence on that which surrounds it, in humility that the human child is a creature among creatures. At the same time the new life is recognised as already a part of this community of life, not an object for use, or training or neglect by other human beings, but a life which must be accounted for to the power which is evident in the earth and the sky. The human duality is thus made clear, that those who would be the stewards of the earth and the sky must also accept the protection of the power which causes them to be.

Early in the eighth century a monk of the community of St Peter in Jarrow wrote:

> Britain is rich in grain and timber; it has good pasturage for cattle and draught animals, and vines are cultivated in various localities. There are many land and sea birds of various species, and it is well known for its plentiful springs and rivers abounding in fish. Salmon and eels are especially plentiful, while seals, dolphins and sometimes whales are caught. (Bede, *A History of the English Church and People*, p. 37)

Today it would be difficult to find the land of which the Venerable Bede wrote so lyrically. The 'twenty-eight noble cities' of his time have become vast conurbations, the rivers have suffered from urbanisation, pollution and increasing extraction of water, the open land and forest has been cleared and enclosed with hedges, then the hedges ripped out and vast fields made for new machinery to work in. No land stands still. But what we have done to the land of Britain in the last two hundred years will be hard to justify to succeeding generations.

What we have lost in this process is not only the ability to control our relationship to the environment in practice, but also our vision of what that relationship should be. The human relation to nature in the Bible has two aspects, both shown in the story of the creation in Genesis 2.4–24. The first is that the human being is formed from the earth. 'The Lord God formed a human being from the dust of the ground and breathed into his nostrils the breath of life, so that he became a living creature' (2.7). Adam, the human being as yet undifferentiated into female and male, is formed from the earth, a part of the material creation in the same way as other creatures.

The second is that the other living creatures follow after Adam, who shares in the act of creation by naming them. Adam has responsibility for the 'garden', the original earth, and for all the creatures in it. 'So from the earth he formed all the wild animals and all the birds of the air, and brought them to the man to see what he would call them' (2.19). Adam's task is not merely naming, but a sharing in creation. It is Adam who gives final definition to the natures of the animals which he names.

At this point in the story Adam is in a state of community with the other animals, which is not broken when the human being breaks into male and female for companionship and for sexual reproduction. The web of community with the rest of nature is not broken until the 'fall' by which Eve and Adam seize the responsibility for their own lives. Then the unity of natural knowledge is broken and man and woman have to labour for their food and shelter. In the story of the Flood, the new situation after the waters have subsided is expressed in the covenant with Noah, in which now 'Fear and dread of you will come on all the animals on earth, on all the birds of the air, on everything that moves on the ground, and on all fish in the sea,' because 'they are made subject to you' (Genesis 9.2).

The co-operative power of humanity is now universalised in the power to do anything that is within reach of our invention and skill, but is still, as the later story of the creation insists, a rule that must be 'in the image of God' (Genesis 1.26–28). The human being remains answerable to God for the human stewardship of the earth. Do we still have the possibility to effect this stewardship, or has the 'third chimpanzee' now gone beyond the limit of its ability to survive on the planet earth?

For us today the classical world of 'natural law' has gone for ever. We are committed to a world of flux, of evolutionary change, of relativity. Neither rocks nor living beings are substances in the old sense. As Charles Birch and John Cobb put it, we are concerned, not with 'substance' but with 'event':

> Substance thinking recognised the occurrence of events and undertook to explain them in terms of substances. Event thinking must recognise the existence of relatively enduring 'substantial objects' and undertake to explain them in terms of patterns of interconnectedness among events. From this point of view an atom is not a substantial entity but a multiplicity of events interconnected with each other and with other events in a describable pattern. A mouse is a far more extensive society of events, electronic, cellular and organismic, interconnected in far more complex patterns. (*The Liberation of Life*, p. 86)

The law of nature is not the discovery of a plan and even less the discovery of a set of rules for putting a plan into effect, but a dance. As the Greek Fathers said, life is a *perichoresis*, a dance of the universe led by Christ the Lord of Creation, towards a fulfilment that is not yet seen.

The best word to describe the human location in this dance today is 'precarious'. We have arrived at a point where our own abilities and our own successes are the biggest threat to our own continued successful existence on the planet. Thomas Berry, a Catholic theologian concerned with the study of ecology and spirituality, comments on the changes we have made to the biosphere, including the damage to the ozone layer and the possibility of the 'greenhouse effect', that 'Events in this modality and at this order of magnitude have never taken place in the total course of human history, possibly in the course of earth history ... We are not capable of extinguishing everything, but we are wreaking severe damage on the earth process' (*Befriending the Earth*, p. 5).

The most serious aspect of human activity in the natural world at the present time is our capacity for destroying other species. Jared Diamond comments:

> There are many grounds for pessimism. Even if every human now alive were to die tomorrow, the damage that we have already inflicted on our environment would ensure that its degradation will continue for decades. Innumerable species

already belong to the 'living dead', with populations fallen to levels from which they cannot recover, even though not all individuals have died yet. (*The Rise and Fall of the Third Chimpanzee*, p. 7)

Essentially this destructive power arises from our positive abilities to invent weapons, to build structures and to change environments, not from any specific ill-will. From pre-historical times human beings have hunted other animals to destruction, or changed habitats in ways which meant that other species could not survive. Since evolution is about change as well as about continuity, this was not in itself a problem for most of human history, even though today we must in principle regret the disappearance of any species as something unique and irreplaceable.

It is striking to note that even as late as the first half of this century the Catholic theologian Pierre Teilhard de Chardin, known today for his interpretation of the evolutionary purpose of God, did not see humanity as a threat in this way. Thomas Berry records that 'Once, when someone pointed out to him the destruction of the natural world, Teilhard said that science would discover other forms of life' (*Befriending the Earth*, p. 25). Similarly in the early 1970s, when serious discussion began, through the work of Paul and Anne Ehrlich, Dennis Meadowes and others, about the process of economic growth as a threat to human survival on the planet, the general reaction was to expect to find solutions through further technological development. No such comfort remains today.

The question now is about the possibility of human survival under any circumstances whatever. We start off with one advantage, which is that this universe seems to be designed to support our kind of life. The narrowness of the initial conditions in the first stages of the present state of our universe is now well known. Very small differences from what must actually have occurred would have meant no possibility of organic life on earth. Charles Birch and John Cobb remark that 'A slightly different history in those microseconds could have resulted in the universe being all helium with no hydrogen. Without hydrogen there would have subsequently been no heavy elements which were formed by the fusion of hydrogen nuclei. These heavy elements, such as carbon and iron, are essential for life' (*The Liberation of Life*, p. 190).

In the universe as it is, life has been an emergent force. As Birch and Cobb also say, 'Biologists rightly insist that life is not another thing alongside the entities that make up living things. Instead it is the effectiveness of unrealised possibilities in shaping the actualisation of living things' (p. 189).

It is the emergence of consciousness that has led human beings to ethics and to religion. Birch and Cobb, following H. N. Wieman, argue that chaos and disintegration are widespread in human life because the task of maximising the richness of experience in the world puts human life at the forefront of an evolutionary drive towards the integration of greater complexity, so that 'human life is now the fighting frontier of the progressive integration of universe, so far as we know'. They add that 'There may be other frontiers far in advance of human society in other parts of the cosmos, but we know nothing of them. So far as our knowledge reaches, human society is the utmost cosmic venture toward the creation of richer integrations' (*The Liberation of Life*, pp. 191–2).

John Crook, writing of ethology and psychology in the context of a Zen Buddhist model of understanding, suggests similarly that 'If the wise of the world only remain in the traditional cultures it is not surprising that the young seek their gurus often in strange places. The Western models are simply not enough. Yet these far-away cultures too are threatened as the flux of modern times continues to roll' (*The Evolution of Human Consciousness*, p. 411). To develop the ability to live with this crisis, it seems that we must develop new abilities to construct the self which will allow us to come to terms with change and insecurity.

While Crook himself places his faith in the Zen process of meditation as a training in the development of the self, he recognises also the existence of an equivalent tradition in Christian spirituality. His conclusion is that the changes we need can still be made. 'Wisdom is not out of reach. It requires a recalibration of the ego. The mental equipment is there but unused. Like chimpanzees, who do not know how intelligent they are, we are only dimly beginning to perceive the possibilities of which our minds, operating in society, are capable' (p. 411).

This human capacity for 'religion', in the broadest sense is indeed at the forefront of the current stage of the emergence of life, even though the whole of recorded human history is no more than a moment in the story of the emergence of life on this planet. If moral meaning is to be given to our life on earth at all, then the human capacity for moral judgment must be of some significance in the evolving process, and that capacity depends on our ability to envision the system as a moral whole. As Thomas Berry puts it, 'There is no such thing as "human community" without the earth and the soil and the air and the water and all the living forms. Without these, humans do not exist. There is, therefore, no separate human community.' He adds, 'The large community is the sacred community' (*Befriending the Earth*, p. 43).

The notion of the sacred community is the final interpretative principle of the mandate of heaven. It is more than an embracing of ecological correctness. For those of us who have been brought up in the Western European or North American educational tradition it requires a willingness to reverse our understanding of our own history. As Zygmunt Bauman argues in relation to the Holocaust and to Hiroshima and Nagasaki, 'What is untenable is the concept of our – European – history as the rise of humanity over the animal in man, and as the triumph of rational organisation over the cruelty of life that is nasty, brutish and short. What is also untenable is the concept of modern society as an unambiguously moralizing force …' ('Social Manipulation of Morality', in *Modernity and the Holocaust*, p. 212). Only when we recognise that the normal work of socialisation is in many ways the work of suppressing the challenge of morality can we see that western history is largely a history of a refusal to give the other a human face – the dehumanisation of the enemy within and the external enemy, the religious opponent and the person of a different race.

The first interpretative or hermeneutical principle of a true Christian morality is that of 'justification by grace through faith', the recognition of our own standing before God as that of a redeemed sinner, one who is accepted because the divine love wills it so. The second principle of interpretation is that of the eucharistic community, in which it becomes possible to practise love for another through the reality of the sacramental action. The third principle is that of the sacred community, the recognition that the community for which the divine purpose exists is the totality of the living communities of earth. All life is to be interpreted through these principles and everything else in the Bible is simply commentary upon them.

The performance of this morality, even in speech, is a difficult task. As T. S. Eliot puts it,

Words strain,
Crack and sometimes break, under the burden ...
('Burnt Norton', in *Four Quartets*, p. 12)

Eliot saw the purification of the language as particularly the responsibility of the poet, but it is the responsibility also of the theologian
and the moralist. Above all it is the task of Christian spirituality,
which undergirds all our theological and moral thought. The
refining fire of St John of the Cross, of Dante and of the *Four
Quartets* is the one force which can overthrow the social power of the
language of institutions – whether governments, armed forces,
churches, schools or banks – and make a counter-claim on us on the
most fundamental ground of all, that God is with us, Immanuel.

The sacred community can be only a sentimental notion unless it
is seen also as the source and centre of a power which cleanses the earth
of the impurities of the conventional and of the 'necessities' of
national security and *raison d'etat*. So the mandate of heaven cannot
be anything other than a political challenge, because it represents the
Word of God against all corruption and subterfuge. It is the voice of
that God who, as we often fail to remember, both creates and destroys.
The Old Testament is aware of the potential for destruction:

A voice says, 'Proclaim!'
and I asked, 'What shall I proclaim?'
'All mortals are grass,
they last no longer than a wild
    flower of the field.
The grass withers, the flower fades,
when the blast of the Lord blows on
    them.
Surely the people are grass!
The grass may wither, the flower
    fade,
but the word of our God will endure
    for ever.'
(Isaiah 40.6–8)

The New Testament is aware of the potential for reconstruction:

O wisest love! that flesh and blood
    Which did in Adam fail,

> Should strive afresh against their foe,
> Should strive and should prevail.

These lines from the hymn 'Praise to the Holiest in the height' point to a doctrine which has been, so to speak, undernourished in recent times, the thought of Christ as the 'Second Adam', who recapitulates human history. For the way forward today must be through a Christology, a doctrine of Christ, that can cope with the whole complex of problems that surrounds human existence, from the problems of birth and death and of our sexual lives to the problem of the integrity of creation. St Irenaeus, who was bishop of Lyons in the second century, wrote of the divine rescue as an act which took up the whole human experience, indeed the whole of the created order, into the Godhead in order to make all things new. What failed in the first creation now succeeds, still in human flesh, but in Jesus of Nazareth human flesh is glorified and made capable of bearing the full glory of God.

The true glory of God acts on earth not in power but in weakness:

> He was in the form of God; yet he laid no claim to equality with God, but made himself nothing, assuming the form of a slave. Bearing the human likeness, sharing the human lot, he humbled himself, and was obedient, even to the point of death, death on a cross! Therefore God raised him to the heights ... (Philippians 2.6–9)

Alongside this hymn in Philippians can be placed the hymn of Colossians, 'He is the image of the invisible God; his is the primacy over all creation' (1.15). In refusing to be other than he is, the true representative of God, standing in non-violent resistance to false claims, Jesus exerts authority over the whole creation.

The return to a 'theology of creation' required by our new awareness of the nature of our relation to other living things, which we see as the ecological crisis, should not become the cause of a return to the teaching of God as maker at the expense of the knowledge of Jesus as saviour. Rather our understanding of creation has to be taken up into a wider understanding of salvation as the continuously creating and saving action of the Holy Trinity. Too often we think of God (the Father!) as creating the world and then sitting back to see how it goes on. The notion of 'Trinity', however, is an affirmation of relationship. In the Holy Trinity the three equal persons pursue the patterns of activity which create the cosmos. In the full nature of God these activities are beyond our understanding. Human speech cannot encompass the intention and activity of the Holy Trinity. What we know is that the created order, the known 'universe', is the outcome of these activities. In the Trinity the creation is known to us as both loving and purposive. In Jesus we see that the creation of the universe involves both personal intention and personal love. As the theology of the Orthodox Church expresses it, in the creation we experience God's 'energies', the power which comes from God, not God's 'essence' the unseen inner nature of the Holy Trinity, but we know also that the energies of God express as much of that essential nature as can be taken on board by our human nature.

The universe therefore can be seen as something to be cared for in its own right, irrespective of any purely human purposes. Within this outpouring of the energies of the Trinity the revelation in Jesus Christ is testimony to the fact that the energy of God can wholly inhabit the human sphere and that the human can fully represent to the creation the nature of the divine activity through which the universe is created.

The revelation of Jesus Christ therefore is not only the salvation *of* human beings, but also the saving act offered *to* human beings, to become part of the divine action, the divine 'economy' of saving and remaking this universe. For the cosmos depends entirely on the self-unfolding action which lies within it as a gift which comes from the Holy Trinity. The human being is invited to become the priest of this creation, the microcosm through which the macrocosm is revealed in its full glory. For the Christ is not only the bearer of the Godhead in human flesh but also the sign of the fullness of the process to which the cosmic unfolding moves as an end. The glory of the cosmos is to become wholly loved, the whole creation one act of love, which continually changes yet continually remains the same:

> History, then, is the springtime of the Spirit. It is the time for ploughing by repentance and for sowing seed by heeding the word of God. History is certainly not the final reality, but neither is it a meaningless illusion. It is to be taken as seriously as the field to be ploughed in which the seed is to be scattered.

But ultimately it is not the field and the plant that matter, but the grain or fruit which is borne on the plant and which will be gathered together in the final harvest. The new metahistorical existence, the new creation, into which the whole of humanity has to be reborn through death and resurrection, has already been inaugurated through Christ's death, resurrection, and ascension. He has assumed all humankind into himself, and exalted it to the right hand of God. (Paulos Gregorios, *The Human Presence*, p. 67)

The movement from the sowing of the seed to the harvest is the work of Christ the mediator, the Lord of the Dance who brings the divine *perichoresis*, the constant inter-relating activity of love, into the cosmos and into the human microcosm. In Christ the dance becomes visible, so that the lost can be found, the weak become strong, the spoiled become whole and the impossible be accomplished. This divine Dance is danced in the church, in the time of the liturgy, the eucharist, which makes divine life manifest there on earth. Whenever Christians gather to celebrate the Lord of the cosmos who is the Lord of the Dance, we affirm that the material is capable of bearing God, that it has indeed already borne God, but also that this same transformation indicates the future of the cosmos, that bread, wine, water, human beings and all the elements of creation are always to be transformed and renewed by the divine energies which are gift and miracle and promise.

The notion of 'Trinity', therefore, is not an abstract theological idea, but a simple formula – as simple as the formula of relativity theory, $E = MC^2$ – and as powerful in resolving difficulties. In the formula 'Trinity' we know that we and all the cosmos are already saved, made whole and able to act against all the odds in love. The divine *perichoresis* is the most practical of all formulae, and the most fundamental – the most difficult to 'see' but the most simple to 'do'. 'I made your name known to them, and will make it known, so that the love you had for me may be in them, and I in them' (John 17.26). Nothing less than the affirmation of the whole of the creation as being already 'in Christ' will save us and give us the energy which we need to save the creation. Nothing less than this affirmation of divine energy is the task of the church. For God's inner nature as 'the social Trinity' is impenetrable to us except through the experience of the 'cosmos' as the 'church' writ large. Unless the church now understands this as the task which defines its own nature, it has no purpose on earth. This is not to say that the task is easy, nor that it is solely a Christian task, but that as a Christian task the mandate of the church is to become itself the microcosm, the creation in its true glory.

REFERENCES

Chapter 1: The Divine Order

Aronson, Ronald, *Jean-Paul Sartre: Philosophy in the World*, Verso 1980.

Bonhoeffer, Dietrich, *Ethics*, SCM Press 1978.

Brunner, Emil, *The Divine Imperative*, Lutterworth Press 1937.

Buber, Martin, *I and Thou*, T. & T. Clark 1987.

Camus, Albert, *The Plague*, Penguin Books 1978.

Countryman, L. William, *The Truth about Love*, SPCK 1993.

Crook, John Hurrell, *The Evolution of Human Consciousness*, Oxford University Press 1980.

Curran, Charles, *Faithful Dissent*, Sheed & Ward 1987.

Diamond, Jared, *The Rise and Fall of the Third Chimpanzee*, Vintage 1992.

Fletcher, Joseph, *Situation Ethics*, SCM Press 1966.

Gula, Richard M., 'Natural Law Today', in Charles E. Curran and Richard A. McCormick (eds), *Natural Law and Theology*, Readings in Moral Theology, No. 7, New York / Mawah: Paulist Press 1991, pp. 369–91.

Kent, John, *William Temple*, Cambridge University Press 1992.

McDonagh, Enda, *Invitation and Response*, Dublin: Gill & Macmillan 1972.

Niebhur, Helmut Richard, *Christ and Culture*, New York / London: Harper & Row 1951.

Niebuhr, Reinhold, *Moral Man and Immoral Society*, New York: Charles Scribner's Sons, 1932.

Polkinghorne, John, *Science and Creation*, SPCK 1988.

Pope John Paul II, *Veritatis Splendor*, encyclical letter 'Regarding Certain Fundamental Questions of the Church's Moral Teaching', 6 August 1993, Catholic Truth Society 1993.

Pope Paul VI, *Humanae Vitae*, encyclical letter 'On Human Life', 25 July 1968, Catholic Truth Society 1968.

Sartre, Jean-Paul, *Existentialism and Humanism*, Eyre Methuen 1980.

Smuts, Barbara B., *Sex and Friendship in Baboons*, New York: Aldine de Gruyter 1985.

Tillich, Paul, *Love, Power and Justice*, Oxford University Press 1960.

Wilkins, John (ed.), *Understanding Veritatis Splendor*, SPCK 1994.

Chapter 2: The Mandate of Human Dignity

Bauman, Zygmunt, *Modernity and the Holocaust*, Polity Press 1991.

Berger, Peter, *Invitation to Sociology*, Penguin Books 1966.

Brown, Roger, *Social Psychology*, The Free Press 1986.

Campbell, James, *Talking at the Gates: A Life of James Baldwin*, Faber & Faber 1991.

Crook, John Hurrell, *The Evolution of Human Consciousness*, Oxford University Press 1980.

Cohen, Arthur, 'In Our Terrible Age: The *Tremendum* of the Jews', in Elizabeth Schüssler Fiorenza, *The Holocaust as Interruption*, *Concilium*, vol. 175, October 1984, pp. 11–16.

Cohn-Sherbok, Dan, *Jewish Faith and the Holocaust*, Centre for the Study of Religion and Society, the University of Kent at Canterbury, Pamphlet Library No. 17, 1988.

Dawe, Alan, 'Theories of Social Action', in Tom Bottomore and Robert Nisbet (eds), *A History of Sociological Analysis*, Heinemann 1979, pp. 362–417.

Dawidowicz, Lucy, *The Holocaust and the Historians*, Harvard University Press 1981.

Diamond, Jared, *The Rise and Fall of the Third Chimpanzee*, Vintage 1992.

Douglas, Mary, *Purity and Danger*, Ark Paperbacks 1986.

Durkheim, Emile, *The Division of Labour in Society*, Macmillan 1984.

Durkheim, Emile, *The Elementary Forms of Religious Life*, Allen & Unwin 1915.

Education for All, Report of the Committee of Inquiry into the Education of Children from Ethnic Minority Groups, under the Chairmanship of Lord Swann, HMSO, Cmnd 9453, 1986.

Falconer, Alan, 'Theological Reflections on Human Rights', in Alan Falconer (ed.), *Understanding Human Rights*, Dublin: Irish School of Ecumenics 1980, pp. 196–223.

Freire, Paulo, *Pedagogy of the Oppressed*, Penguin Books 1972.

Küng, Hans, 'Towards a World Ethic of World Religions', in Hans Küng and Jürgen Moltmann (eds), *The Ethics of World Religions and Human Rights, Concilium*, 1990/2, SCM Press 1990, pp. 102–19.

Leech, Kenneth, *Struggle in Babylon*, Sheldon Press 1988.

MacBride, Sean, 'The Universal Declaration – Thirty Years After', in Alan Falconer (ed.), *Understanding Human Rights*, Dublin: Irish School of Ecumenics 1980, pp. 7–20.

Marx, Karl, 'Alienated Labour', in Eugene Kamenka (ed.), *The Portable Karl Marx*, Viking Press / Penguin Books 1983, pp. 131–46.

Marx, Karl, 'Manifesto of the Communist Party', in Eugene Kamenka (ed.), *The Portable Karl Marx*, Viking Press / Penguin Books 1983, pp. 203–41.

Moore, Wilbert E., 'Functionalism', in Tom Bottomore and Robert Nisbet (eds), *A History of Sociological Analysis*, Heinemann 1979, pp. 321–61.

Multicultural Education, Report of the Board of Education Committee on Education to the General Assembly of the Church of Scotland 1990.

The New Black Presence in Britain: A Christian Scrutiny, A Statement by The British Council of Churches' Working Party on Britain as a Multi-Racial Society, Community and Race Relations unit of the British Council of Churches 1976.

Racism in Theology and Theology Against Racism, Report of a consultation organised by The Commission on Faith and Order and The Programme to Combat Racism, Geneva: World Council of Churches 1975.

Riches, David, 'The Phenomenon of Violence', in David Riches (ed.), *The Anthropology of Violence*, Basil Blackwell 1986, pp. 1–27.

Rose, E. J. B. (ed.), *Colour and Citizenship*, Institute of Race Relations, Oxford University Press 1969.

Ruether, Rosemary Radford, *Gaia and God*, SCM Press 1993.

Russell, Lord Russell of Liverpool, *The Scourge of the Swastika*, Corgi Books 1956.

Shapiro, Susan, 'Hearing the Testimony of Radical Negation', in Elizabeth Schüssler Fiorenza, *The Holocaust as Interruption, Concilium* vol. 175, October 1984, pp. 3–10.

Sheppard, David, *The Black Experience in Britain*, Christian Action 1981.

Six, Jean François, *Church and Human Rights,* St Paul Publications 1993.

Tajfel, Henri and Dawson, John L. (eds), *Disappointed Guests,* Oxford University Press 1965.

Thubron, Colin, *Behind the Wall,* Penguin Books 1988.

Wiesel, Elie, *Night, Dawn, Accident,* Robson Books 1974.

Chapter 3: The Mandate of the Sanctity of Life

Anderson, Ray S., *Theology, Death and Dying,* Basil Blackwell 1988.

Birch, Charles and Cobb, John B. Jnr, *The Liberation of Life,* Cambridge University Press 1981.

Bishop, Jerry and Waldholz, Michael, *Genome,* Simon & Schuster 1991.

Buchanan, Keith, 'The Ultimate Arrogance: Genetic Engineering and the Human Future', in *New Blackfriars,* vol. 69, No. 812, January 1988, pp. 35–44.

D'Entrèves, A. P., *Aquinas: Selected Political Writings,* Basil Blackwell 1948.

Duncan, A. S., Dunstan, G. R., and Welbourn, R. W. (eds), *Dictionary of Medical Ethics,* Darton, Longman & Todd 1981.

Glover, Jonathan, *Causing Death and Saving Lives,* Penguin Books 1977.

Häring, Bernard, *Medical Ethics,* St Paul Publications 1974.

Higginson, Richard, 'The Fetus as a Person', in *Abortion in Debate,* Church of Scotland Board for Social Responsibility, Quorum Press 1987, pp. 37–48.

Human Fertilisation and Embryology Act 1990, HMSO 1990.

Jonas, Hans, 'The Right to Die', in T. S. Shannon (ed.), *Bioethics,* Mahwah, NJ: Paulist Press 1987, pp. 195–208.

Kass, Leon R., ' "Making Babies" Revisited', in T. S. Shannon (ed.), *Bioethics,* Mahwah, NJ: Paulist Press 1987, pp. 453–80.

Mahoney, John, *Bio-Ethics and Belief,* Sheed & Ward 1984.

Norman, Edward, 'AIDS and the Will of God', in James Woodward (ed.), *Embracing the Chaos,* SPCK 1990, pp. 82–9.

O'Donovan, Oliver, *Begotten or Made?,* Oxford University Press 1984.

Pattison, Stephen, 'To the Churches with Love', in James Woodward, *Embracing the Chaos,* SPCK 1990, pp. 8–19.

Pope John Paul II, *Veritas Splendor*, encyclical letter 'Regarding Certain Fundamental Questions of the Church's Moral Teaching', 6 August 1993, Catholic Truth Society 1993.

Report of the Committee of Inquiry into Human Fertilisation and Embryology (The Warnock report) HMSO, Cmnd 9314, 1984.

Suzuki, David and Knudston, Peter, *Genethics*, Unwin Paperbacks 1990.

Veith, Frank K., 'Brain Death', in T. S. Shannon (ed.), *Bioethics*, Mahwah, NJ: Paulist Press 1987, pp. 171–94.

Chapter 4: The Mandate of Love

Abercrombie, Nicholas and Warde, Alan, *Contemporary British Society*, Polity Press 1988.

Ariès, Philippe, 'The Indissoluble Marriage', in Philippe Ariès and André Béjin, (eds), *Western Sexuality*, Basil Blackwell 1985, pp. 140–57.

Attenborough, David, *Life on Earth*, Collins / BBC 1979.

Avis, Paul, *Eros and the Sacred*, SPCK 1989.

Bell, Alan P., and Weinberg, Martin S. (eds), *Homosexualities*, Mitchell Beazley 1978.

Bowlby, John, *Child Care and the Growth of Love*, Penguin Books 1953.

Coleman, Peter, *Gay Christians*, SCM Press 1989.

Countryman, L. William, *Dirt, Greed and Sex*, SCM Press 1989.

Curran, Charles, 'Natural Law', in Charles Curran, *Directions in Fundamental Moral Theology*, University of Notre Dame Press 1985, pp. 119–72.

Dobash, R. Emmerson, and Dobash, Russell P., *Violence Against Wives*, Open Books 1980.

Dobash, R. Emmerson, and Dobash, Russell P., *Women, Violence and Social Change*, Routledge 1992.

Dominian, Jack, *Marriage, Faith and Love*, Darton, Longman & Todd 1981.

Donaldson, Margaret, *Children's Minds*, Fontana 1978.

Dormor, Duncan J. (ed.), *The Relationship Revolution*, One Plus One 1992 (Central Middlesex Hospital, London NW10 7NS).

Elliot, Faith Robertson, *The Family: Change or Continuity?*, Macmillan 1986.

Erikson, Erik H., *Childhood and Society*, Penguin Books 1965.

Friedan, Betty, *The Second Stage*, Abacus 1983.

Fromm, Erich, *The Art of Loving*, Unwin Books 1962.

Gaudium et Spes, 'The Pastoral Constitution on the Church in Today's World', Second Vatican Council, 7 December 1965, Catholic Truth Society 1966.
The complete texts of the Council are published in Austin Flannery (ed.), *The Documents of the Second Vatican Council*, Fowler Wright Books 1975.

Giddens, Anthony, *Sociology*, second edition, Polity Press 1989.

Gilligan, Carol, *In a Different Voice*, Harvard University Press 1982.

Hudson, Liam and Jacot, Bernadine, *The Way Men Think*, Yale University Press 1991.

Moberly, Elizabeth R., *Homosexuality*, James Clarke 1983.

Oppenheimer, Helen, *Marriage*, Mowbray 1990.

Parsons, Susan, 'Feminist Reflections on Embodiment and Sexuality', in *Studies in Christian Ethics*, vol. 4, No. 2, 1991, T. & T. Clark, pp. 16–28.

Pope Paul VI, *Humanae Vitae*, encyclical letter 'On Human Life', 25 July 1968, Catholic Truth Society 1968.

Social Trends 17, Central Statistical Office, HMSO 1987.

Chapter 5: The Mandate of Justice

Balasuriya, Tissa, *The Eucharist and Human Liberation*, SCM Press 1979.

Bauman, Zygmunt, *Modernity and the Holocaust*, Polity Press 1991.

Boff, Leonardo and Boff, Clodovis, *Introducing Liberation Theology*, Burns & Oates 1987.

Brown, Robert McAffee, 'The Significance of Puebla for the Protestant Churches in North America', in John Eagleson and Philip Scharper, (eds), *Puebla and Beyond*, Maryknoll, NY: Orbis Books 1979, pp. 330–46.

Camara, Helder, *Spiral of Violence*, Sheed & Ward 1971.

De Waal, Esther, *A World Made Whole*, Fount Paperbacks 1991.

Elliott, Charles, *Praying the Kingdom*, Darton, Longman & Todd 1985.

Ellul, Jacques, *To Will and to Do*, Philadelphia, PA: Pilgrim Press 1969.

Evangelization in Latin America's Present and Future': Final Document of the Third General Conference of the Latin American Episcopate, Puebla de Los Angeles, Mexico, 27 January–13 February 1979, in John Eagleson and Philip Scharper (eds), *Puebla and Beyond,* MaryKnoll, NY: Orbis Books 1979, pp. 122–285.

Faith in the City, Report of the Archbishop of Canterbury's Commission on Urban Priority Areas, Church House Publishing 1985.

Fetters of Injustice, Report of an Ecumenical Consultation on Ecumenical Assistance to Development Projects, Geneva: World Council of Churches 1970.

Forrester, Duncan B., and Skene, Danus, *Just Sharing,* Epworth Press 1988.

Freire, Paulo, *Pedagogy of the Oppressed,* Penguin Books 1972.

Gaudium et Spes, 'The Pastoral Constitution on the Church in Today's World', Second Vatican Council, 7 December 1965, Catholic Truth Society 1966.

George, Susan, *A Fate Worse Than Debt,* Penguin Books 1989.

Gosling, David, *A New Earth,* CCBI 1992.

Granberg-Michaelson, Wesley, *Redeeming the Creation,* Risk Book Series, Geneva: World Council of Churches 1992.

Gutiérrez, Gustavo, *A Theology of Liberation,* revised edition, SCM Press 1988.

Harrington, Michael, *Socialism, Past and Future,* New York: Arcade Publishing 1989.

Hawthorn, Geoffrey, *Enlightenment and Despair,* Cambridge University Press 1987.

Lernoux, Penny, 'The Long Road to Puebla', in John Eagleson and Philip Scharper (eds), *Puebla and Beyond,* Maryknoll, NY: Orbis Books 1979, pp. 3–17.

Lochman, Jan Milic, *Christ and Prometheus?* Geneva: World Council of Churches 1988.

MacIntyre, Alasdair, *After Virtue,* Duckworth 1981.

Moltmann, Jürgen, *Theology of Hope,* SCM Press 1967.

Moltmann, Jürgen, *The Way of Jesus Christ,* SCM Press 1990.

Niebuhr, Reinhold, *Moral Man and Immoral Society,* New York: Charles Scribner's Sons 1960.

North–South: A Programme for Survival, Report of the Independent Commission on International Development Issues, under the Chairmanship of Willy Brandt, Pan Books 1980.

Novak, Michael, *The Spirit of Democratic Capitalism*, IEA Health and Welfare Unit 1991.

Oppenheim, Carey, *Poverty: The Facts*, Child Poverty Action Group 1990.

Plant, Raymond, *Modern Political Thought*, Basil Blackwell 1991.

Pope Leo XIII, *Rerum Novarum*, encyclical letter 'On the Condition of the Working Classes', 15 May 1891, Catholic Truth Society 1960.

Pope Paul VI, *Populorum Progressio*, encyclical letter 'On Fostering the Development of Peoples', 26 March 1967, Catholic Truth Society 1967.

Preston, Ronald H., *The Future of Christian Ethics*, SCM Press 1987.

Rawls, John, *A Theory of Justice*, Oxford University Press 1973.

Resources and Man, A Study and Recommendations by the Committee on Resources and Man of the Division of Earth Sciences, National Academy of Sciences – National Research Council, San Francisco: W. H. Freeman 1969.

Ryan, Alan, *Property and Political Theory*, Basil Blackwell 1984.

Sen, Amartya, *Resources, Values and Development*, Basil Blackwell 1984.

Sen, Amartya, 'Beneconfusion', in J. Gay Tulip Meeks, *Thoughtful Economic Man*, Cambridge University Press 1991, pp. 12–16.

Sider, Ronald J., *Rich Christians in an Age of Hunger*, new edition, Hodder & Stoughton 1990.

Song, C. S., *The Tears of Lady Meng*, Risk Book Series, Geneva: World Council of Churches 1981.

Walzer, Michael, *Spheres of Justice*, Basil Blackwell 1983.

Ward, Barbara, and Dubos, René, *Only One Earth*, An unofficial report commissioned by the Secretary-General of the United Nations Conference on the Human Environment, Penguin Books 1972.

Witvliet, Theo, *A Place in the Sun: An Introduction to Liberation Theology in the Third World*, SCM Press 1985.

Chapter 6: The Mandate of the Church

Barrett, C. K., *Church, Ministry and Sacraments in the New Testament*, Paternoster Press 1985.

Barbé, Dominique, *A Theology of Conflict and Other Writings on Nonviolence* Maryknoll, NY: Orbis Books 1989.

Bauman, Zygmunt, *Modernity and the Holocaust,* Polity Press 1991.

Bede, *A History of the English Church and People,* Penguin Books 1968.

Bennett, Lerone, Jnr, *What Manner of Man: Martin Luther King Jnr,* Chicago: Johnson Pub. Co., 1965.

Berry, Thomas, with Thomas Clarke SJ, *Befriending the Earth,* Mystic, CT: Twenty-Third Publications 1991.

Birch, Charles and Cobb, John B., Jnr, *The Liberation of Life,* Cambridge University Press 1981.

Blake, William, *Blake: Poems and Letters,* selected by Jacob Bronowski, Penguin Books 1958.

Bonhoeffer, Dietrich, *Ethics,* SCM Press 1978.

Crook, John Hurrell, *The Evolution of Human Consciousness,* Oxford University Press 1980.

Dewey, John, *Democracy and Education,* The Free Press 1966.

Diamond, Jared, *The Rise and Fall of the Third Chimpanzee,* Vintage 1992.

Eliot, T. S., *Four Quartets,* Faber & Faber 1944.

Freire, Paulo, *Cultural Action for Freedom,* Penguin Books 1972.

Freire, Paulo, *Pedagogy of the Oppressed,* Penguin Books 1972.

George, K. M., 'Towards a Eucharistic Ecology', in Gennady Limouris, *Justice, Peace and the Integrity of Creation,* Geneva: World Council of Churches 1990, pp. 45–55.

Hartshorne, Charles, 'Tillich's Doctrine of God', in Charles Kegley and Robert Bretall (eds), *The Theology of Paul Tillich,* New York: Pilgrim Press 1982, pp. 198–232.

Herbert, George, *The Poetical Works of George Herbert,* T. Nelson & Sons 1864.

Lossky, Vladimir, *The Mystical Theology of the Eastern Church,* James Clarke 1957.

Merton, Thomas, *The Sign of Jonas,* Hollis & Carter 1953.

Moltmann, Jürgen, *The Way of Jesus Christ,* SCM Press 1990.

Mott, Michael, *The Seven Mountains of Thomas Merton,* Sheldon Press 1986.

Paulos Gregorios, *The Human Presence: An Orthodox View of Nature,* Geneva: World Council of Churches 1978.

Schmemann, Alexander, *For the Life of the World,* St Vladimir's Seminary Press 1973.

Shik, Oh Jae, 'Justice with Peace: From Whose Perspective?', in D. Premand Niles, *Between The Flood and the Rainbow*, Geneva: World Council of Churches 1992, pp. 153–63.

Thomas, R. S., *Selected Poems 1946–1968*, Bloodaxe Books 1986.

Thomas, R. S., *Later Poems 1972–1982*, Macmillan 1984.

Tillich, Paul, *Love, Power and Justice*, Oxford University Press 1960.

Torrance, Thomas F. (ed.), *The School of Faith: The Catechisms of the Reformed Church*, James Clarke 1959.

Zahn, Gordon, *In Solitary Witness: The Life and Death of Franz Jägerstätter*, Springfield, IL: Templegate 1986.

INDEX OF BIBLICAL REFERENCES

INDEX OF NAMES

INDEX OF SUBJECTS